Entrepreneurial Complexity

T0330886

Entrepreneurial Complexity

Methods and Applications

Edited by

Matthias Dehmer
University of Applied Sciences Upper Austria
Steyr School of Management
Department of Operations Management
Nankai University, Tianjin, China
UMIT, Hall in Tyrol, Austria

Frank Emmert-Streib
Tampere University, Finland

Herbert Jodlbauer
University of Applied Sciences Upper Austria
Steyr School of Management
Department of Operations Management

CRC Press
Taylor & Francis Group
Boca Raton London New York

CRC Press is an imprint of the
Taylor & Francis Group, an **informa** business

A CHAPMAN & HALL BOOK

CRC Press
Taylor & Francis Group
6000 Broken Sound Parkway NW, Suite 300
Boca Raton, FL 33487-2742

First issued in paperback 2020

ISBN 13: 978-0-367-65659-1 (pbk)
ISBN 13: 978-0-8153-7001-7 (hbk)

Library of Congress Cataloging-in-Publication Data

Names: Dehmer, Matthias, 1968- editor. | Emmert-Streib, Frank, editor. | Jodlbauer, Herbert, 1965- editor.
Title: Entrepreneurial complexity : methods and applications / [edited by] Matthias Dehmer, Frank Emmert-Streib and Herbert Jodlbauer.
Description: Boca Raton, FL : CRC Press, 2018.
Identifiers: LCCN 2018047228 | ISBN 9780815370017
Subjects: LCSH: Entrepreneurship–Mathematical models. | Management science–Mathematical models.
Classification: LCC HB615 .E577854 2018 | DDC 658.4/21–dc23
LC record available at https://lccn.loc.gov/2018047228

Visit the Taylor & Francis Web site at
http://www.taylorandfrancis.com

and the CRC Press Web site at
http://www.crcpress.com

To Ilie Burdujan

Contents

Preface

Understanding entrepreneurial complexity has been a key issue for being a successful business leader. Essential reasons for the entrepreneurial complexity are: eco-systems are moving fast, many technological innovations are rushing into the markets, digital transformation of the whole society is taking place quickly, people are being over-loaded with data, decreasing transaction, switching and marginal cost, scarcity of high-qualified employees, raw materials and energy is commonplace, dynamic net-works are growing worldwide and so forth. Also, social systems are changing radically and new mobility concepts are arising. Political systems, legal requirements, welfare systems, environmental issues and other aspects also contribute to the complexity to be managed by an enterprise.

In this book, models to describe entrepreneurial complexity and its drivers are presented and approaches for complexity reduction as well as for mastering complex systems are discussed. A wide range of business topics is covered focusing on activities, processes, transactions, services and strategy of an enterprise. We put the emphasis on describing accurate complexity methods by focusing on stability, robust-ness, sustainability and other properties thereof. The reader of the book acquires knowledge how to run, manage, lead and improve a complex economical system. The target group of the book is twofold: First, scientists and scholars of different fields such as economy, computer science and applied mathematics who are interested in extend-ing the entrepreneurial convexity research and, second, entrepreneurs and business leaders of all branches who aim to deal with their complexity factors efficiently.

Many colleagues have provided us with precious input, help and support before and during the formations of the present book. Particularly, we would like to thank Ilie Burdujan, Danail Bonchev, Werner Dehmer, Dragan and Sanja Stevanovic, Zengqiang Chen, Andreas Holzinger, Yongtang Shi, Jin Tao, Andrey A. Dobrynin, Boris Furtula, Ivan Gutman, Bo Hu, Xueliang Li, D. D. Lozovanu, Abbe Mowshowitz, Fred Sobik, Shailesh Tripathi, Kurt Varmuza, Chengyi Xia, Yusen Zhang, Dongxiao Zhu, and apologize to all whose names have been inadvertently omitted. Also, we would like to thank acquiring editor, Khan Sarfraz and editorial assistant, Callum Fraser from CRC Press for their excellent support in publishing this book. Matthias Dehmer thanks the Austrian Science Funds for supporting this work (project P30031).

This book is dedicated to Ilie Burdujan (University of Agronomical Sciences and Veterinary Medicine "Ion Ionescu de la Brad" in Iasi, Romania) who unfortunately passed away in 2017. Ilie was a great friend, very loyal, inspiring in discussions and very passionate towards his work. This book shall be a memento to Ilie.

Finally, we hope that this book helps to establish a better understanding of entrepreneurial complexity and contributes to some implementation of addressed concepts and methods in real-world application. We wish our readers new insights and ideas for further research as well as implementation work.

Matthias Dehmer
Frank Emmert-Streib
Herbert Jodlbauer

Editors

Matthias Dehmer is a professor at the University of Applied Sciences Upper Austria, Steyr School of Management and UMIT – The Health and Life Sciences University in Austria. He also holds a guest professorship at Nankai University, College of Artificial Intelligence in China. His research interests are in graph theory, complex networks, complexity, data science, machine learning, big data analytics, and information theory. In particular, he is also working on machine learning-based methods to design new data analysis methods for solving problems in manufacturing and production.

Frank Emmert-Streib is a professor at Tampere University, Finland, heading the Predictive Society and Data Analytics Lab. His research interests are in the field of data science, machine learning and network science in the development and application of methods from statistics and machine learning for the analysis of big data from genomics, finance, social media and business.

Herbert Jodlbauer is a professor at the University of Applied Sciences Upper Austria, Steyr School of Management and also acts as a director of studies of the bachelor study program Production and Management and the master study program Operations Management. Furthermore, he leads the trans-faculty institute of Smart Production. His research is primarily concerned with production planning, time continuous production models, financial valuation of production related decision-making as well as digitalization.

Contributors

Ahmed Musbah Aboyssir
School of Islamic Management
Universiti Sains Islam
Nilai, Malaysia

Adekiya Adewale
Department of Business
Administration and
    Entrepreneurship
    Bayero University
Kano, Nigeria

Katarzyna Awruk
Faculty of Psychology
University of Economics and
    Human Sciences
Warsaw, Poland

Martin Döring
Universität Hamburg
Institute of Geography
Hamburg, Germany

Helmholtz Zentrum Geesthacht
Institute of Coastal Research
Geesthacht, Germany

María del Rocío Gálvez-García
Dpt. de Métodos de Investigación y
Diagnóstico en Educación
Facultad de Ciencias de la Educación
Universidad de Sevilla
Sevilla, Spain

Ineta Geipele
Institute of the Civil Engineering
    and Real Estate Economics
Faculty of Engineering Economics
    and Management
Riga Technical University
Riga, Latvia

Konrad Janowski
Faculty of Psychology
University of Economics and
    Human Sciences
Warsaw, Poland

Kyriaki I. Kafka
Department of Economics
National and Kapodistrian
    University of Athens
Athens, Greece

Linda Kauškale
Institute of the Civil Engineering and
    Real Estate Economics
Faculty of Engineering Economics
    and Management
Riga Technical University
Riga, Latvia

Panagiotis E. Petrakis
Department of Economics
National and Kapodistrian
    University of Athens
Greece, Stadiou

Beate M.W. Ratter
Universität Hamburg
Institute of Geography
Hamburg, Germany

Helmholtz Zentrum Geesthacht
Institute of Coastal Research
Max Planck, Geesthacht

María Fe Sánchez-García
Dpt. de Métodos de Investigación y
Diagnóstico en Educación
Facultad de Ciencias de la
   Educación II (Orientación
   Educativa, Diagnóstico e
Intervención Psicopedagógica)
Facultad de Educación, UNED
Madrid, Spain

John T. Scott
Department of Economics
Dartmouth College
New Hampshire, USA

Marcin Waldemar Staniewski
Faculty of Management and Finance
University of Economics and
   Human Sciences
Warsaw, Poland

Magdalena Suárez-Ortega
Dpt. de Métodos de Investigación y
Diagnóstico en Educación
Facultad de Ciencias de la Educación
Universidad de Sevilla
Sevilla, Spain

Diana Süsser
Universität Hamburg
Institute of Geography
Hamburg, Germany

Barbara Weig
Universität Hamburg
Institute of Geography
Hamburg, Germany

Chapter 1

Entrepreneurs for Renewables
Emergence of Innovation and Entrepreneurship in Complex Social Systems

Diana Süsser, Barbara Weig, Martin Döring and Beate M.W. Ratter

1 Introduction

The main contribution of this chapter lies in the investigation of the emergence of innovation and entrepreneurship in complex social systems, exemplarily in the context of community-based renewable energy. We, hence, theoretically consider 'entrepreneurial complexity' as the emergence of innovation processes and entrepreneurship in complex and social systems arising from multifarious and intertwined behaviours. Our study aims to examine the factors and processes underlying the renewable energy transition in rural communities.

Complex realities define our daily life: complex processes work in nature, and complex structures define our social environment. Complexity is inherent in decision-making and connected behaviours, complexity issues revolve around technologies, complexity innate in different policies, etc. The nature of complexity also applies to how our economic system works since it consists of the complex actions and interactions between individual entrepreneurs, national and international companies, whole societies and the politics governing them. Within this multifaceted situation, innovation and an emerging entrepreneurship are of increasing importance because they are driven by different actors stemming from the public, the economy and policy. Furthermore, the landscape of economy is characterised by entities such as big companies (stock-noted companies), by small- and medium-sized enterprises (SME) and so-called start-ups. Start-ups – as the naming suggests – take up an increasing role when it comes to the provision of sustainable solutions in order to solve environmental challenges such as climate change. In the present context of the energy transition in Germany, many new green tech companies, energy consulting businesses, renewable energy innovation laboratories and hubs, as well as further green energy initiatives emerged in the last two decades. Based on entrepreneurial thinking, innovative individuals and collectives who develop(ed) or want(ed) to promote sustainable business solutions and business models initiated those companies and initiatives. Local agents of the energy transition, who invested time, money and their intellectual capacities, are here called *energy-preneurs*.

While big cities are well known for being hotspots for start-ups, incubators and co-working, innovations and entrepreneurship, the potentials of rural areas are often underestimated or remain in many cases unknown or hidden. However, the *Energiewende* – the energy transition in Germany – became common for spatially emphasising the local and social relevance of community-based origins of energy transition. Thus, the importance of citizens and communities for a successful and sustainable energy transition has been recognised from the onset in public and political debates [1–3]. The transition towards a renewable energy supply, however, involves local innovation processes which induce and lead to the transformation of places, communities, villages and cities. Despite the different geographies inherent in and relevant for energy transition [4], the focus in the present study lies on one important pillar: community-led transition towards renewable energy in terms of wind farms, solar panels, geothermal plants and biogas plants.

The concept of community-based renewable energy – also called community renewables – has theoretically and practically been used to define small-scale and local renewable energy-generating social groups, which hold high degrees of project ownership and collective benefits [5–8]. Two dimensions are crucial for defining its character: the process dimension – considering who develops and is involved in the project – and the outcome dimension – looking at the kind of benefits created in the course of the project and for whom [7]. With regard to the process of project development, the literature is primarily devoted to the question which aspects are influencing the acceptance of and participation in projects. Highlighted key aspects are the importance of place meanings and attachments [9–11] and the trustworthy embedding of local entrepreneurs [12,13]. In addition, financial support mechanisms, a more localised and participatory development process and opportunities for local ownership, were identified as being essential to increase awareness and acceptance [5,14,15], and to support the deployment of renewable-energy technologies [16–18]. Regarding the real outcome of alternative energy installation projects, the success in generating community benefits is found to be dependent on the local involvement of people [7,19], the social and economic capacities of key local entrepreneurs [20] and the community control of the projects [21,22]. Moreover, a fair process and distribution of community benefits have been identified to foster the acceptance of renewable energy projects [15,22,23].

Given the increasing relevance of community renewables and their inherent 'complexities', we conceptualise methodologically entrepreneurs as agents, the relations among them including their surrounding social system, different social and other proximities among them, and the capitals set up in the course of the process of renewable energy deployment. Relations with further external systems were also taken into consideration where they emerged in the course of the empirical investigation of the qualitative data gathered and appeared to be of further analytical value. Taking the aspects previously outlined into account, our overarching research question is:

> What are the underlying factors of and which processes led to the emergence of community-based innovation and entrepreneurship in the context of renewable energy technologies?

To answer this question, we first investigate and analyse the convergence of the theoretical concepts of complex social systems, innovation and entrepreneurship. Our conceptual exploration of structures and behaviours demonstrates how innovation and entrepreneurship arise and how they are embedded in social, complex systems. In the second part, we empirically apply and test our theoretical reflections in the community of Reußenköge – a pioneering energy community in North Frisia, Germany. An empirical analysis of the main characteristics of innovation and entrepreneurship in Reußenköge (Germany) is provided. The study is based on a mixed-method and qualitative approach which has been applied in the context of interviews with citizens inside and in the surroundings of the community. Finally, in the discussion and conclusion, we present and discuss the key results of the investigation and provide an outlook.

2 Exploring Conceptual Convergences: Complex Social Systems, Innovation Theory and Ideas of Entrepreneurship

Complexity theory addresses multifarious kinds of processes in the 'real world' out there [24]. It holds the potential to offer an analytically structured but at the same time process-open understanding of how systems behave, change and evolve in certain contexts, under particular circumstances and over time [25]. In this sense, complexity theory does not follow a reductionist epistemology formulating restrictive or even functionalist position about a certain system and its constitutive elements, but aims at an evolutionary, interactive and comprehensive explanation based on the concept of emergence [26]. Consequently, the complex systems' approach emphasises the analysis of the interplay between functional elements and characteristics that can lead to different system states on different levels by defining system components, disclosing pathways and analysing their multifaceted relations.

Such a general understanding provides the complexity-related background for our research question: What contributes to the emergence of community-based innovation concepts in renewable energy technologies? The conceptual rationale underlines the relevance of analytical units such as agents, the importance of their characteristics and their non-linear and dynamic relations. The crucial question arises, how and why do community-owned wind turbines materialise and stand in the landscape? To better understand this process, the analytical approach is complemented with elements taken from the theory of the diffusion of innovation and the characteristics of a Bourdieusian understanding of entrepreneurship and entrepreneurs. These elements theoretically go together with the aforementioned analytical units inherent in complex social systems. Hence, Rogers' [27] four analytical categories of the diffusion of innovation provide an analytical tool which holds the potential to supply an improved and comprehensive understanding of the structural characteristics underlying the diffusion of innovation while economic, social, cultural and symbolic forms of capital [28] will assist in investigating the main characteristics of actors and their relations and exemplify the features of an entrepreneurship that enabled the implementation of renewable energy technologies. These elements will be successively outlined and theoretically integrated in an analytical toolkit at the end of this contribution.

2.1 Characteristics of Complex Social Systems

To begin with, a system can generally be defined as a composition (etymologically derived from the Greek term *systema*) of different heterogeneous elements and their relations which can clearly be distinguished from its surrounding environment [29]. A system is thus characterised by specific boundaries which are not per se given, but have to be defined according to a research question or an analytical perspective taken. The analytical boundary to be set between a system and its surrounding environment represents a heuristic to be defined by the scientist and requires a considerable effort to be determined [30]. Most (if not all) systems represent so-called open entities, meaning that they are linked and engaged in an exchange of information, energy and matter with their external environments [31].

Changing this rather broad perspective and looking into a system itself, one can see that it is composed of a variety of elements which interact and form mutual relations securing its functional consistency. The variety and multiplicity of these relations define and shape the connections between constitutive elements and enable multiple possibilities of emergencies and non-linear feedbacks. This theoretically implicates the possibility that the behaviour of one element in the system can lead to reactions among other elements, which then might or might not adapt their behaviour and by doing so influence other elements, change their relational properties and can result in a system change [32]. Repeated interaction can, furthermore, turn into iterative interaction which changes the probability of future events in a system without making them (entirely) predictable [33]. This kind of complexity, which is called behavioural complexity, arises from processes between the elements of a system [34] and is of special analytical interest here since – what we call – an emerging entrepreneurship among entrepreneurs is based on these processes of interaction among different elements of a system. Their study is supposed to assist in unravelling the social dynamics and the behavioural changes provoking innovation and resulting in the emergence of community renewable energy. Consequently, the constituting elements, relations, structures and processes need to be examined by exploring local entrepreneurs. It requires the conceptual study and analysis of their interactions and relationships within their local and social environment [34,35].

One important structural characteristic within a system is emergence. Emergence is conceived as the capability of a complex system to generate new characteristics, patterns or functions on the macro level through a change of interaction of elements on the micro level. Such a bottom-up understanding of emergence goes together with a top-down concept in which changes on the system level yield feedback effects on the behavioural elements [36] and their functional relations. Hence, emergence has to be understood as a multifarious reshaping of relations among the elements themselves and on different system levels probably resulting in a changed or altered system state. Such occurrences and underlying processes cannot be predicted or controlled [31] because there is – metaphorically speaking – no steersman who sets the course. The interaction of the elements and the feedback between the elements among different system levels can after all produce a reshaping of functional relations among system elements resulting in surprising, unpredictable and unplanned structures and forms of order [37]. The materialisation of a system of community renewable energy – as in our case – can therefore be understood as such an emergent structure.

To go on, path dependency represents another important characteristic of complex social systems. It can be understood as an established way of how a system, its elements and relations maintain system-constituting functions, and by doing so secure the system's integrity. It represents a historically and experientially established way of acting or functioning in a system-related way. The conception of path dependency could consequently be framed as a 'path-dependent sequence of [...] changes [bearing] [...] important influences upon the eventual outcome [which] can be exerted by temporally remote events, including happenings dominated by chance elements rather than systematic forces' [38, page 332]. Such a more or less traditional understanding of path dependency [38–42] is based on the assumption that path-dependent processes inevitably lead to non-ideal equilibrium states called 'lock-in' which can only be overcome by exogenous shocks. These shocks are conceived as abrupt events of any kind that introduce system changes and lead to an altered or changed path. Contrary to this understanding of exogenous shocks for change, evolutionary concepts of path dependency in complex social systems [43–45] challenge this understanding and highlight the idea of gradual and incremental changes. Thus, elements, system components and sub-systems possess their own path dependencies working against the backdrop of slow evolutionary and co-evolutionary processes followed by structural changes on the micro and macro level [46]. Hence, functional and structural change does not exclusively rely on shocks from the outside. On the contrary, the endogenous dimension can also lead to sudden emerging structures, be they shock-wise or slow in character, as revealed by a complexity perspective: interaction on the micro level instigates endogenous processes of layering, conversion and recombination [45] which result in change on the macro level. Consequently, path-dependent and connected processes are a subject of a continuous momentum stimulating permanent interaction and learning to avoid systemic lock-ins as it occurred in the change from agriculture as a single business to an agricultural business combined with renewable energy generation in our case-study.

The agents are the system's elements which are undergoing change and ensuing path dependency, and in our context, we conceive them as heterogeneous decision-making individuals. Generally seen, agents are characterised as possessing limited knowledge about the whole system, its behaviour and the different functionalities implicated in it [35]. They act locally, are influenced by their personal characteristics, life experiences, norms, values and the social status [47] describing properties of their relations with other agents and indirectly influencing the behaviour of the whole system. Such features enable a single agent to (re)act and reflect on macrostructures [29] and intentionally target a certain objective with all resources available, even though she or he cannot intentionally realise a specific development of a social system [30,32] due to its inherent complexity. As a result, complex social systems can also be called complex adaptive systems [48] because their agents are able to reflect, learn and adapt to new situations. This is carried out on the grounds of past experiences which assist in generating prognosis and strategies for the future [49] as we will see in the analysis of our community system and its agents.

Finally, learning as an important characteristic in complex adaptive systems strongly depends on the proximity between the respective agents of a system. Based on the findings of the French 'proximity dynamics group' [50–52], five important dimensions of proximity in terms of learning are defined [53]: geographical, cognitive, social, institutional and organisational proximity appear to foster interaction on the one hand and thereby support learning processes on the other hand. Thus, geographical proximity enables agents to meet face-to-face whilst cognitive proximity refers to a common or shared knowledge base. Organisational proximity originates from socio-hierarchical structures within organisations such as administration or firms, whereas social proximity arises through relations built upon social ties such as friendship or family relationships. Especially the last two dimensions foster trust and prevent uncertainty and opportunism while institutional proximity entails a shared set of norms and values. All of these dimensions or relational characteristics are important in one way or another, but none is sufficient on its own to enhance the process of learning [53]. Hence, too much proximity can harm interaction and learning processes because excessive cognitive proximity hampers the exchange and processing of new information while too much organisational proximity entails inflexible, rigid hierarchies and dependencies or asymmetric power relations [53]. Consequently, a dynamic balance of geographical, cognitive, social, institutional and organisational proximity and distance is envisaged to fostering interaction and learning processes which, in turn, enable systemic change in terms of innovation [53].

Therefore, an understanding of how entrepreneurs including their entrepreneurship did get the innovation of community-based renewable energy technologies going requires the analytical concepts of system, emergence, path dependency, agent and proximity to perform an investigation from a complex social system's perspective. The community (see Figure 1), in our view, represents a social system which – taking the inner perspective – consists of agents (the individuals of the community and also the entrepreneurs to be analysed) holding different kinds of proximities with other agents characterising their relations and being embedded in a socio-historical path dependency. In addition, the community and its agents should also be envisaged as connected to and being part of the surrounding economic, political and social systems with which it mainly converges on the level of agents. However, not in every community system an innovative subsystem of entrepreneurs evolves. Therefore, which factors enable this development in terms of community-owned wind turbines and individually owned solar panels? To answer this question, there is a need to conceptually integrate the notion of grassroots innovation which provides a schematic of the innovation process and helps to better assess developmental stages.

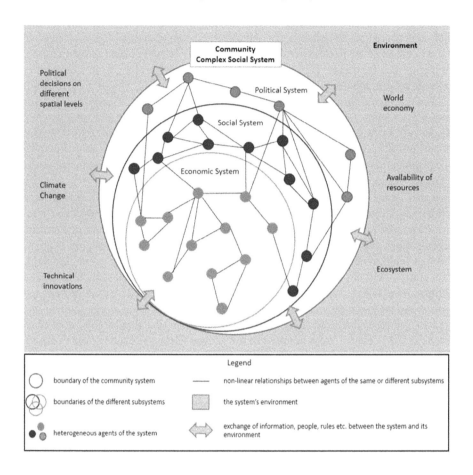

FIGURE 1: Community as complex social system

2.2   Grassroots Innovation in a Complex Social System

Innovation represents a notion that implicates connotations of improvement, renewal and technological or social progress. In the context of a complex social systems approach, it subliminally holds strong ties with concepts such as agent, proximity, path dependence and emergence because a theory of innovation builds on them. But what actually is innovation? A widely accepted notion of innovation has been developed by Rogers [27] who defines innovation as an object, idea or practice which is perceived as new by an individual agent within society, and which is communicated over time and adopted by individuals or agents within a context or system. Although most concepts of innovation refer to new products or technologies, innovation, represents more than just technology [54] or its implementation as it can be envisaged as a succession of sequences in the context of a social process. This aspect is reflected in Roger's [27] definition of innovation which ranges from individually perceived novelty to societal distribution comprising the non-linear and complex stages of invention (research in different areas and develop new products), innovation (further development, testing and launch of a product) and diffusion (bringing the product to the market). This more or less process-related perspective of innovation has, however, be complemented by the social dimension contained in it. Here, the focus is set on the role and behaviour of civil society and its individuals in terms of accepting and adopting new technologies through processes of negotiation and discussion. This means that agents probably accept the fact that for example carbon emissions boost climate change and start adopting the practice of car-sharing to avoid emissions emerging from the individual use of cars. But reality provides another picture as it makes clear that the service of car sharing is more and more distributed among cities while the cultural acceptance and social willingness of individuals to immobilise their own car remain limited.

Considering the development of renewable energies technologies, they followed the process of invention, innovation and diffusion. Especially from the diffusion process evolved another perspective on development within civil society called *grassroots innovation*. This notion has been developed by Seyfang and Smith [6] who define it as:

> the networks of activists and organisations generating novel bottom-up solutions for sustainable development; solutions that respond to the local situation and the interests and values of the communities involved. In contrast to mainstream business greening, grassroots initiatives operate in civil society arenas and involve committed activists experimenting with social innovation as well as using greener technologies.
>
> [6, page 585]

The notion of grassroots innovation is based on a different rationale of innovation as it implicates dispersed and bottom-up developments which are characterised by collective activities and a rhizome-like spread across the social system. Based on widely distributed social interaction on a system's micro level – and in the context of socially constituted values, social norms and needs [55] – different kinds of phenomena or even problem solutions can emerge and affect the system's macro level. One has yet to bear in mind that such developments do not result from intentional activities of a single agent, but should be conceived as system-specific and collective achievements [56,57]. Thus, grassroots innovation first emerges as niche of innovation, second, facilitates the social diffusion of innovations, and third leads to system changes [58]. Community renewable energy could exactly be seen as such a process because the previously mentioned aspects are elements of this development providing a framework for explaining the emergence and implementation of renewable energy technologies [8,13,59–61].

From a social complexity perspective of grassroots innovation, the adoption of innovation represents an interesting object of research because such an approach enables the systematic analysis of systems, emergence, path dependencies, agents and proximities involved in an innovation process. Simply put, the process of human decision-making about the adoption of a certain technology is complex because agents make individual and collaborative decisions based on a variety of interacting factors such as attitudes, preferences, experiences, norms and values. Diffusion occupies an important position in this context because '[…] an innovation is communicated through certain social channels over time among members of a social system' [27, page 5]. The conceptual rationale underlying this process [27] can be divided into the analytical categories of (i) the innovation and its characteristics, (ii) the communication channels through which information is disseminated, (iii) the time along which innovation decisions are made and (iv) the social system in which the innovation is diffused and in which it spreads [27]. Innovations are, in turn, saturated with characteristics [27] such as the relative advantage (evaluation of the innovation), aspects of compatibility (perceived consistency of the innovation with existing values, past experiences and needs), the complexity of the innovation (perceived ability to understand the innovation and to use/implement the innovation), the tinkering with the innovation (prior experimentation with innovations) and the observability (visibility of results of an innovation to others). It becomes apparent that the diffusion of an innovation such as wind energy is a multi-layered and interactive social process among agents of a system that can lead to a system change. But what are the features of local entrepreneurs that boost an innovation and interact with it?

2.3   Entrepreneurship and Entrepreneurs in the Framework of Complex Social Systems Approach

In recent years, the analytical notions of entrepreneurship and entrepreneurs as change agents, origins and/or sources of innovation have received considerable attention in the context of research on sustainable development ranging from policy change to the implementation of renewable energy technologies [6,62–66]. This development co-occurred with the aim to challenge positivist approaches of entrepreneurship that predominantly explored individual's cognitive abilities and intellectual capacities to identify overlooked business opportunities [67] or the exploitation of market niches [68,69]. Contrary to these strands of research, studies devoted to critically deconstruct the prevalent reification or personification of the ingenious entrepreneur [70, page 85] were and are devoted to finding and defining the new place of entrepreneurship and entrepreneurs within postmodern capitalist societies [71]. Here, different approaches showed how a broader social and cultural embedding of entrepreneurs, the application of different kinds of resources and the execution of entrepreneurial bricolages [72] contribute to a socio-cultural reframing of the concept of entrepreneurship [73]. Following these insights, entrepreneurship was reconceptualised as a socially intertwined set of practices in the context and fabric of business, society and culture [74,75] highlighting the socially embedded nature of entrepreneurs [76] distributed in complex processes of agency and among different system levels [77].

In line with these developments and against the background of a complex social systems approach, ideas emerged that entrepreneurs do have to navigate their businesses through social and cultural contexts [78] fulfilling certain social rules and cultural norms constructed in and maintained by social, political, cultural, economic and geographical systems surrounding them. Such insights provide food for thought about our research question because the emergence of a specific kind or type of entrepreneur and entrepreneurship is considerably characterised and influenced by his or her social, cultural or symbolic and economic capital [29], and the different fields or systems the entrepreneur is situated in. A combination of a complex social systems approach with Pierre Bourdieu's theory of practice [79,80] seems to be promising as it holds the potential to bring about analytical concepts which provide a structural under-standing about the processes underlying and propelling entrepreneurship and entrepreneurial behaviour. According to Bourdieu, society could be framed as a plurality of intersecting social fields or systems (hereafter system) in which different forms of economic, social, cultural and symbolic capital perform a relational positioning work for and of each individual or agent (hereafter agent) [29]. This means that the position of various agents in a social system depends, on the one hand, on the specific social profile a system holds and, on the other hand, on the proportionate importance of the different capitals working in it. The relevant combination of capitals hence delineates a social position or differing proximities of the agent in the system to other agents, defines the power she or he possesses in the system's hierarchy and partially characterises her or his odds in power struggles.

Analytically seen, economic capital represents the most familiar form of capital among the different kinds of capitals. Bourdieu describes it as different kinds of things or abstract entities that can immediately be converted into money such as patents, stocks, real estates and valuable materials. Social capital yet differs from economic capital in the sense that it describes the different relational networks, social contacts and relationships an individual can draw on to enlarge his or her sphere of social influence and power. Social capital hence embraces different degrees of group membership through which an agent can get access to a social institution such as a university, a political party or a business company. The gaining and maintenance of social capital requires constant work and is closely related to and often combined with cultural capital. The notion of cultural capital in turn designates the knowledge and the intellectual skills of an actor in a system that assists her in achieving a social position, gaining status and acquiring legitimacy. The term cultural capital is analytically subdivided into embodied cultural capital (an individual's knowledge and rhetoric mastery), objectified cultural capital (a person's property in terms of culturally valuable objects) and institutionalised capital (university degrees or professional qualifications). Both social and cultural capital can be converted into economic capital, and their combination is often supported by symbolic capital that describes a 'degree of accumulated prestige, [reputation,] celebrity or honour and is founded on [...] recognition [...]' [81, page 7]. Symbolic capital framed as respectability and honourableness often goes hand in hand with social and cultural capital, and all capitals combined characterise the relations and proximities in any kind of social system.

To better understand the conditions of how and why a certain type of entrepreneur emerges, the notions of field and habitus offer further analytical concepts that converge with complex social systems theory. The notion of field – what we already called system for the sake of terminological consistency – designates according to Bourdieu and Wacquant [82] a pre-structured and historically grown network of social relations where different kinds of actors deploy their capitals and struggle for power in view of a certain issue. Ex negativo seen, the ontological status of system cannot be reduced to a certain spatial conception, profession or business segment because a social sub-field or sub-system should be conceived an intangible and intersecting entity which is constituted through and maintained by its interacting agents. Fields intersect – such as systems – with other fields or systems while the constant practices of agents deploy different combinations and kinds of capital safeguarding its social rationale. In doing so, dominant and dominated actors establish networks of power which define a field's code of conduct.

It is against such a backdrop that an entrepreneur has to develop and skilfully perform his or her system-related code of conduct called habitus [80]. It comprises cognitive dispositions, embodied practices and capitals with which an agent acts in a system. Hence, the habitus represents a historically constituted, experienced and constantly updated guideline for adequate social behaviour that could also be framed as a socially binding path dependence of agents in a social system. In view of entrepreneurial practices and legitimacy of the habitus – to be understood as a modifiable and non-static behavioural structure – is a mean to develop compliance with a field and its agents. This means that it provides a socially generated code of conduct that offers the opportunity of bringing something new into a system causing change in the power networks, the practices and the composition of the system. This has happened in our study area with the slow change from agriculture as a prevailing practice to generating an income from selling generated renewable electricity and renewable energy planning consultancy. A certain degree of conformity among entrepreneurial farmers deploying their social, cultural and symbolic capitals secured the habitual integrity of the social system while the start of the wind energy business resulted, as we will see in the empirical section, in a partial re-composition of the social system. How these changes could comprehensively be analysed still remains to be answered. We therefore turn now to the conceptual integration of the different but intersecting concepts outlined in the previous sections.

2.4 Integrating Concepts of Complex Social Systems, Innovation Theory and Ideas of Entrepreneurship

In the previous sections, we depicted different theoretical approaches which were conceived to provide relevant conceptual tools and points of entry for our study. We started with an outline of the basic analytical units of complex social systems theory. Here, we introduced the analytical concepts of system, agent, proximity, path dependence and emergence which are of vital importance for analysing the specific characteristics and structural elements of an entrepreneurship that led to the emergence of community-led renewable energy. The community was heuristically conceptualised as a system in which the group of entrepreneurs represents a subsystem. Different agents and their proximities constitute the subsystem generating a path dependency to be envisaged as a collectively generated liability for any kind of social action to be taken. Conceptual convergences between the notion of path dependency and the concept of habitus were detected which both contain the idea of a historically generated and socially binding way of societal conduct in a system or field.

The same also holds true for the notions of system and field: both appeared to hold strong convergences in the fact that fields and systems represent an analytical heuristic developed by the scientist picturing them as intangible entities which are constituted by and maintained through the interacting social forces and a variety of capitals of different actors or agents of the field/system. Here, further commonalities can be identified with a grassroots understanding of innovation which describes the ability of a system change based on emergence. Strongly based on its agents, their characteristics, the relationships among them and with their surrounding environment, surprising and unpredictable innovations can emerge. The notion of system, in addition, structurally converges with the aforementioned concepts and considers the social system as an important and intangible object to be analysed in the context of the diffusion of innovation. Hence, Rogers' [27] analytical categories of innovation and its characteristics, the communication channels to be understood as interactive feedback loops among agents through which information is disseminated, and the time along which innovation decisions are made, provide a schematic by which the whole process of innovation can be segmented and described. A final commonality exists in the concept of agent in system theory and actor in a Bourdieusian approach because both notions – at least in our context – conceptualise the individual as the decisive object of research. The singular concept of diverse forms of capital, however, differs from approaches in innovation theories and the study of complex social systems as it not only provides the possibility to study the different kinds of proximities among agents, but to qualitatively characterise these relations in terms of what capitals exist and are set out to introduce an innovation in the system. Our hypothesis is that proximities, capitals and path dependency in and among agents strongly interact and can help to, at least to some extent, reveal the social structures underlying and processes propelling the emergence of the community-based innovation of renewable energy generation.

3 Case Study of a Renewable Energy Transition in the Northern German Municipality of Reußenköge

3.1 Embeddedness

To empirically analyse the theoretical concepts presented before, we choose the community of Reußenköge as case study. The community represents our spatial and analytical unit to investigate the emergence of entrepreneurship by undertaking qualitative and quantitative research in the context of the energy transition. Situated on the idea of a community-based renewable energy generation and the development of community renewables as an innovation concept, renewables became a business opportunity in this municipality. We, thus, explored the factors that contributed to the emergence of renewables, and studied the development from idea to concept by tracing the distribution of the concept among members of the municipality and beyond it. Analytical focus was put on entrepreneurial agents as engines of innovation, and their transformation from agriculturalists to *energy-preneurs*, who restructured their existing businesses and founded locally based companies.

3.2   Case Study of Energy Community Reußenköge

Germany has become well known for declaring the *Energiewende* (energy transition). Since the start of the new millennium, Germany has experienced a strong diffusion of renewable-energy technologies, which started off with early development in wind turbines and later investments in solar installations, biogas plants and geothermal plants. This development was driven by strong technological progress, individuals who wanted to become energy independent and political encouragement. The Electricity Feed-In Act (Energieeinspeisegesetz) and the later introduction of the Renewable Energy Sources Act (*Erneuerbare Energien Gesetz*) established a political priority for renewable electricity and a feed-in compensation [83]. The German energy transition is characterised by actor diversity. Nevertheless, the energy transition is largely *citizen energy*. Almost 50% of the installed renewable-energy power in Germany is owned by citizens as private owners or through types of collective ownership [84]. Regionally located citizens, such as private individuals and commercial or agricultural sole traders became joint owners of wind or solar farms and undertook considerable investments in locally managed renewables [85].

Historically seen, the 'energy revolution' in Germany has begun in Northern Germany, with the first installation of a wind turbine in the Kaiser-Friedrich-Koog and early investments of citizens in individual wind turbines and soon after in collectively managed so-called *citizen wind farms (Bürgerwindparks)*. The coastal municipality of Reußenköge (Figure 2) has been chosen as a research site here because it has experienced early and continuous developments in renewable-energy technologies, and thus, represents an excellent showcase example for the processes underlying successful energy transition.

Geographically seen, Reußenköge borders along the German North Sea Coast and is characterised by a 12-km-long dike protecting the hinterland from being flooded at high tide and during storm surges. The municipality is politically independent, although it has an association of administrations with the department of Middle North Frisia. The approximately 332 inhabitants [86] live in six polders – land reclaimed from the sea and settled during the last 100 years [87]. The surrounding marsh landscape is mainly characterised by very fertile marshland resulting in extensive agricultural use.

Over the last three decades, Reußenköge developed from an average agricultural site into a so-called 'model-region' for renewable energy generation. One of

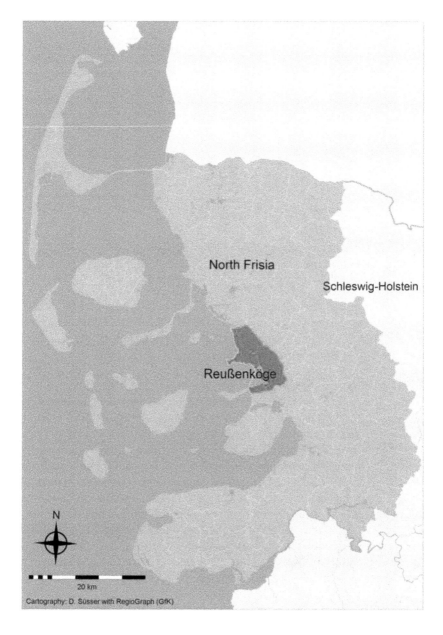

FIGURE 2: Case study area: Municipality of Reußenköge, and the district of North Frisia located in the federal state of Schleswig-Holstein

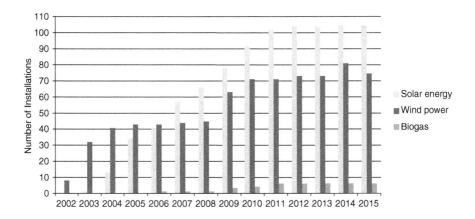

FIGURE 3: Development of community-based renewables in Reußenköge.
Data source: DGS, 2015 [89] (data status: 24.08.2015).

the first wind turbines on the German North Sea Coast was built here in 1983 [88]. It represents the starting point of a continued development of community-based renewable energy. After the beginning of the new millennium, the existing six community-owned wind farms were merged into one community wind farm while one solar farm was built and many inhabitants installed solar panels and biogas plants on their premises, barns and houses (see Figure 3).

Today, Reußenköge produces 408,204 MWh/year which is approximately 130 times more electricity than the municipality consumes [89] (see Table 1) and one of the highest rates in North Frisia. Developments of renewable-energy projects in Reußenköge and other regions of North Frisia were and are typically local, non-commercially motivated, community-led and driven by locally based enterprises. Diverse community-based citizen's energy projects that have been implemented are based on individual investments, e.g. private solar installations and biogas plants, or on collective investments in the form of private limited companies (GmbH & Co. KG.) and cooperatives (eG). All in all, Reußenköge represents a good showcase example for the successful development of renewables in North Frisia and beyond as it displays typical processes, structures and characteristics underlying most community-led renewable energy projects.

---

4   Methodological Requirements: A Mixed-Methods Approach for Analysing Complex Social Systems

To empirically investigate the structures of an emergent entrepreneurship and how it contributed to the development of community-based innovation concepts

TABLE 1: Key energy data of the community of Reußenköge. Note: data from 2015 and covers only electricity generation subsidised after EEG. The electricity demand was guessed based on the average data of the electricity demand in Germany.

Electricity demand: 2,641 MWh/year
Renewable energy production: 408,204 MWh/year
Solar electricity: 8,311 MWh/year; 105 installations, 8 MW (peak)
Wind power: 386,524 MWh/year; 75 installations; 152 MW (peak)
First wind turbine of 1983:

Biomass: 13,368 MWh/year; 8 installations; 1 MW (peak)

Data source: DGS, 2015 [89].

from the perspective of complex social systems theory, an interrelated and integrated methodological approach was applied. This approach was based on the building block of a thorough literature review and followed by a series of qualitative semi-structured interviews with a representative sample of interviewees. Then, a household survey was conducted and finally complemented by expert-interviews. The mixed-methods approach performed here consisted in getting a deep and comprehensive understanding of the social system Reußenköge and the role of entrepreneurship and entrepreneurs played in the course of the innovation process to community-based renewable energy. Consequently, our study focus was placed on the social characteristics and capitals of local entrepreneurs and their impact on triggering the process of energy transition. We therefore methodologically zoomed in on entrepreneurs as agents, the relations among them and their relations with the surrounding social system and its agents, the prevalent proximities among them and the capitals deployed in the course of the implementation process. Relations with further external systems were also taken into consideration if they emerged in the course of the empirical investigation and were of analytical value.

In detail, we started our data collection with a systematic literature review comprising policy documents, reports, the local and regional media coverage in print and online data-bases, thematically relevant websites, existing grey literature, book publications and journals devoted to the history of the municipality Reußenköge and the district of North Frisia. The discourse analytical rationale [90] applied to the written documents [91] provided the first analytical step and offered rich insight into the structural patterns of the local and regional discourses revolving around and the semantic content structuring the topic of energy transition in Reußenköge. The analysis assisted in defining and disentangling the different systems interacting in the context of energy policy on local, regional and supra-regional levels.

Then, semi-structured qualitative interviews were conducted. They form the empirical backbone of our study and were primarily used to explore the structure of people's framings and representations of social actions and entrepreneurial behaviours motivating the transition of community-based innovation in terms of renewable energy technology. Coincidentally – but interestingly though – the data generated also provided us with the personally perceived processes and their assessment of the development from the traditional business of agriculture to a mixed-business approach in renewable energy and the apparent possibility of starting new companies. A first set of interviews was conducted in spring 2014 with a representative number of inhabitants living in Reußenköge. Interview partners were found during the literature review and partially due to personal recommendation. They were selected according to their social function and position within the municipality, their profession, gender and age accurately representing the average social structure of the municipality. Interviewees were aged between 37 and 75 while eight of them were born in the municipality and most of them were local entrepreneurs in the field of agriculture and more or less strongly connected with community-based renewable energy. The professions or social roles covered by the interviewees ranged from the local council, farmers, dike masters, volunteers in local associations such as the voluntary fire-brigade or the country women to managers of community wind farms. The thematic focus during interviews was explicitly set on personal opinions trying to avoid any kind of expert view whatsoever. This enabled us to trace who in the municipality was perceived as an entrepreneur, innovator or pioneer, how these agents were connected to the emergence of wind and solar power and in what way they were contextualised in terms of their specific proximities, particular capitals and path dependency.

We started our qualitative investigation with two preparative meetings with the mayor and the local council of Reußenköge. This provided us with a contextualised field access to the municipality and allowed local support for our research endeavour. For the interviews, a semi-structured interview guide-line was developed based on five thematic strands. These consisted of questions revolving around people's place attachment in the municipality of Reußenköge and in the region of North Frisia, social life and interaction in the municipality, people's framings and experiences of climate change, personal measures taken to prevent climate change in the community and an assessment of communal adaptation and mitigation measure taken. All interviews were transcribed verbatim and structurally analysed according to the requirements as outlined in grounded theory [92,93]. The empirical work included an open and axial coding of themes emerging during the process of analysis as well as a deductive and process-related development of analytical categories from the interview data gathered. This procedure was performed to avoid any preconceptions and problems of a vicious circle. Initially, one interview was co-analysed and a grounded coding was performed based on the interpretive understanding of the first and third authors of this paper working independently on the interview. This approach was conceived as productive and chronologically applied to the following 14 interviews. In the course of the analysis, all categories were collaboratively elaborated, refined and – if necessary – transferred into new or other categories. This provided a structural and content-oriented schematic of the discourses and perceptions revolving around climate change, adaptation and mitigation measures and the implementation of renewable energy. Based on this background, proximities, capitals and path dependencies of agents were separately examined in a second analysis with the help of an in-depth reading of different categories and a cooperative step-by-step analysis. For the coding and categorisation of the qualitative interviews, the analysis software MAXQDA (1989–2015) was used [94] while the second round of analysis was performed in the course of the composition of this book chapter.

Following the first phase of qualitative data gathering, a standardised household survey was conducted in August 2014 in Reußenköge with the aim to get a representative overview over the system and its components. The survey was hence distributed with the intention to receive community-wide information about inhabitant's attitudes, values, personal experiences and behaviour concerning climate change and especially renewable energy technologies. The framework was developed against the conceptual background and results taken from the qualitative analysis and especially addressed decision-making factors underlying the implementation of renewable energy technologies, innovation characteristics and the role of entrepreneurship. The questionnaire incorporated closed and open questions focussing on the basic parameters of what, why, how and when. Thematically, queries were related to measures to counteract climate change and the development of renewables in the municipality. The basic rationale of the questionnaire consisted in the attempt to reveal past actions and motivational factors for the past adoption or rejection of wind and solar energy which strongly contrasts with other studies predominantly addressing future issues, planned behaviours or the general willingness to do something [e.g., 14,17,95]. At the end of each survey, each participant was given the possibility to add additional points of interest not covered.

Generally speaking, the survey was designed as a self-completion survey personally distributed to the 110 households in Reußenköge. The person in each household with the soonest birthday was asked to fill in the questionnaire in order to gain a random participation along gender and age while a time of two weeks was given to return it. Questionnaires could either be returned by (i) placing it under the doormat or leave it on the front door knob in a bag, (ii) put it in a closed envelope and put it in the post box of the mayor or (iii) send it via mail to the first author's work address. On a fixed date after two weeks, all questionnaires were personally collected during another research visit in the region. As a result, 51 completed questionnaires were returned which equals a return rate of 46%. A first analysis showed that with 31 males and 20 females participated in the survey (see Table 2). Furthermore, the sample revealed the average age of the majority of respondents as lying between 45 and 65. For the main number of respondents, Reußenköge was their first place of residence while almost all participants were homeowners and about half of them also owned agricultural land.

To compare, substantiate and systematically extend the findings of the first two rounds of data gathering, a second round of semi-structured qualitative interviews – in this case expert interviews [96,97] – were undertaken in spring 2015. Here, emphasis was put on external developments and emergent structures which led to interviewing eight local politicians in six other energy communities in North

TABLE 2: Demographic statistic of the household survey, N=51, Reußenköge, 2014

	Number	**%**
Gender		
Female	20	39
Male	31	62
Age		
Under 25 (1990)	1	2
25–35 (1980–1989)	5	10
35–45 (1970–1979)	3	6
45–55 (1960–1969)	13	25
55–65 (1950–1959)	10	20
65+ (1949)	17	33
n/a	2	4
Housing arrangement		
Tenant	5	10
Owner	45	88
n/a	1	2
Owner agricultural land	25	49
Owner further buildings	4	8
Resident		
Main	49	96
Secondary	2	4
Building feature		
Under monument		
Protection	7	14

Frisia. Interview partners can be subdivided into two local entrepreneurs of renewable-energy companies being members of and active in a political party, two mayors who had to face local resistance during the implementation of community projects, a nature conservationist and three politicians from the local and the regional government. To better understand the motives and impacts of community renewable energy, the semi-structured interview guide mainly contained questions on local activities to cope with climate change and an assessment of the (non)development of renewables in each municipality and the federal state of Schleswig-Holstein. All expert interviews conducted were transcribed verbatim in order to familiarise the analysts with the content, to help them to develop adequate analytical categories and to compare analytical themes between the two sets of interviews [98]. The data analysis was performed by making use of the categories developed within the first set of interviews, but with an open eye on newly emerging categories. Under chronological analysis of all expert interviews, the overall categories of both data sets were further elaborated, extended and integrated. This procedure provided results in terms of interactions between the communities and our study area Reußenköge.

All in all, the mixed methods approach chosen here enabled us to generate conceptually interrelated and mutually enhancing sets of data to be analysed from the perspective of complex social systems theory. The data sets complement each other and helped to develop a structured perspective on the different systems inherent in and surrounding Reußenköge whilst they also provided important data about entrepreneurship and the entrepreneurs within the municipality itself. Most valuable are both sets of semi-structured qualitative interviews which helped us to explicitly tackle the social framing of the constitutive elements such as the entrepreneurial agents, their different proximities in the municipality and beyond, the capitals deployed in the innovation process and prevailing path dependencies. All these data and their analysis assist in disclosing the main characteristics of an entrepreneurship boosting community-owned wind power in Reußenköge. They, moreover, hold the potential to empirically explain why a development such as community-owned renewable energy emerged and finally materialised in terms of wind turbines, solar installations and biogas plants.

---

5 Empirical Findings: Grassroots Innovation and Energy-Preneurs for a Community-Based Energy Transition

The energy transition of the electricity sector in Germany originated – to a large extend – in local places, communities and rural areas. Different factors and processes led to such a development. We investigated how technological innovations of renewable energy technologies were discovered by individuals within the community, transformed into social innovation concepts, utilised and adopted by individuals within the community, diffused within the community and resulted in local businesses. To better understand the emergence of the community-based innovation concepts and the connected entrepreneurship in renewable energy technologies in Reußenköge, we investigated how renewable energy innovations were diffused among the community system and its agents over time. For this to be done, we analysed the characteristics of local agents and the relations and interactions among them, while accounting also for the influences of surrounding system environment as it has already been indicated. The model of an energy community system, including the innovative subsystem of entrepreneurs in Reußenköge, is illustrated in Figure 4. This figure serves here as a visualisation of our study framework.

We empirically analyse the role of proximities, capitals, path dependency and social interactions underlying the diffusion process and resulting in an

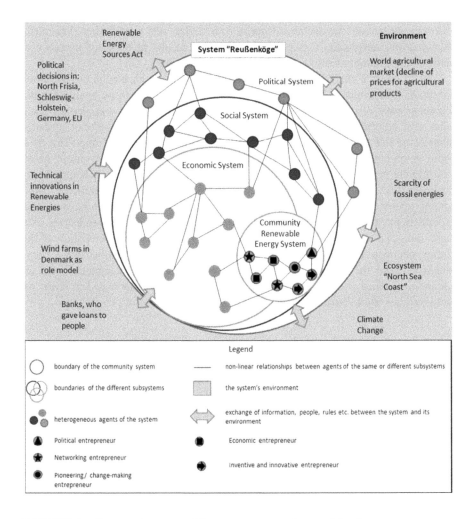

FIGURE 4: Community renewable energy as complex social sub-system

entrepreneurship propelling community-based renewables. The statements by the interviewees are citied as follows: region (IR=Reußenköge; IN=other North Frisian municipality), interviewee number (#X) and line (XX-XX).

5.1   Origin of Grassroots-Based, Social Innovation

Reußenköge is a coastal municipality, which was and still is characterised by the common history of land reclamation, dike building, the businesses of agriculture and tourism. Both dike building and agriculture were found to be deeply engrained historical activities, involving historically grown interactions between the inhabitants, which also mattered for the development of renewables. Hence, past experiences with coastal protection provide the roots of social interactions and adaptability. People framed the claiming of land, colonising of polders and past handling of natural hazards as innovative and adaptive, compared it to today's deployment of renewables. Interviewees developed a historical bond between the innovative energy of past generations who collaboratively reclaimed and settled land and who implement renewable energy technologies today:

> We have been always pioneers/innovators for something new. If you build a dike, you are a pioneer.
>
> (IR_#12:75–76)

This quote underlines the adaptive capacity of the local population. Adaptive implicates that people are able to observe the environment, to respond efficiently to natural hazards and to make long-term plans for coastal protection under rising sea levels, but are also able to build a strategy for the local management of wind energy. This adaptive capacity is based on the local social and cultural capital grounded in collective experiences and actions characterising the state of the art of the system of Reußenköge.

Considering the origin of community-based renewables, local farmers and other locally-based entrepreneurs were the first becoming interested in wind turbines. Interviewees framed the critical situation in agriculture that you could not earn much money with it anymore and thus, critically to secure the subsistence. This slowly emerging shock for the long-established path dependency of system was, however, partly driven by external factors: the changes in German agricultural policy and a local look to Denmark, where interviewees discovered wind turbines on farms and brought them in their backyard:

> But the origin of wind energy in Reußenköge was that one farmer implemented the first wind turbine in 1983. That was a 65 kW-mill, Vestas from Denmark. [...] And he was driving through Denmark and saw such a mill and thought that's also something for me.
>
> (IR_#1:201–205)

Denmark thus functioned as role model in the early 1980s. One interviewee, however, mentioned that '*you could [however] not earn money* [with wind energy] *at that time*' (IR_#15:270–271). This fact changed only in 1991 with the introduction of the Electricity Feed-In Act (Energieeinspeisegesetz). The Feed-In Act and the later Renewable Energy Sources Act (*Erneuerbare Energien Gesetz*) changed existing path-dependencies by introducing economic capital. It offered the possibility for individuals to benefit from the feed-in compensation through the production of renewable electricity [83,99], and thus started a broad funding of renewables. Interviewees mentioned that the wind energy movement in the community started in the early 1990s:

> 93 started the movement in the community that everybody wanted to have a windmill. By that time, the local council luckily said now we are ordering that and now we do it only together. Nobody can do anymore alone. Till that date, we got 7 or 8 mills in the backyards of farmers – like as I had one. [...] And then there were so many in planning that we would have got uncontrolled growth. And that was the birth of the community wind farm movement in Reußenköge.
>
> (IR_#8:51–57)

As nicely reflected in this quote, the grassroots-based innovation concept for a local renewable energy generation by, in and for local citizens was based on the early development of individual wind turbines on the land of farmers. This process exemplifies that local people overcame their historically established and engrained path dependency in the business of agriculture through the interest in wind turbines and, potentially, emerging economic advantages. The openness for change was based on a shift in the system driven by the interaction of social, cultural and economic capitals, and consequently supported by the local council, the mayor and local banks, who gave loans to the people for the investment in wind mills:

> And in the end, all the banks have supported it, 'yes we do that'. I know some from the neighbourhood – that is not a joke now – they went to their house bank and said: 'I got a leather jacket and outside is parking my car. That's all what I got. But I want to have a windmill'. [...] So for sure you have to mention the banks in Bredstedt, surely also the mayors and the local council in that relation.
>
> (IR_#4:193–200)

The interviewee here mentions the support for investments in renewables outside and inside the community, which holds true until today. As highlighted by most interviewees, the concept of community renewable energy is based on active participation, collective ownership and shared benefits (IR_#8:63–65). Due to the new nature of this community-led development process, the concept can be conceived as a social innovation, driven by individual farmers – abandoning an established path dependency and developing a new one – and different kinds of capitals for economic and intangible collective investments in wind energy.

5.2 Entrepreneurs for Renewables

To get a better understanding about the contextual factors influencing the emergence and diffusion of community renewables, the interviews have been analysed with regard to statements about the role and characteristics of entrepreneurs prompting community-based energy transition. Local entrepreneurs are used as analytical units here who are conceived to conceptually personify and reflect the characteristics of the local entrepreneurship in community renewables. Our findings indicate that local entrepreneurs who are referred to as pioneers and innovators by the interviewees actively contributed to the transition towards community renewable energy in Reußenköge. All interviewees directly or indirectly stated important characteristics of energy-preneurs, which are not mutually exclusive, but may emerge in a combined fashion in one person and shape local entrepreneurship. These characteristics materialise in eight analytical categories, which define energy-preneurs and characteristics of the local entrepreneurship: grounded, collaborative, innovative, change making, economic, communicating, networking and political.

First, the interview results indicate a considerable importance of entrepreneurship as being locally grounded. 'Grounded entrepreneurship' is conceived as rooted in agriculture and in the local place as an essential ingredient for implementing community renewables because they share the same socio-historical context and experience:

> And I do have the advantage that I am a farmer, do have a farm here and do still agriculture. And I am grounded, so to speak. I don't reside somewhere in the city.
>
> (IR_#8:94–96)

The shared cultural and social capital of all people involved is mainly based on the geographical, social and cognitive proximity and was found to play a vital and integrating role in generating social credibility and trust in relation to the implementation of community-based renewables.

Furthermore, our research indicates that the common grounding of inhabitants with its inherent code of contact or habitus, proximities and capitals results in a collaborative thinking and positive community view which is represented by 'collaborative entrepreneurs'. Our results exhibit that community renewable energy, as an innovative concept for local energy transition, emerged basically as a collective and socially integrative effort. One interviewee emphasised the importance of the collaborative – the 'We' – by indicating, *'We are proud here in the North, that we are the pioneers. We have built the first community wind farms here*' (IR_#8:303–305). For every wind farm in Reußenköge, the community opened up the possibility to participate with '*equal right, equal rents [...], equal interests of shareholders*' (IR_#8:63–65). This integrative and collaborative procedure of community renewables represents a social and not a legal 'consensus' informally accepted all over the municipality (IR_#10:263–264). The requirement of the social willingness and legitimacy speaks for a high social and cultural capital structuring the system as a whole: collective engagement and individual participation are only possible in the context of this prerequisite and consequently bear a considerable impact on the acceptance of renewable energy technologies because people develop social bonds via the technology and share the common purpose of renewable energy generation. Thus, people create social and cognitive proximities to other members of community renewables as well as to the technology itself. In addition, an integrative thinking of entrepreneurs characterised by a long-term and municipality perspective emerges when it comes to revenues of renewable energy technologies. Interviewees highly value concepts of how locally generated profits were reinvested in the infrastructure of the municipality creating further social and cultural capital and enabling social and cognitive proximity. The creation of local value and the investment of economic capital in terms of money are conceived as important to provide a sustainable livelihood for inhabitants and the municipality as a whole. What became apparent was that community collaboration appeared to be important, but it required locally emplaced entrepreneurs who discover and socially exploit proximities and capitals.

Local energy transition in Reußenköge appeared to be characterised by an 'inventive and innovative entrepreneurship' that started with renewable energy technologies from an innovative and visionary point of view, continued with 'change making entrepreneurs' who distribute products and concepts as well as 'economic entrepreneurs' who transformed their existing business or even started a new business. Inventors were the first who identified and explored new opportunities inherent in renewable energy technologies, partially motivated by a pending change in path dependency due to the critical situation in agriculture. These agents were locally framed as individualists who started with the vision to become energy independent taking a high financial risk. While looking for new independence, they stepped away from the 'old path'. Hence, their innovativeness is one basic characteristic of their entrepreneurship based on their willingness to take risks and to create new economic, social and cultural capital also affecting social and cognitive proximities. A strong character and devotion to their project seems to be important in order to deal with refusal, problems and, sometimes, to fight for their visions to become real. However, our results also indicate that an 'inventive and innovative entrepreneur' is characterised by his or her foresight of local challenges and the anticipation of technical needs which he or she can turn into cultural capital. Interviewees stated an ongoing search, hunt or even habitus for new innovations by local entrepreneurs. Moreover, entrepreneurs actively contribute to the diffusion of renewable energy technologies. They possess a self-confidence based on social and cultural capital that can make a change happen, develop ideas and push projects actively forward. In this context, to counteract climate change represents an important, but not the utmost motivation. One interviewee mentioned moral and ideological aspects by recounting '*[that] several followed, who did that seriously for ideological reasons*' (IR_#15:270–271). Besides the individualistic perspective and innovativeness of entrepreneurs, a general openness for change in the municipality itself was imperative for enabling technological and social change. This is mirrored in the quote of one interviewee, who said that individuals, but also the municipality of Reußenköge as a whole, is '*able to think outside the box*' (IR_#3:20). This implies that the scope of the community can be conceived as an open system beyond its own place because it is based on high social capital inherent in it. Subsequently, community-owned renewables developed into an innovative and applicable concept that also developed into local renewable energy companies. Renewable energy consulting and planning companies were founded by 'change-making entrepreneurs', who '*deal with, belief in and promote renewable energies*' (IR_#4:136–137). Moreover, local people made use of incentives for investments in wind, photovoltaic and biogas plants, providing an important economic income to private households and farms. One interview expressed this aspect:

> And the wind energy has a large significance; economically for many companies. There are many companies, who can only exist because of the wind energy.
>
> (IR_#3:207–209)

The entrepreneurial thinking in the municipality was complemented by local people's willingness to socially and economically invest in local companies, to reinvest in them and the municipality. This led to the enrichment of the economic and social capital, on the one hand, and developed into social and cognitive proximities the community is nowadays based on, on the other hand. Considering the economic benefits for many rural municipalities, one interviewee said,

> [they] have no money, and you can see that they try to throw the sheet anchor by building a community wind farm. Because a community wind farm is sustainable, also the only demonstrable instrument, which can diminish the threat to the financial future, because [the municipality] gets the trade tax and because the citizens get their payouts, and because the farmers get their rent.
>
> (IN_#5:107–112)

Thus, many municipalities perceive renewables as the future creating social and economic capitals. Activities of 'economic entrepreneurship' have added local economic values, such as new jobs and communal infrastructures, while social capital in terms of fairness and respect have proven to be important when it comes to how the municipality deals with wind energy. This created an atmosphere of trust that enabled an economic management without fear of financial inequality and socially envy. One interviewee summarised the local benefits by saying that beyond the civic participation, '*main advantages of renewables are a decentralised energy supply, through decentralised structures [...] where also added values stay decentralised*' (IR_#15:380–381). Thus, 'decentralisation' embodies physical as well as socioeconomic structures. The benefits of such concepts applied by the companies in Reußenköge raised awareness also in other regions, referring to an openness of systems and system interaction. Local companies consequently 'export' the concept of community renewables as service to other areas in the world and actively help with socially and financially implementing projects. It thus becomes apparent that the concept of a change-making and economically thinking entrepreneurship is an export success that generates social, cultural and economic capital.

In order to enable and maintain community renewables, communication both inside the municipally and outside the municipality (the system) was revealed as important. We found a strong interpersonal exchange about different topics such as agriculture and renewable energy. Nevertheless, information provision and education were conceived as important requirements for people's understandings for the necessity of renewable energy technologies and for creating acceptance. 'Communicative entrepreneurship' was perceived as the ability and responsibility to inform about the importance of renewables for mitigating climate change and to be clear about local potentials of different renewable energy technologies. One interviewee underlined the importance of transparency and the communication of project plans for the creation of trust and acceptance:

> Yes, that it is transparent and understandable, what we want, and no mistrust arises. And this works quite well. And sometimes there are countering voices or other opinions, but you have to talk about it.
>
> (IR_#8:148–150)

The interview results furthermore reveal that local entrepreneurs offer community information events in their enterprises for providing information about current developments of renewable energy technologies and to receive opinions about possible plans. For example, during the interview phase, one interviewee informed us about the idea of wind farm owners to merge the six community wind farms into one big wind farm. This idea was taken into consideration to increase social cohesion between the wind farm owners and to remove differences in the revenues of the wind farms, which finally may have led into social envy (IR_#4). In the end, many rounds of discussion and information events resulted in a positive voting for merging the wind farms [100]. This activity brought not only the wind farms symbolically closer together, but it also represents the proximity generated between the wind park owners. In addition to the internal communication, networking as one element of social capital can be seen as an important entrepreneurial characteristic for exchange and the creation of new ideas. For example, one interviewee outlined that interns bring in outside experiences and can instigate the allocation or re-arrangement of capitals that positively challenge the path dependency of existing business structures and transform society. Through social networks in other regions, entrepreneurs were able to perceive the community from outside, to get '*another view on the municipality than before*' (IR_#15:56–57) and to develop new ideas. Moreover, the 'networking entrepreneur' was characterised by his involvement in associations in order '*to place this comprehensive theme [of renewables] and to provide solutions*' (IR_#15:298–299) to local challenges in community and business contexts. This engagement and the social proximity with agents in other systems and in the own system proved to be of direct relevance for the political involvement of entrepreneurs as they could considerably contribute to the development of administrative and policy structures. Hence, entrepreneurs could also be identified as political actors – holding a 'political entrepreneurship' – who create local politics and advise policy on a regional and national level. First, findings in the interviews show the importance of local politics for the development of community-based renewable energy. Looking back to the start of community-owned wind farms, the local council and the mayor have been found to be essential for planning the first wind farm. They dealt with procedures slightly challenging the path dependency by changing land development plans, establishing development plans and adopting a collective approach. In brief, entrepreneurs were found to play an important role in advising local councils, if they were not even part of the council. Beyond the local level, grassroots innovations required reliable energy governance that is based on 'pulling' incentives. In order to be perceived, local farmers transformed to political actors, as one interviewee described:

> By now, the farmer has become a political representative, so to speak. Nobody who is interfering in politics, but a consultant, who is going to the federal association of wind energy (BWE) and also consults politics, yes.
>
> (IR_#3:207–209)

We, furthermore, found that 'political entrepreneurs' also represent the community externally and pursue lobbyism in order to create awareness for local benefits and create for support of community renewable energy projects. The results indicate the importance of supportive governance and reliable foundation of investments but also indicate that proximities and different kinds of social and cultural capital are basic ingredients for implementing renewable energy technologies. Emerging discussions about a revision of the German Renewable Energy Act of July 2014 have already yielded impacts on the fear of people about changing regulations and possible impacts on future financing of larger renewable-energy projects: to divert economic capital might bear an impact on other forms of capital and proximities.

In view of the presented eight entrepreneurial characteristics, the role of interactions between the people became already apparent. Thus, the next section is devoted to the role of the social momentum for driving the development of community renewable energy.

5.3   Social Interactions Driving Community Renewables

The interviewees stated citizen participation in the development as the core of the concept of community renewables. With support by the local council, citizens sat together and planned the first community-owned wind farm. The inhabitants of Reußenköge conceived it extremely important that the implementation and ownership of renewables was and still remains in the hands of local people and their municipality. This common interest in community-owned wind farms formed a shared meaning of place, strongly connected to the idea of it as a source for renewable-energy generation, collective action, social proximity, shared social capital and renewables-connected identity:

> But we have many common interests and this is bonding, too. For example the interest in operating collectively renewable energy in form of wind farms for more than 20 years.
>
> (IR_#7:35–36)

The collective planning and implementation of wind turbines was even found to lead to a dispersed and commonly shared 'entrepreneurial spirit' that connects local people and provides social cohesion. Given the importance of the social dimension of the development processed, we investigated in more detail the importance of social interactions on the individual adoption behaviour. Interviewees and the household survey revealed the importance of direct communication and social norms.

To start with, different occasions for face-to-face communication within the community have been found to be important for the adoption of renewables. The interviewees mentioned direct communication to inform other community members as relevant. The survey results underline the importance of direct communication as a source of information on renewables. Personal communication with other inhabitants was perceived as 'very important' or 'rather important' by 40% for solar and 74% for wind energy. The interviews exhibit a high level of social proximity between the people within the whole municipality. However, the communication was higher among the people living in the same polder, often equivalent to the streets. The so-called opinion leaders were the people who 'lead in influencing others' opinions' by providing information and advice [27, page 300]. Almost half of the households (11 for solar and 8 for wind energy) stated to sought personal advice either for solar panels or for wind turbines. Regarding solar panels, approximately 52% of the households, who adopted a solar panel, also gave advice to others, but only about 22% stated clearly giving advice again. In the case of wind energy, approximately 73% of the households stated that they gave advice for the investment in a community wind farm, while an even a higher number (about 84%) would give advice again. Moreover, 74% of the households stated information events as very important or rather important for receiving information about wind energy in municipality. Even in the case of solar energy, the information event was perceived as important by 30% of the households. The interviews underlined the importance of community meetings to get informed about developments and participation opportunities in the community.

Moreover, social norms are conceived as important arrangements of tolerable behaviour and serve as a habitus for individual behaviour [27]. The interviews exhibit the importance of the community of common interest as motivation to invest in order to be part of it. Also the survey results indicate the importance of social pressure for household behaviour (compare Figure 5). Observations of developments in the community were seen as very important or rather important information sources for 36% of the households, in the case of solar panels, and 70% of the households, in the case of wind turbines. Furthermore, people were asked whether their investments were motivated by the observation of others, referred to the acceptance of social norms. About 40% and 48% of the households 'totally' or 'rather' agreed in the case of solar panels and wind turbines, respectively, which indicates that a social path dependency is conceived as important.

The importance of social interactions did, however, not end with the boundary of the community system. The inhabitants of Reußenköge perceived themselves as a model community which could offer advice to other municipal systems, too.

> And so it always goes further on. We have implemented some projects in France. Tomorrow we go to Ireland. The farmers were here already. Those are farmers too. The chemistry works and we want to operate it together.
>
> (IR_#8:110–113)

The interest in the concept of community renewables by other communities showed to the people '*that [they] hit overall the bull's eye with the concept of citizen's participation*' (IN_#8:337–338). Nowadays, locally grounded planning companies share their expertise and offer the implementation of the existing concepts in other regions.

5.4   Diffusion Patterns of Community Renewables

Based on the importance of social interaction for driving the adoption, we considered more closely the individual adoption and societal diffusion of wind turbines and solar panels in Reußenköge. The interviewees underlined the importance of so-called pioneers and innovators of the community-based electricity generation, while others adopted renewables later on or never. One local expert in North Frisia stated in an interview that about one-third of the people support renewables, another third follow current trends, while one-third will never participate. In the case-study of Reußenköge, the survey results have also been analysed in respect to different household types and were divided based on the adoption year and attitudes regarding renewables. A relatively low number of innovators (# of 8) and opponents (# of 3) were found, while the majority could be categorised as supporters (# of 17) and followers (# of 22). The survey represents however only a sample of 50 households, and the grouping was done indicative.

(a)

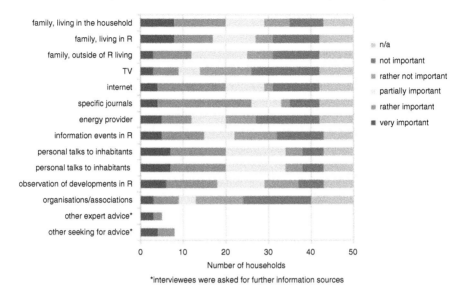

FIGURE 5: Importance of information sources for the decision about the adoption or rejection of renewables; a) for solar panels and b) for wind turbines. Household survey results in Reußenköge (N=50)

(b)

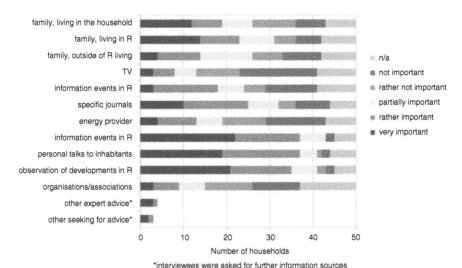

For wind turbines, we found that the majority of the households adopted wind turbines by becoming part of a community wind farm:

> In the first group we were 28 [owners] and in the last 238 [owners] or something like that.
>
> (IR_#8:60–61)

There are 101 partners/owners in the 'Bürgerwindpark Reußenköge GmbH und Co. KG' [101] of the 120 households in the municipality. It indicates that about 84% of the households invested in a wind turbine. One interviewee stated that *'[t]here are a few, which are not involved, and although they had the possibility'* (IR_#9:187–188). Regarding the possible participation phases, the findings reveal six 'waves' of participation in community wind: *'And at the end of the day, we have six community wind farms. 6 participation rounds so to say'* (IR_#8:59–60). These 'waves' of adoption, however, extend over several calendar years (Figure 6). In 2016, there were over 80 wind turbines in Reußenköge [100]. A second phase of repowering is currently planned until 2020 [102].

For solar panels, slightly less than half of the households adopted them. The survey revealed that 45% of the households, who did not state to live in a house under monumental protection, adopted solar panels. According to the

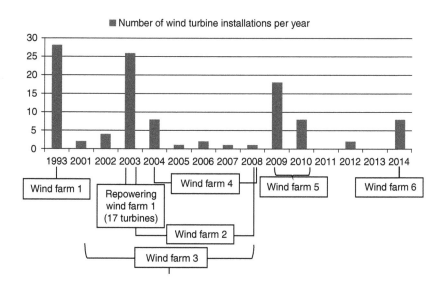

FIGURE 6: Diffusion of wind turbine installations in Reußenköge based on founded operating companies of wind farms (wind farms 1–6), based on the interviews (IR) and data from DGS, 2015 [103] (data status 24.08.2015). Note: 1993 is the year where the wind farm was connected to the grid.

statistical data by the DGS [103], 50 of the 120 households adopted solar panels. This equals to 42% of the households. Interviewees stated that solar panel adoption rates rapidly increased: '*But then the spark jumped over and all solarised their roofs*' (IR_#15:260). The statistical data by the DGS [103] show high adoption rates in 2004 and 2005 and a steady increase from 2006 until 2011 (Figure 7).

The patterns of the diffusion of wind turbines and solar panels reveal lower adoption rates at the beginning, a quick distribution after the change to the new millennium and a satisfaction later on. In terms of community wind farms, high adoption rates could be found due to the innovative concept of collective investment in wind energy, in different open participation rounds. As a result, more and more members of the community decided over the years to participate, leading almost to an exploitation of suitable wind sites. In the upcoming years, repowering – the change of older wind turbines with less capacity to new, high-capacity wind turbines – will play a higher role. Considering solar panels, the adoption rates were low at the beginning and increased rapidly later on. Many houses – which are not under monumental protection – have solar panels today. Under the currently decreasing subsidy rates for photovoltaic technologies, a full exploitation of the remaining rooftop is not to be expected.

5.5   From Entrepreneurial Spirit to Companies in Reußenköge

The interviews revealed a shared and dispersed 'entrepreneurial spirit' in Reußenköge, which connects local people. This mentality is characterised by a collectively shared mind-set and habitus that people in Reußenköge 'still have visions' (IR_#13:176) and are, thus, willing to contribute to the innovative

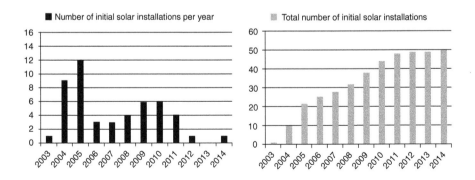

FIGURE 7: Diffusion of initial solar installations in Reußenköge; secondary installations, etc. in the same household are not illustrated: initial installations per year (left), total installed number (right), based on the data from DGS, 2015 [103], initial installation based on the street names (data status 24.08.2015)

character of the place they feel attached to. This entrepreneurial spirit transformed – based on several proximities and deploying different capitals – into the
foundation of the community wind farm Reußenköge, the foundation of two new
renewable energy development companies, and the collaborative and socially
integrative realignment of many existing companies.

The community wind farm of Reußenköge (Bürgerwindpark Reußenköge GmbH
& Co. KG) is a private limited company. As a result of a positive voting by the wind
farm owners, there was a fusion of six independent wind farm to one big wind farm in
2015, which consists at the moment of about 80 turbines [100]. The project planning
was implemented by the socially and geographically proximal company *Dirkshof*,
while the private limited company is the operator. About 90 of the local citizens
are member of the community wind farm or operator of their own wind farm, which
indicates that the technology holds a socially integrating force [102]. One interviewee
in Reußenköge highlighted the value of the wind farm by saying '*that the whole
municipality has one big company [of community wind farms] in the end*'
(IR_#12:21). This statement highlights the organisational and social proximity which
is created between the people through the collectedly led and owned wind turbines.
Considering the economic effects, all citizens who invested collectively in wind turbines
or individually in other renewables, such as photovoltaic and biogas, were able to
increase their income. Sixty-one percent of the surveyed households in Reußenköge
'strongly' agreed that they benefit personally from wind energy, while 67% 'strongly'
agreed that wind energy is an important source of income. Furthermore, almost 60% of
the surveyed households 'strongly' agreed that wind energy has a community benefit
and thus generates social capital. Thus, one interviewee summarised: '*And the idea of
community wind farms is super. It implies that, for example, all members of the
municipality profit from the windmills, and not individuals*' (IR_#1:301–303). This fact
highlights the social and economic capital inherent in community wind farms.

Beyond these aspects, two important companies in the business of renewable
energy are to be highlighted in Reußenköge: the *Dirkshof* and *GP Joule*. The
Dirkshof is an expert company for wind energy since 1989 and counts to the
vanguard of the community wind farm movement. Nowadays, the company
counts to one of the most important contractors in the wind business. '*The roots
of the engagement in natural energy-sourcing lies, since the year one, in the
ecological agriculture*', states the company on its website and emphasises its
local anchoring [100]. Together with the Fraunhofer Institute for High Frequency
Physics and Radar Techniques, the Dirkshof develops a concept for a modern
obstruction light, needed for windmills higher than 100 meters. The Parasol
Radar System offers an adequate and environmentally friendly alternative to the
red blink light. After the successful development and high investment costs, the
serial production is about to start [100]. The related company is the PARASOL
GmbH & Co. KG, also based in Reußenköge. GP Joule is another company
based in Reußenköge, which understands itself as partner for all areas of renewables. '*Origin, authenticity, trust, joie de vivre, fair play, quality, success and
innovation*' are the core values shaping the company, according to its philosophy
stated at the companies' website [104]. GP Joule has nowadays five locations in

Germany and four in North America. The GP Joule group includes moreover the miniJoule solar plants and devices to-go, and, H-Tech Systems for research in the area of renewable energy, e.g. solar storage, GP Joule is about to implement the biggest pilot project for green hydrogen mobility in Germany [104]. The two companies provide an example of the success of community-based companies and the continued energy to invent new solutions.

This development of local renewable energy companies is not exclusive for Reußenköge. Also, in other municipalities, companies have been founded often with a specific economic focus. Interestingly, many entrepreneurs described that they consciously decided to settle their company in a local municipality: *'because [they] want to show that you can also provide attractive and interesting jobs away from cities'* (IN_#8:111–113). Local employment opportunities have been assessed as highly relevant for rural areas with low prospects:

> We always talk about resources and about income and about creating awareness, and I think it comes to show that alone the wind branch in Germany [...] has now created about 140.000 jobs.
>
> (IN_#5:706–709)

Those people are employed in project development, service, energy logistics, system solutions and so on. As exemplary demonstrated in North Frisia, community renewables are a door opener for new companies in the renewable-energy business and promote the realignment of existing companies that result in new communal income opportunities and new local employment opportunities. It is therefore not surprising that the implementation of the concept of community renewables, which *'is strongly driven by [...] local companies, who work on that and plan it [and]] also employ many'* (IR_#13:173–174), has been assessed as highly beneficial for municipalities and other regions.

---

6   Discussion

Community renewable energy arose from entrepreneurial spirit of individuals, was shaped by different capitals and proximities between local individuals, and developed into grassroots-based innovation concepts that have led to the active participation of many citizens in Reußenköge and to the generation opportunities beyond the community.

We depicted different theoretical approaches which provided relevant conceptual tools for our study. Complex system theory served as basis to structure and to define the boundaries of our system under consideration [30]. Here, we introduced the analytical concepts of system, agent, proximity, path dependency and emergence which are of vital importance for analysing the specific characteristics and structural elements of an entrepreneurship that led to the emerging innovation of community renewables. The community was heuristically conceptualised as a system in which the group of energy-preneurs represents a subsystem. Different agents and their respective relations described by different forms of proximities and capitals constitute the subsystem generating a path dependency to be envisaged as a collectively generated liability for any kind of social action to be taken. The concept of different forms of capital, furthermore, offered the possibility not only to study the different kinds of proximities among agents, but also to qualitatively characterise these relations in terms of what capitals exist and are set out to introduce an innovation in the system. Conceptual convergences between the notion of path dependency and the concept of habitus were detected, both containing the idea of a historically generated and socially binding way of societal conduct in a system.

The same also holds true for the notions of system and field: both appeared to hold strong convergence in the fact that fields and systems represent an analytical heuristic developed by the scientist picturing them as intangible entities which are constituted by and maintained through the interacting capitals and proximities of different actors or agents of the field/system. Here, further commonalities can be identified with a grassroots understanding of innovation. The notion of system structurally converges with the aforementioned concepts and considers the social system as an important object to be analysed in the context of the diffusion of innovation. Moreover, Rogers' [27] analytical categories of innovation and its characteristics, the communication channels through which information is disseminated and the time along which innovation decisions are made provide a good guideline to structure and describe innovation processes. The approach of complex social systems helped us to disentangle and trace subliminal characteristics of entrepreneurship nestling in entrepreneurs and innovation from a sociological point of view. Subsequently, we empirically tested our theoretical approach in the case study of Reußenköge.

Empirically, we analysed the different factors and processes that led to the emergence of community renewable energy. With the case study of Reußenköge, we were able to provide in-depth evidence about the relevance of the social setting for enabling grassroots innovation and the multifaceted social factors underpinning local entrepreneurship. We emphasised the characteristics of the individual agents and their social interactions, while we found also indications for the influence of interactions between different subsystems and of external factors (see Figure 4). Those system elements such as capitals, proximities, path dependency and emergence are the core of complexity theory. Thus, complexity theory helped us to structurally disentangle and conceptually classify the findings from the empirical study. Nevertheless, our empirical study was not conceptualised to implement a holistic systems analysis. Our empirical study focused on local citizens, their characteristics and the interaction among them that finally led to a successful and sustainable renewable-energy transition. We, furthermore, applied qualitative and quantitative methods to investigate the community of Reußenköge with the aim to get a detailed description of the system structures and processes, on the one hand, and to get a higher sample with statistically comparable data, on the other hand. This approach proved to be suitable for understanding the importance of agents, social interactions and the community environment for the emergence of community renewable energy (Chapter 5). Nevertheless, further studies could take a more structured focus by concentrating just on one analytical category and its interaction with different subsystems and the external factors driving development.

Our empirical findings most importantly revealed the relevance of the socio-cultural embeddedness of local agents in terms of social, geographical and cognitive proximities and the relevance of social and cultural capital. Furthermore, we could demonstrate the relevance of agents acting in the community, of interactions between community agents and of external factors influencing the development of community renewables in Reußenköge. The importance and characteristics of those three main factors are discussed in more detail.

6.1   Community Renewables Need Diverse, Strong Local Entrepreneurs and Leaders

The development of renewables in Reußenköge is found to be facilitated by the support of local entrepreneurs and the local political authorities. The entrepreneurship can be differentiated in our eight entrepreneur categories: grounded, collaborative, inventive and innovative, change making, economic, communicating, networking and political aspects. Those diverse characteristics of local entrepreneurship and their inherent capitals and proximities appeared to be relevant for the creation of trust and support for community renewable energy. In contrast to studies by Hayward et al. [105] and Rogers [106], our findings reveal the importance of grounded and locally attached project leaders and the direct management by community members. While sustainable energy studies highlight the challenge of responsibility and leadership in project development [107, page 14], in our study, a few people took action and promoted the implementation of renewables by deploying different sorts of capitals, and proximities challenging the established path dependency or habitus. Entrepreneurship became even a spirit and became a local mentality based on a past path dependency. The findings of this research furthermore indicate that these local entrepreneurs might be able and willing to support community renewables in other regions where local leaders and knowledge are absent. It would, however, require project support in order to facilitate local resources and empower communities [14]. In line with a previous study [5], trust to local leaders and entrepreneurs is crucially based on local embeddedness of people who bring projects forward.

6.2   Community Renewables Emerges Out of a Collaborative Community with Shared Visions

Our empirical findings sustain the idea that community renewable energy is a collective achievement, as discussed by Tanimoto [56] and van de Ven [57], based on the support of locally grounded entrepreneurs and the local political authorities. Most importantly, the development process should be based on local participation in and ownership of projects and community benefits generated. While we found, as another study did [10], a strong scepticism towards new technologies at the beginning of the implementation process, our study indicates that a high level of participation in community renewable energy takes advantage from an approach that is locally grounded, collectively shared, participatory and politically supported. This approach brought the legitimation for something new – for the community-based renewables – among most citizens. Community renewables have been invented, collectively realised, implemented and sustained in local municipalities and by local people, providing opportunities to and benefits for people, communities, local places and regions beyond the local renewable-energy generation and supply. This fact is underlined by the multifaceted capitals and proximities inherent in community renewable energy. The cultural and social capital – in terms of collaboration and collective action – allowed them to transform it into economic capital benefiting communities and enterprises at different levels. The importance of the social momentum of community renewables became clear, which is expressed by open participation opportunities, fair shares of revenues and investments in the social gentrification. Beyond a single municipality, other municipalities can potentially benefit from the experiences and learning, and embrace the opportunity for support by the development of community renewables. In sum, community-based renewables mobilise citizens from being pure energy consumers to become active and engaged energy producers or even 'prosumers', probably creating a new habitus of community-based energy generation that holds the potential to develop into an energy citizenship [108].

6.3 Community Renewables are Influenced by External Support and Push Factors

The community renewable energy transition in Reußenköge resulted from a mix of endogenous and exogenous influences. Along with the internal factors, the empirical findings revealed different, external environmental, economic and political factors framing the development of renewables. The natural system 'North Sea Coast' is found to shape the people till today. The interviewees were and are used to adapt to storms and floods. This leads to a certain path dependency. People stay where they are, even though the natural surrounding places them at risk from time to time. However, they learned to live with nature and its risks, by keeping together and adapting to new challenges. This capability helped them by establishing community renewable energy transition in Reußenköge. Although climate change might not be the main motivation driving the development of renewable-energy projects in North Frisia, the public debate and political relevance of climate change partly catalysed them together with the Renewable Energy Act. In line with Rogers et al. [106] and Seyfang and Smith [109], our findings indicate that clear policy ambitions and support can support successful implementation and preservation of community renewable energy but that the so-called social on the ground including its agents, proximities, capitals, path dependencies and potentials for emergence play a vital role. These aspects are of vital importance because they characterise the grounded characteristics which should always be taken into consideration in the context of energy politics: the social is atleast as much important as economic aspects.

7 Conclusion

Based on our theoretical analysis and empirical application of the identified factors and processes driving the emergence of innovation and entrepreneurship in social, complex systems, we could identify important characteristics transitioning communities towards a collective renewable energy generation. The data analysed designate community renewable energy as an innovative concept that is invented by locally based entrepreneurs but collectively realised and implemented for people, local communities and in places. Moreover, community renewable energy offers the possibility to develop the entrepreneurial thinking and activities into locally and socially grounded business opportunities in agriculture or through the foundation of local consulting companies for renewables that boost the further diffusion of renewables beyond a single community.

The convergence between the concepts of complex social systems, innovation theory and entrepreneurship enabled us to conceptually explore and empirically disclose the importance of entrepreneurs, certain characteristics of entrepreneurship, and social interactions in and beyond the community for the emergence of community renewable energy. The well-known diffusion of innovation theory framework [27] has proven to be useful for analysing the process of adoption and diffusion of renewables. Envisaging Rogers' analytical categories as descriptive units helped us to structure the process of innovation diffusion from an overarching point of view. Analytical emphasis was put on the complex social system of Reußenköge in which the innovation is diffused. Here, the concepts system, agent, proximity, path dependence, capital and emergence were used as analytical categories to investigate how the subsystem of entrepreneurs and their entrepreneurship manage not only to diffuse, but also to collaboratively implement the innovation of community-owned wind energy. Energy-preneurs were at the heart of our analysis and emerged to be more than just economically acting individuals. The importance of the social in economic development became apparent. As inherent in innovation theory, also Bourdieu contains a social momentum that is proven to be useful for understanding the role of social structures characteristics, interactions and processes. It became apparent that the entrepreneurial practices conform to social path dependency while changing it at the same time. This is a tricky endeavour because the sensitive application of different kinds of capital in the context of various proximities among different agents is a main characteristic of the everyday mangle [110] of innovation an entrepreneur is situated in. There is more at work in the entrepreneurship of innovation than accumulating economic capital. Based on our theoretical findings, we tested them exemplarily on the community-based energy transition.

The mixed methods and grounded approach applied, provided us in-depth information on the relevance of local agents, interactions among them and impacts from outside the community influencing the transformation towards a renewable energy community. Coming back to our research question what factors and processes led to the emergence of community-based innovation concepts and entrepreneurship in renewable energy technologies, our empirical research leads us to the conclusion of three main factors that pushed the early and inventive deployment of renewables:

1. Entrepreneurs, who hold divers and complementary characteristics, are needed to invent innovative concepts, to apply and implement the concepts with as many inhabitants as possible, and to spread the word within the community and beyond.

2. The community-based adoption and diffusion requires a social system with high social, cultural and economic capitals and well-balanced proximities, being able to be open for new developments, with knowledge, high adaptive capacity and a common vision.

3. External factors, such as political funding schemes, the technical progress in renewable energy technologies, the deployment of renewables in other regions, and the support by the regional banks, enabled the development.

In conclusion, the findings presented here conceptually and empirically illustrate the importance of a locally grounded energy transition implemented by, in and for localities and communities. For further development of renewables, two important aspects should be considered: First, an understanding of the social, complex system – where community renewables are created and implemented – can provide a deeper understanding of the structures and processes for the emergence of community renewables, and second, an in-depth understanding of entrepreneurship and local entrepreneurs – by whom community renewables are created and implemented – can improve structural aspects about the emergence and success of community renewable energy. Thus, it can be concluded that local entrepreneurial spirit, relations among agents, described by proximities, different capitals and path dependencies affect the emergence of grassroots innovations of renewables. To support further diffusion of community-based energy transition, energy policies and funding schemes should recognise the local embeddedness of projects, the characteristics and capitals of local citizens and communities, and the effects beyond a single community. Furthermore, energy policies and funding schemes must be designed in a way that they socially, economically and legally empower local citizens and communities in driving the energy transition, to become actively involved and to enable them to benefit locally and collectively from the local energy generation.

References

1 HM Government(Ed.) (2010): The coalition: our programme for government: freedom, fairness, responsibility. London: Cabinet Office.
2 Ethikkommission(Ed.) (2011): Deutschlands Energiewende – Ein Gemeinschaftswerk-für die Zukunft. Available online atwww.nachhaltigkeit.info/media/1326189452phpeJ PyvC.pdf?sid=mmu7l010t8ns9tej2ng35r0fg2.
3 Department of Energy and Climate Change (DECC)(Ed.) (2014): Community energy strategy: Full report. Available online atwww.gov.uk/government/uploads/system/ uploads/attachment_data/file/275163/20140126Community_Energy_Strategy.pdf.
4 Bridge, G.; Bouzarovskib, S.; Bradshawc, M.; Eyred, N. (2013): Geographies of energy transition: space, place and the low-carbon economy. In Energy Policy53, pp. 331–340.
5 Walker, G.; Cass, N. (2007): Carbon reduction, 'the public' and renewable energy. Engaging with socio-technical configurations. In Area39 (4), pp. 458–469.
6 Seyfang, G.; Smith, A. (2007): Grassroots innovations for sustainable development. Towards a new research and policy agenda. In Environmental Politics16 (4), pp. 584–603.
7 Walker, G.; Devine-WrightP. (2008): Community renewable energy. What should it mean? In Energy Policy36 (2), pp. 497–500.
8 Süsser, D.; Kannen, A. (2017): 'Renewables? Yes, please!': perceptions and assessment of community transition induced by renewable-energy projects in North Frisia. Sustainability Science12(4), pp. 563–578.
9 Manzo, L.C.; Perkins, D.D. (2006): Finding common ground. The importance of place attachment to community participation and planning. In Journal of Planning Literature20 (4), pp. 335–350.
10 Devine-Wright, P. (2011): Place attachment and public acceptance of renewable energy: a tidal energy case study. In Journal of Environmental Psychology31 (4), pp. 336–343.
11 Devine-Wright, P.; Howes, Y. (2010): Disruption to place attachment and the protection of restorative environments. A wind energy case study. In Journal of Environmental Psychology30 (3), pp. 271–280.
12 Walker, G.; Devine-Wright, P.; Hunter, S.; High, H.; Evans, B. (2010): Trust and community. Exploring the meanings, contexts and dynamics of community renewable energy. In Energy Policy38 (6), pp. 2655–2663.
13 Süsser, D.; Döring, M.; Ratter, B.M.W. (2017): Harvesting energy: place and local entrepreneurship in community-based renewable energy transition. In Energy Policy101, pp. 332–341.
14 Rogers, J.C.; Simmons, E.A.; Convery, I.; Weatherall, A. (2008): Public perceptions of opportunities for community-based renewable energy projects. In Energy Policy36 (11), pp. 4217–4226.
15 Walker, B.J.A.; Wiersma, B.; Bailey, E. (2014): Community benefits, framing and the social acceptance of offshore wind farms: an experimental study in England. In Energy Research & Social Science3, pp. 46–54.
16 Toke, D.; BreukersS.; Wolsink, M. (2008): Wind power deployment outcomes: how can we account for the differences? In Renewable and Sustainable Energy Reviews12, pp. 1129–1147.
17 Gormally, A.M.; Pooley, C.G.; Whyatt, J.D.; Timmis, R.J. (2014): "They made gunpowder … yes down by the river there, that's your energy source": attitudes towards community renewable energy in Cumbria. In Local Environment 19 (8), pp. 915–932.

18 Bauwens, T.; Gotchev, B.; Holstenkamp, L. (2016): What drives the development of community energy in Europe? The case of wind power cooperatives.In Energy Research & Social Science2016 (13), pp. 136–147.Available online athttps://ssrn.com /abstract=2714847.

19 Feldman, M.P.; Kogler, D.F. (2010): Stylized facts in the geography of innovation. Hall, B.H.; Rosenberg, N. (Eds.): Handbook of the economics of innovation. Vol. 1.1st ed.Amsterdam: Elsevier(Handbook of development economics series, 1).

20 van der Horst, D. (2008): Social enterprise and renewable energy: emerging initiatives and communities of practice. In Social Enterprise Journal4, pp. 171–185.

21 Aitken, M. (2010): Wind power and community benefits: challenges and opportunities. In Energy Policy38, pp. 6066–6075.

22 Cowell, R.; Bristow, G.; Munday, M. (2011): Acceptance, acceptability and environmental justice. The role of community benefits in wind energy development. In Journal of Environmental Planning and Management54 (4), pp. 539–557.

23 Gross, C. (2007): Community perspectives of wind energy in Australia: the application of a justice and community fairness framework to increase social acceptance. In Energy Policy35, pp. 2727–2736.

24 Manson, S.M.; O'Sullivan, D. (2006): Complexity theory in the study of space and place. In Environment and Planning A38(4), pp. 677–692.

25 Martin, R.; Sunley, P. (2007): Complexity thinking and evolutionary economic geography. In Journal of Economic Geography7(5), pp. 573–601.

26 Johnson, S. (2002): Emergence: the connected lives of ants, brains, cities, and software. New York: Scribner.

27 Rogers, E.M. (2003): Diffusion of innovations. 5th ed.New York: Free Press.

28 Bourdieu, P. (1986): Forms of capital. Richardson, J. (Ed.): Handbook of theory of research for the sociology of education. Vol. 1.1st ed.Westport: In Greenwood Press, pp. 241–258.

29 Foster, J. (2005): From simplistic to complex systems in economics. In Cambridge Journal of Economics29 (6), pp. 873–892.

30 Casti, J.L. (1994): Complexification: explaining a paradoxical world through the science of surprise. New York: Harper Collings Publisher.

31 Manson, S.M. (2001): Simplifying complexity: a review of complexity theory. In Geoforum32(3), pp. 405–414.

32 Cilliers, P. (1998): Complexity and postmodernism – understanding complex systems. London, New York: Routledge.

33 Urry, J. (2005): The complexity turn. In Theory, Culture & Society22(5), pp. 1–14.

34 Ratter, B.M.W. (2013): Surprise and uncertainty – framing regional geohazards in the theory of complexity. In Humanities2 (1), pp. 1–19.

35 Ratter, B.M.W. (2012): Complexity and emergence? Key concepts in non-linear dynamic systems. Glaser, M (Ed.): Human-nature interactions in the anthropocene. Potentials of social-ecological systems analysis. 1.publ. New York, NY, London: Routledge. (Routledge studies in environment, culture, and society, 1).

36 Martin, R.; Sunley, P. (2011): Forms of emergence and the evolution of economic landscape(Papers in Evolutionary Economic Geography, Nr. 11.16). Available online athttp://econ.geo.uu.nl/peeg/peeg1116.pdf.

37 Lewin, R. (1993): Die Komplexitätstheorie – Wissenschaftnach der Chaosforschung. Hamburg: Hoffmann und Campe.

38 David, P.A. (1985): Clio and the economics of QWERTY. In The American Economic Review75 (2), pp. 332–337. Available online at: www.jstor.org/stable/1805621.

39　Arthur, W.B. (1989): Competing technologies, increasing returns, and lock-in by historical events. In The Economic Journal99 (394), pp. 116–131.

40　Arthur, W.B. (Ed.) (1994): Increasing returns and path dependence in the economy. Ann Arbor: University of Michigan Press.

41　David, P.A. (2001): Path dependence, its critics, and the quest for 'historical economics'. Garrouste, P.; Ioannides, S. (Ed.): Evolution and path dependence in economic ideas. Cheltenham, Northampton: Edward Elgar Publishing, pp. 15–40.

42　Grabher, G. (1993): The weakness of strong ties – the lock-in of regional development in the Ruhr area. Grabher, G. (Ed.): The embedded firm. London, New York: Routledge, pp. 255–277.

43　Martin, R. (2010): Roepke lecture in economic geography – rethinking regional path dependence: beyond lock-in to evolution. In Economic Geography86 (1), pp. 1–27.

44　Martin, R. (2011): Regional economics as path-dependent systems: some issues and implications. Cooke, Ph.et al. (Eds.): Handbook of regional innovation and growth. Cheltenham, Northampton: Edward Elgar Publishing, pp. 198–210.

45　Martin, R.; Sunley, P. (2006): Path dependence and regional economic evolution. In Journal of Economic Geography6 (4), pp. 395–437.

46　Weig, B. (2016): Resilienz komplexer Regionalsysteme. Brunsbüttelzwischen Lock-in und Lernprozessen.Wiesbaden: Springer Fachmedien Wiesbaden GmbH.

47　Portugali, J. (2006): Complexity theory as a link between space and place. In Environment and Planning A38 (4), pp. 647–664.

48　Beinhocker, E. (2007): Die Entstehung des Wohlstands – Wie Evolution die Wirtschaftantreibt. Landsberg am Lech: mi-Fachverlag.

49　Gell-Mann, M. (1994): The quark and the Jaguar. London: Little, Brown and Company.

50　Torre, A.; Gilly, J.-P. (1999): On the analytical dimension of proximity dynamics. In Regional Studies34 (2), pp. 169–180.

51　Torre, A.; Rallet, A. (2005): Proximity and localization. In Regional Studies39 (1), pp. 47–60.

52　Torre, A. (2014): Proximity relationships and entrepreneurship: some reflections based on an applied case study. In Journal of Innovation Economics & Management2 (14), pp. 83–104.

53　Boschma, R. (2005): Proximity and innovation: a critical assessment. In Regional Studies39 (1), pp. 61–74.

54　Schumpeter, J.A. (1942): Capitalism, socialism, democracy. New York/London: Harper.

55　Hargadon, A.; Douglas, Y. (2001): When innovations meet institutions: Edison and the design of the electric light. In Administrative Science Quarterly46 (3), pp. 476–501.

56　Tanimoto, K. (2012): The emergent process of social innovation. Multi-stakeholders perspective. In IJIRD4 (3/4), p. 267.

57　van de Ven, H. (1993): Special theoretical issue: the development of an infrastructure for entrepreneurship. In Journal of Business Venturing8 (3), pp. 211–230.

58　Seyfang, G.; Hielscher, S.; Hargreaves, T.; Martiskainen, M.; Smith, A. (2014): A grassroots sustainable energy niche? Reflections on community energy in the UK. In Environmental Innovation and Societal Transitions13, pp. 21–44.

59　Howells, J.; Bessant, J. (2012): Introduction. Innovation and economic geography: a review and analysis. In Journal of Economic Geography12 (5), pp. 929–942.

60　Hargreaves, T.; Hielscher, S.; Seyfang, G.; Smith, A. (2013): Grassroots innovations in community energy. The role of intermediaries in niche development. In Global Environmental Change23 (5), pp. 868–880.

61　Süsser, D. (2016) People-powered local energy transition. Mitigating climate change with community-based renewable energy in North Frisia.Hamburg: Dissertation

University of Hamburg. Available online athttp://ediss.sub.uni-hamburg.de/volltexte/2016/8034/pdf/Dissertation.pdf.
62 Isaak, R. (1999): Green logic: ecopreneurship, theory and ethics. West Hartford: Kumarian.
63 Larson, A. (2000): Sustainable innovation through an entrepreneurship lens. In Business Strategy and the Environment9 (5), pp. 304–317.
64 Young, W.; Tilley, F. (2006): Can business move beyond efficiency? The shift toward effectiveness and equity in the corporate sustainability debate. In Business Strategy and the Environment15 (6), pp. 402–415.
65 Schaltegger, S.; Wagner, M. (2011): Sustainable entrepreneurship and sustainability innovation: categories and interactions. Business Strategy and the Environment20 (4), pp. 222–237.
66 Magnani, N.; Maretti, M., Salvatore, R.; Scotti, I. (2017): Ecopreneurs, rural development and alternative socio-technical arrangement for community renewable energy. In Journal of Rural Studies51, pp. 33–51.
67 Messeghem, K. (2003): Strategic entrepreneurship and managerial activities in SMEs. In International Small Business Journal: Researching Entrepreneurship21 (2), pp. 197–212.
68 Caputo, R.; Dolinsky, A. (1998): Women's choice to pursue self-employment: the role of financial and human capital of household members. In Journal of Small Business Management30 (6), pp. 8–17.
69 Auerswald, P. (2008): Entrepreneurship in the theory of the firm. In Small Business Economics30 (2), pp. 111–126.
70 Schumpeter, J. (1934): The theory of economic development. An inquiry into profits, capital, credit, interest, and the business cycle. Harvard: Harvard University Press.
71 Valliere, D.; Gegenhuber, T. (2014): Entrepreneurial remixing: bricolage and postmodern resources. In The International Journal of Entrepreneurship and Innovation15 (1), pp. 5–15.
72 Baker, T.; ReedN. (2005): Creating something from nothing: resource construction through entrepreneurial bricolage. In Administrative Science Quarterly50 (3), pp. 329–366.
73 Chell, E. (2007): Social enterprise and entrepreneurship. Towards a theory of the entrepreneurial process. In International Small Business Journal25 (1), pp. 5–26.
74 Low, M.; Abrahamson, E. (1997): Movements, bandwagons, and clones: industry evolution and the entrepreneurial process. In Journal of Business Venturing12 (6), pp.435–457.
75 Nicholson, L.; Anderson, A. (2005): News and nuances of the entrepreneurial myth and metaphor: linguistic games and entrepreneurial sense-making and sense-giving. In Entrepreneurship: Theory and Practice29 (2), pp. 153–172.
76 de Clercq, D.; Voronov, M. (2009): Toward a practice perspective of entrepreneurship: entrepreneurial legitimacy as habitus. In International Small Business Journal27 (4), pp. 395–419.
77 Garud, R.; Kanøe, P. (2003): Bricolage versus breakthrough: distributed and embedded agency in technology entrepreneurship. In Research Policy32 (2), pp. 277–300.
78 Welter, F. (2011): Contextualising entrepreneurship – conceptual challenges and ways forward. In Entrepreneurship: Theory and Practice35 (1), pp. 165–184.
79 Bourdieu, P. (1977): Outline of a theory of practice. Cambridge: Cambridge University Press.
80 Bourdieu, P. (1990): The logic of practice. Stanford, CA: Stanford University Press.
81 Bourdieu, P. (1993):The field of cultural production. Cambridge: Polity Press.

82 Bourdieu, P.; Wacquant, L. (1992): An invitation to reflexive sociology. Cambridge: Polity Press.

83 EEG, Gesetzfür den Vorrang Erneuerbarer Energien. BGBl I 2000, 305. (2000).Available online atwww.gesetze-im-internet.de/bundesrecht/eeg/gesamt.pdf.

84 Agenturfür Erneuerbare Energien (AEE)(Ed.) (2014): Renews Kompakt. Akteure der Energiewende. Großteil der Erneuerbaren Energienkommtaus Bürgerhand.With assistance of Redaktion: Ryotaro Kajimura, Nils Boenigk V.i.S.d.P.: Philipp Vohrer. Available online atwww.unendlich-viel-energie.de/media/file/284.AEE_RenewsKompakt_Buer gerenergie.pdf.

85 InstitutfürZukünftigeEnergiesysteme (IZES)(Ed.) (2015): Nutzeneffekte von Bürgerenergie – Einewissenschaftliche Qualifizierung und Quantifizierung der Nutzeneffekte der Bürgerenergie und ihrermöglichen Bedeutungfür die Energiewende. Eva Hauser, Jan Hildebrand, Barbara Dröschel, Uwe Klann, Sascha Heib, Katherina Grashof. Available online atwww.greenpeace-energy.de/fileadmin/docs/pressematerial/IZES_2015_ 09_10_B%C3%BCE-Nutzen_Endbericht.pdf.

86 Statistisches Amtfür Hamburg und Schleswig-Holstein(Ed.) (2015): Bevölkerung der Gemeinden in Schleswig-Holstein, 2. Quartal 2015. Fortschreibung auf Basis des Zensus 2011 (A I 2 - vj 4/13 SH). Available online atwww.statistik-nord.de/fileadmin/Doku mente/Statistische_Berichte/bevoelkerung/A_I_2_S/A_I_2_vj_152_Zensus_SH.pdf.

87 Kunz, H.; Panten, A. (1997): Die Köge Nordfrieslands. Bräist/Bredstedt, NF: Nordfriis-kInst(NordfriiskInstituut, Nr. 144).

88 Pingel, F. (2005): 100 Jahre Cecilienkoog: 1095–2005. Bedtesdt/Bräist: Nordfriisk Instituut.

89 DGS, Deutsche Gesellschaftfür Sonnenenergiee. V.(Ed.) (2015a): EnergyMap. Gemeinde Reußenköge. Available online atwww.energymap.info/energieregionen/DE/105/119/477/ 23038.html, checked on Data status: 8/3/2015.

90 Wodak, R.; Meyer, M. (2001): Methods of critical discourse analysis. London: Sage.

91 Prior, L. (2003): Using documents in social research. London: Sage.

92 Charmaz, K. (2014): Constructing grounded theory. 2nd ed.London, Thousand Oaks, CA: Sage(Introducing qualitative methods).

93 Corbin, J.M.; Strauss, A.L. (2015): Basics of qualitative research. Techniques and procedures for developing grounded theory. 4th ed.Los Angeles: Sage.

94 VERBI Software – Consult – Sozialforschung GmbH. (1989–2015): MAXQDA. Software for qualitative data analysis. Berlin, Germany.

95 Baxter, J.; Morzaria, R.; Hirsch, R. (2013): A case-control study of support/opposition to wind turbines. Perceptions of health risk, economic benefits, and community conflict. In Energy Policy61, pp. 931–943.

96 Gläser, J.; Laudel, G. (2010): Experten interviews und qualitative Inhaltsanalyseals Instrumenterekonstruierender Untersuchungen. Wiesbaden: VS-Verlag.

97 Bogner, A.; Littig, B.; Menz, W. (Eds.) (2005): Das Experteninterviews: Theorie, Methode, Anwendung. Wiesbaden: VS-Verlag.

98 Fielding, N.; Thomas, H. (2008): Qualitative interviewing. Gilbert, N. (Ed.): Research-ing social life. 3rd ed. London: SAGE Publications Ltd, pp. 123–144.

99 BMUB(Ed.) (2009): Renewable Energy Sources Act (EEG) 2009. Available online atwww.bmub.bund.de/fileadmin/bmu-import/files/english/pdf/application/pdf/ eeg_2009_en_bf.pdf.

100 Dirkshof(Ed.) (2017): Bürgerwindpark Reußenköge. Available online atwww .dirkshof.de/windparks/windpark-reussenkoege/.

101 Creditreform (2016): Bürgerwindpark Reußenköge GmbH & Co. KG. Information. Available online atwww.firmenwissen.de/az/firmeneintrag/25821/209028

102 Fachagentur Windenergie an Land (2017): Bürgerwindpark Reußenköge. Available online atwww.fachagentur-windenergie.de/beteiligung/datenbank-goodpractice/projekt/reussenkoege.html.

103 DGS, Deutsche Gesellschaft für Sonnenenergiee. V.(Ed.) (2015): EnergyMap. Gemeinde Reußenköge. Die EEG-Anlagen der Region "Reußenköge". Available online atwww.energymap.info/energieregionen/DE/105/119/477/23038.html, checked on Data status: 8/24/2015.

104 GP Joule (2017): Websitewww.gp-joule.de/.

105 Hayward, C.; Simpson, L.; Wood, L. (2004): Still left out in the cold: problematising participatory research and development. In Sociologia Ruralis44 (1), pp. 95–108.

106 Rogers, J.C.; Simmons, E.A.; Convery, I.; Weatherall, A. (2012): Social impacts of community renewable energy projects. Findings from a woodfuel case study. In Energy Policy42, pp. 239–247.

107 Smith, J.; Blake, J.; Grove White, R.; Kashefi, E.; Madden, S.; Percy, S. (1999): Social learning and sustainable communities. An interim assessment of research into sustainable communities projects in the UK. In Local Environment4 (2), pp. 195–207.

108 Devine-Wright, P. (2007): Energy citizenship: psychological aspects of evolution in sustainable energy technologies. Murphy, J. (Ed.): Governing technology for sustainability. Hoboken: Earthscan, pp. 63–86.

109 Seyfang, G.; Park, J.J.; Smith, A. (2013): A thousand flowers blooming? An examination of community energy in the UK. In Energy Policy61 (0), pp. 977–989.

110 Pickering, A. (1995): The mangle of practice: time, agency, and science. Chicago: University of Chicago Press.

Chapter 2

Entrepreneurial Network Effects
Empirical Observations of Entrepreneurial Networks in a World of Complexity[1]

John T. Scott

1 Introduction: The Context for Entrepreneurial Networks

This chapter describes a method for identifying entrepreneurial networks and discusses evidence of the effects of entrepreneurial networks identified with that method. An entrepreneurial network, as defined in this chapter, is a group of entrepreneurs or entrepreneurial firms interacting in a set of activities in order to improve their performance.[2] Formally, as defined and explained herein, an entrepreneurial network is a probabilistically significant intersection of the leaf nodes of the two-level directed rooted tree that depicts a network of activities of one entrepreneurial agent, with the leaf nodes for another agent's network. For the set of entrepreneurial firms interacting in an entrepreneurial network, we observe a dimension of their conduct and performance beyond firm and industry effects – namely, we observe entrepreneurial network effects.

Hébert and Link [1] review and analyze the long history of scholarly contributions to our understanding of entrepreneurs and entrepreneurship, and based on their review, they identify [1, pp. 100–101] the many roles that have been associated with entrepreneurs – innovator, bearer of risk and uncertainty, enterprise owner, decision-maker, industrial leader, manager, supplier of financial capital, organizer and coordinator of economic resources, allocator of resources among alternatives, employer of factors of production, contractor, arbitrageur – and identify the scholars whose work emphasized the various, often overlapping, roles.[3]

The industrial organization and technological change literatures have typically focused on the firm effects and industry effects that are present in the behavior and performance of firms. A firm that is diversified into many different industrial activities might have a managerial and operations group with exceptional talent and orientation toward innovation, and regardless of the industry where those talents are applied, the firm's behavior and performance would be highly innovative – a firm effect. An industry might have exceptional opportunities for innovation, and for a firm operating in the industry, its behavior and performance would be expected to be more innovative than would be the case in an industry with less opportunity – an industry effect. Firm and industry effects might entail static performance given available technologies and products or dynamic performance as process and product innovations emerge.[4]

This essay focuses on entrepreneurial network effects – effects, beyond the firm and industry effects, that reflect the interaction of some entrepreneurs and entrepreneurial firms within groups of activities. Section 2 provides an overview of firm, industry and entrepreneurial network effects. Section 3 explains a method for identifying entrepreneurial networks. Section 4 discusses evidence showing that the entrepreneurial network effects are distinguishable from the firm and industry effects in both behavior – illustrated with research and development (R&D) spending and with patent citations – and in performance – illustrated with total factor productivity growth. Section 5 concludes that the use of the method for identifying entrepreneurial networks can enable more powerful hypothesis tests about those networks.

---

2   Firm, Industry, and Entrepreneurial Network Effects. Dimensions of Behavior and Performance

Griliches [2, pp. 6–7] discusses the importance of firm and industry effects in research and development (R&D) behavior in the following observations.[5]

> Given the fact that many of the major R&D performing firms in the United States are large, diversified, and conglomerate, it is interesting to ask: Is their R&D behavior primarily determined by the industrial location of their "lines of business" (division or establishment) or does a common "company" R&D policy exist? Without an affirmative answer to the last part of this question there would be grave doubts about the applicability of various R&D optimizing models which relate to such firmwide variables as the cost of capital or their managerial style. Luckily Scott [3] does provide an affirmative answer. In his data (473 companies, 259 different four-digit level FTC lines of business, and a total N of 3387) he can observe the variation in the R&D to sales ratio (R/S) within firms across their various lines of business. He finds

that approximately half of the overall variance in R/S can be accounted for by common company effects, common industry effects, and their interaction, in roughly equal parts. Thus, there appear to be significant differences in company R&D policy above and beyond what would have been predicted just from their differential location within the industrial spectrum.

Griliches [2, pp. 6–7]

The firm effects are strong evidence of what is called the "resource-based view" of the firm in the field of strategic management.[6] The industry effects are strong evidence that technological opportunity, among other things (appropriability conditions, for example), varies across industries [4–6] as reviewed in [7, pp. 84–85]. But there is another important dimension to the data with an important effect on behavior and performance – namely the entrepreneurial network effects. They are the focus of this essay. Not only can the attributes of a firm create a measurable effect on behavior (for example, a positive increment to the R&D to sales ratio) and performance (for example, a positive increment to productivity growth) in each of the firm's activities above and beyond the effects typically associated with the particular activities themselves. Not only are there typical effects (say for R&D intensity or for productivity growth) associated with various industries. But, additionally, there are discernable effects of entrepreneurial networks for the entrepreneurial agents that participate in those networks. Entrepreneurial networks can help entrepreneurs exploit opportunities for profit in the context of "static" stories about the allocation of resources with given technologies and demands, as well as in the context of the "dynamic" stories about R&D and technological change and new products and processes. As Hébert and Link [1] explain, the scholarship about entrepreneurs and their roles in the economy covers the gamut of relatively static and relatively dynamic aspects of economic performance.

In Section 3, we turn to the issue of identifying entrepreneurial networks in a complex world. Leyden and Link [8] emphasize that the process of forming and working within such networks "is inherently and irremediably an uncertain one" (p. 476). In Section 4, we describe evidence of entrepreneurial network effects for networks identified using the method described next in Section 3.

---

3 Identifying Entrepreneurial Networks. A Probabilistic Method

Figure 1 depicts an entrepreneurial agent – an entrepreneur or entrepreneurial firm – choosing among various activities. Entrepreneurial firms provide the means through which entrepreneurs achieve and put into effect the various roles [1, pp. 100–101] played by entrepreneurs as described in Section 1. Thus, the entrepreneurial firm reflects what Hébert and Link [1, p. 98] call "the traditional concept of the entrepreneur operating through the medium of the firm."

Figure 1 depicts a very simple graph or network for an individual entrepreneurial agent. As Emmert-Streib [9, p. 1] explains, in applications of graph theory, graphs can represent physical, biological, or sociological objects. Emmert-Streib [9, pp. 1–2] explains that although *graph* and *network* are often used interchangeably, the former represents mathematical objects, while the later represents real-world objects. Thus, Figure 1 represents a *network* for an entrepreneurial agent. The network is a connected set of objects, each represented by a node, with the connections between the nodes called edges. As an abstraction, the graph in Figure 1 is a two-level *rooted tree* with some *edges* removed and with the 'top' or root node denoting the entrepreneurial agent and the 'bottom' or leaf nodes denoting the activities in which the entrepreneur can participate.[7] The edges that are shown link the agent to the activities actually chosen; some edges, connecting the agent to activities not chosen, have been removed.

In this section, we shall define an *entrepreneurial network* as the probabilistically significant intersection of the set of linked leaf nodes for the connected tree (excluding the nodes for which edges are removed in the encompassing unconnected tree) for one entrepreneurial agent with the set of linked leaf nodes for another agent, and we shall explain a method for identifying the probabilistic significance of the intersection.

The approach presented in this chapter – an approach developed in [10–13] – identifies an entrepreneurial network with a probabilistic measure based on the idea that entrepreneurial agents in the network will have purposively sought to combine the entrepreneurial network's activities to gain the advantages of that network.[8]

Let n denote the number of activities in which an entrepreneur or entrepreneurial firm could choose to participate. For any pair of entrepreneurial agents, s is the number of activities chosen by one of the agents, while $t \leq s$ is the number of activities chosen by the other agent. Let g denote the number of activities that the two agents have in common, and let $C_{x,y}$ denote the combination of

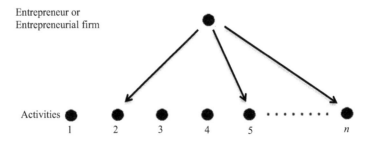

FIGURE 1: Activities chosen by an entrepreneurial agent.

x things taken y at a time where $C_{x,y} = x!/(y! (x-y)!)$ with $x!$ denoting x factorial, the product of the integer x with all the positive integers smaller than x.

Then, the probability measure of the similarity of the activities of the two entrepreneurial agents is given by the following formula:

$$probsim = 1 - \sum_{f=0}^{g} p(f) = 1 - \sum_{f=0}^{g} \frac{C_{t,f} C_{n-t,s-f}}{C_{n,s}}$$

The formula gives the probability *probsim* that the entrepreneurial agents would have more activities in common than they actually do if their choice of activities were random.[9] $C_{n,t}$ has been canceled from the numerator and the denominator of the combinatorial expression for $p(f)$. Then, given a particular set of t activities for one agent, $C_{t,f}$ denotes the number of different combinations of f activities in which the two agents could meet. Next, conditional on the two agents meeting in a particular f activities, $C_{n-t,s-f}$ is the number of possibilities for s minus f activities that do not coincide with the t activities of the other entrepreneurial agent. $C_{n,s}$ is the total number of ways that the agent with s activities can chose s activities. Thus, $p(f)$ gives the proportion of all possible cases taken by those cases where the two agents meet in f activities. The summation of $p(f)$ from $f = 0$ to t equals 1.

The probability *probsim* measures inversely the similarity of the set of activities for the two entrepreneurial agents, and it also is a formal measure of the significance of the meetings across the activities that the agents could choose. For example, the second column of Table 1 illustrates the case illustrated in Figure 2 where there are six possible activities, so $n = 6$, and where one of the agents chooses four of the activities while the other chooses three. Against the null hypothesis that the agents choose their activities randomly, the probability that they meet more than twice in the six activities is 0.2. The probability that they meet more than three times is of course zero.

The probability measure provides a formal way to scale the number of observed meetings to reflect the fact that some overlap would occur simply by chance. Agents with more activities would by chance meet more than agents with fewer activities, and yet as a proportion of the agents' activities, the smaller number of meetings may be more significant and have more influence on behavior. A deeper reason for using the probabilistic measure of similarity is that if the agents are deliberately pursuing the opportunities of an entrepreneurial network, we expect them to meet more than would happen by chance. The probability measure of similarity of activities identifies the presence of purposive pursuit of the advantages of an entrepreneurial network.

In the hypothetical example discussed above, the two agents chose four and three activities among the six possible activities. Consider in contrast the pair of agents illustrated in the third column of Table 1 and in Figure 3. Each of the agents chooses just one of the six activities. The probability that they would meet more than once is of course zero. If, in fact, these two hypothetical pairs met twice

TABLE 1:   Two distributions for the probability,
$p(f)$, of overlapping activities when $n = 6$.

f	$p(f; s = 4, t = 3)$	$p(f; s = 1, t = 1)$
0	0.0	0.83
1	0.2	0.16
2	0.6	0.0
3	0.2	0.0
4	0.0	0.0
5	0.0	0.0
6	0.0	0.0

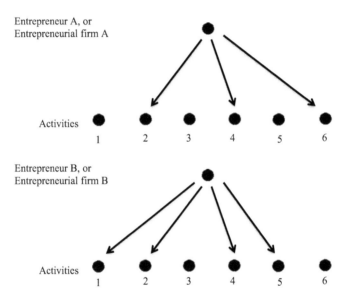

FIGURE 2: Activities chosen by entrepreneurial agents A and B.

and once respectively, the probabilistic inverse measure of overlap in activities is
0.2 for the pair that meets twice in activities, but the measure is 0.0 for the pair
that meets once. Thus, using the probabilistic measure, a pair of agents with fewer
overlapping activities could have greater similarity than a pair with more overlapping activities. Ideally, the importance, the significance, of the overlaps rather
than the number of overlaps is measured.

An entrepreneurial network encompassing the g activities where the two entrepreneurial agents meet exists with confidence level equal to $100(1 - \textit{probsim})$%. So,
for example, using the information in Table 1, we see that for the entrepreneurial

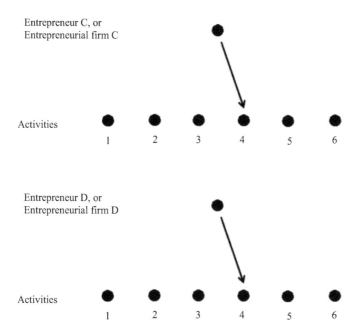

FIGURE 3: Activities chosen by entrepreneurial agents C and D.

agents A and B depicted in Figure 2, activity network {2, 4} exists with confidence level 80%, and for entrepreneurial agents C and D depicted in Figure 3, the activity network {4} exists with confidence level 100%. Alternatively, we could say that the network of activities identified for A and B is significant at the 0.20 level, while the network identified for C and D is significant at the 0.00 level.

4   Testing Hypotheses about Entrepreneurial Networks. Examples

In [11], the procedure described in Section 3 is used to identify entrepreneurial networks spanning different types of R&D activities of large firms. In the context of this chapter, we think of those large firms with significant R&D activities as entrepreneurial firms. Thus, in [11], the examples of entrepreneurial networks and the hypothesis tests about those networks are for entrepreneurial firms that are large firms. Although "[s]uccessful firms tend to grow, and larger firms tend to be dominated by rigid rules of conduct" [1, p. 98], the large firms can still be entrepreneurial, reflecting the behavior and the results of entrepreneurs "operating through the medium of the firm" [1, p. 98] in the various roles attributed to entrepreneurs.

Scott and Pascoe [11] find what we are calling entrepreneurial network effects in behavior and performance. They find that the firms within a network have R&D investments that are systematically different from the investments of firms in the same activities but not in the network, and those differences are systematically related to the pursuit of profits. Spillovers of knowledge from R&D across the activities in a network would be expected to affect productivity, and we would expect to find a higher correlation between R&D intensity and the rate of growth in total factor productivity when the R&D investment and the productivity are observed for the sets of related activities in the entrepreneurial networks. In fact, examining the relation between R&D investment and total factor productivity growth across what Section 3 calls the entrepreneurial networks of activities rather than across the individual activities, Scott and Pascoe find that the estimated marginal product of R&D is somewhat more than two-and-a-half times as large and the proportion of variance explained by the regression of total factor productivity growth on R&D intensity increases by almost four times.

Scott [13–15] also presents evidence supporting the hypothesis that entrepreneurial firms share knowledge within entrepreneurial networks of activities identified with the method of Section 3. Other things are controlled for, including the effects associated with the industry and technology areas in which each firm of a pair of observed firms operates. Then, given those controls, for a given pair of firms, each firm is about nine times more likely to use (as reflected in citations of the other's patents) the other's invention insights when the pair share an entrepreneurial network identified by their meeting to a highly significant extent in their sets of innovation markets—that is, their entrepreneurial activities as defined in Section 3. Scott [15, p. 250] describes the result as follows:

> The model controls for the firms' numbers of patents, the science linkage of their patents, their product market diversification (as indicated by the industries where they have sales), their innovation market diversification (as indicated by the product categories where they have patents), their locations in product and innovation markets, and the significance of the congruence of their product market operations and their innovation market operations.... [Sharing of knowledge] is evidenced by the greatly increased frequency of mutual citations apart from the effects associated with particular locations in the product and innovation markets. Imagine two firms that have completely congruent operations in *product* markets. Then even after controlling for the effect of that congruence, and even after sweeping out the effects associated with the particular locations in product and innovation markets, with the closeness to science and size of the patent portfolios, and with the diversification in product and innovation markets, the additional effect of significant congruence in innovation markets increases the expected citations by about nine... times.
>
> (italics in original)

5 Conclusion: Implications and Agenda for Future Research

This chapter has distinguished entrepreneurial network effects from the firm effects and industry effects that have been the focus of much of the literature about the economics of technological change and the economics of industrial organization. A method of identifying entrepreneurial networks is described, explained, and illustrated with hypothesis tests about entrepreneurial network effects engendered by those networks. In a world of complexity, observations of networks will typically be noisy in the sense that many similarities such as contacts of agents in activities will occur by chance. The method described in this chapter allows the identification of the similarities that resulted because of purposive behavior by the agents; and hence, it provides a way to identify the networks among the noisy observations. The method could be applied to identify the social networks of entrepreneurial agents more generally (or other types of networks) and allow more powerful hypothesis tests about the effects of the broader social networks that enable successful entrepreneurship (or other types of activity).

On the agenda for future research is the description of more complex entrepreneurial networks. In this chapter, entrepreneurial networks are defined as the probabilistically significant intersection of the set of activities chosen by individual entrepreneurial agents, with each agent's set of activities depicted with a network that is a very simple two-level directed rooted tree. For future research, each agent could be described with a more complex generalized tree, and then more complex entrepreneurial networks could be described. With entrepreneurial networks understood as arising out of more complex characterizations of the networks describing each entrepreneurial agent, classes of entrepreneurial networks could be developed, and then entrepreneurs could be characterized by using a graph-theoretic approach.

Notes

1 The author, John T. Scott, wishes to thank Matthias Dehmer for many helpful suggestions that improved this chapter.

2 An "entrepreneurial network" in the sense defined here is less encompassing than the social networks created by entrepreneurs as described by Leyden and Link [8, p. 483], who observe: "Social networks are created by entrepreneurs to aid in deciding which innovation to pursue and in searching for that innovation....Social networks are composed of bonds between individuals and/or organizations with varying types of knowledge." Such interactive bonds entail "complexity." The interactions of entrepreneurs entail complexity in the sense used in the literature about complexity in science and technology. Complexity is described by Antonelli [16, p. 3]: "Complexity is emerging as a new unifying theory to understand endogenous change and transformation across a variety of disciplines, ranging from mathematics and physics to biology. Complexity thinking is primarily a systemic and dynamic approach according to which the outcome of the behavior of each agent and of the system into which each agent is embedded is intrinsically dynamic and can only be understood as the result of multiple interactions

among heterogeneous agents embedded in evolving structures and between the micro and macro levels."

3 The role of the entrepreneurial agent as an innovator is often associated with Schumpeter [17,18]. Hébert and Link [1] place Schumpeter's contribution in the context of the large literature about entrepreneurs, and Martin and Scott [19] place it in the context of public policy toward innovation.

4 Broadly speaking, taking an astigmatic view, the firm and industry effects in Schmalensee [20] and Scott and Pascoe [21] are focused on static performance, while the effects in Scott [3] are associated with dynamic performance. Schmalensee [20] found the strong industry effects, but he did not find firm effects. As Scott and Pascoe [21] show, the firm effects are present, explain a large amount of the variance in performance, and are highly significant statistically. Using the Federal Trade Commission's (FTC's) Line of Business (LB) Program data as Schmalensee did, Scott and Pascoe do find both the firm effects and the industry effects. Unlike Schmalensee's sample of the FTC LB Program data, the Scott and Pascoe sample consisted "only of firms that (1) reported to the FTC LB Program in all 3 years (1974, 1975, and 1976) for which data were available, and (2) that could be matched to Standard & Poor's Compustat files. Further, all 3 years of data [were]...used...; Schmalensee used only the data for 1975....[F]irm effects in the LB data are extremely sensitive to outliers. The [Scott and Pascoe]...sample...is exceptionally clean with regard to coherent firms since it excludes firms disappearing during the sample period because of mergers and firms for which data could not be reconciled with Standard & Poor's. In addition to examining just one (rather odd) year, Schmalensee used a procedure for sample selection that reduced each firm's number of business units entering the statistics. Estimation of firm effects requires a sufficiently large number of business units for each firm." [7, pp. 231–232].

5 Further discussion of the structure of the data that allowed the estimation of the firm and industry effects is provided in Scott [22].

6 For an appreciation of the resource-based view in the context of an exposition of the foundations of business strategy by a leading strategy practitioner and thinker, see Helmer [23] in general, and in particular the discussion at p. 106 and then throughout Part II of the book.

7 The set of connected nodes in Figure 1 is a "directed rooted tree" as defined in Definition 2.1 in [24, p. 448]. Figure 1 depicts a very simple "ordinary directed rooted tree" for which each of the edges in the graph, or network, "over jumps always just one level" [24, p. 449].

8 The probabilistic measure is one possible measure of the similarity of the graphs depicting the activities of two entrepreneurs or entrepreneurial firms. Dehmer et al. [24, p. 447] "present and analyze an algorithm to measure the structural similarity of generalized trees, a new graph class which includes rooted trees." They also provide a window to the literature about graph similarity. In [9], Emmert-Streib provides an overview of measures of the similarity of networks. This chapter describes an approach to identifying entrepreneurial networks that measures the similarity in the activities of the entrepreneurs or entrepreneurial firms using the methods introduced in [10,11,13]. The measure used is designed to exploit the purposive behavior of the economic agents who choose to combine the activities in the entrepreneurial network to gain the advantages of using the entrepreneurial network.

9 Note that in [10,11], the formulation is somewhat different, giving the probability that the overlap would be as great or greater than it actually is, rather than the probability that it would be greater. In those applications, the number of possible activities was quite large, and with smaller dimensions for the sample space, the measure of the probability of a greater number of meetings allows for better discrimination in the significance of the overlaps in activities. Also, in [10], the pair of agents was selected from a given industry, and then their meetings in other activities were examined. Discussion of the merits of the alternative approaches is provided in [13].

References

1 Hébert, R.F.; Link, A.N. (2009): A history of entrepreneurship. London: Routledge.
2 Griliches, Z. (1984): Introduction. In Griliches, Z. (Ed.): R&D, patents, and productivity. Chicago: University of Chicago Press for the National Bureau of Economic Research, pp. 1–19.
3 Scott, J.T. (1984): Firm versus industry variability in R&D intensity. In Griliches, Z. (Ed.): R&D, patents, and productivity. Chicago: University of Chicago Press for the National Bureau of Economic Research, pp. 233–245.
4 Levin, R.C.; Cohen, W.M.; Mowery, D.C. (1985): R&D appropriability, opportunity, and market structure: new evidence on some Schumpeterian hypotheses. In American Economic Review 75, pp. 20–24.
5 Geroski, P.A. (1990): Innovation, technological opportunity, and market structure. In Oxford Economic Papers 42, pp. 586–602.
6 Geroski, P.A. (1991): Market dynamics and entry. Oxford: Basil Blackwell.
7 Scott, J.T. (1993): Purposive diversification and economic performance. Cambridge, UK: Cambridge University Press.
8 Leyden, D.P.; Link, A.N. (2015): Toward a theory of the entrepreneurial process. In Small Business Economics 44, pp. 475–484.
9 Emmert-Streib, F. (2010): A brief introduction to complex networks and their analysis. In Dehmer, M. (Ed.) Structural analysis of complex networks. New York: Springer Science & Business Media, pp. 1–26.
10 Scott, J.T. (1982): Multimarket contact and economic performance. In Review of Economics and Statistics 64, pp. 368–375.
11 Scott, J.T.; Pascoe, G. (1987): Purposive diversification of R&D in manufacturing. In Journal of Industrial Economics 36, pp. 193–205.
12 Scott, J.T. (1990): Purposeful diversification of R&D and technological advancement. In Link, A.N.; Smith, V.K. (Eds.): Advances in applied micro-economics, Vol. 5. Greenwich, CT: JAI Press, pp. 7–28.
13 Scott, J.T. (2001): Designing multimarket-contact hypothesis tests: patent citations and multimarket contact in the product and innovation markets of the chemicals industry. In Baum, J.A.C.; Greve, H.R. (Eds.): Multiunit organization and multimarket strategy; advances in strategic management, Vol. 18. Oxford, UK: JAI/Elsevier Science, pp. 175–202.
14 Scott, J.T. (2001): Strategic research partnerships: what have we learned? In U.S. National Science Foundation, Division of Science Resources Studies, Strategic research partnerships: proceedings from an NSF workshop, NSF 01-336. Arlington, VA: U.S. National Science Foundation, pp. 195–205.
15 Scott, J.T. (2003): Absorptive capacity and the efficiency of research partnerships. In Technology Analysis & Strategic Management 15, pp. 247–253.
16 Antonelli, C. (2011): The economic complexity of technological change: knowledge interaction and path dependence. In Antonelli, C. (Ed.): Handbook on the economic complexity of technological change. Cheltenham, UK; Northampton, MA: Edward Elgar, pp. 3–59.
17 Schumpeter, J.A. (1934): The theory of economic development, translated by R. Opie. Cambridge, MA: Harvard University Press.
18 Schumpeter, J.A. (1942): Capitalism, socialism, and democracy. New York: Harper.

19 Martin, S.; Scott, J.T. (2000): The nature of innovation market failure and the design of public support for private innovation. In Research Policy 29, pp. 437–447.

20 Schmalensee, R. (1985): Do markets differ much? In American Economic Review 75, pp. 341–351.

21 Scott, J.T.; Pascoe, G. (1986): Beyond firm and industry effects on profitability in imperfect markets. In Review of Economics and Statistics 68, pp. 284–292.

22 Scott, J.T. (2014): The U.S. Federal Trade Commission's line of business program and innovation research. In Science and Public Policy 41, pp. 438–448.

23 Helmer, H. (2016): 7 Powers: the foundations of business strategy. Los Altos, CA: Deep Strategy.

24 Dehmer, M.; Emmert-Streib, F.; Kilian, J. (2006): A similarity measure for graphs with low computational complexity. In Applied Mathematics and Computation 182, pp. 447–459.

Chapter 3

Entrepreneurial Process
The Overbearing Role of Complex Social Network

Adekiya Adewale and Ahmed Musbah Aboyssir

1 Background to the Study

Though, it is a well-documented fact within the entrepreneurship literature that those entrepreneurs who tend to engage in social networking in facilitating core business operations record a significantly higher success than their counterparts who fail to act in this regard. Nevertheless, these studies on social networking, and their relationship with the entrepreneurial process, have been largely focused on the traditional offline social networking, thus providing the need to examine the role of a more complex social networking: the online social media, as it relates to business success. In this regard, this study extends on previous studies by making use of the resource mobilization theory of social media to argue that nascent entrepreneurs would tend to achieve significantly higher business success if they strive to capitalize on the numerous benefits of social media by optimizing the usage of this platform, at each stage of the entrepreneurial process. Specifically, we found that social media platforms, such as LinkedIn, printerest, Twitter, Myspace,

Facebook, Afro-introduction, and Tagged, can aid nascent entrepreneurs in extending their social ties to significant others from a wide range of geographical locations, thereby facilitating the required access to diverse range of social capital needed for business competitiveness. Hence, we drew implications from these and suggest the need for nascent entrepreneurs to capitalize on the technologically enhanced social platform to recognize better entrepreneurial opportunities, to mobilize for better business resources, to improve business formation activities, and to achieve competiveness in both value creation and values offering.

2 Introduction

Entrepreneurship has over the years been highlighted as antecedent in promoting innovation and technological progress, engendering competition, job creation, leading to economic recovery and national prosperity [1]. With the increasing rate of economic and social challenges currently permeating the global landscape, relevant actors in both developed and developing nations are beginning to shift their focus to this concept with the view that it could serve as an appropriate intervention strategies to aid in turning the tides [2]. Nevertheless, the reasons why nascent entrepreneurs usually fail to achieve effective business performance or predictable outcomes may be sufficiently understood by focusing on the critical stages involved in complex entrepreneurial process, constituted by many social actors, other than the entrepreneur [3]. This is due to the fact that the best entrepreneurship ideas were profitable only because the entrepreneurs went through the necessary steps to build a company from scratch [4]. Of note in this regard is the networks approach which visualizes the entrepreneurial process as a set of ties and interactions between the entrepreneurs, informal, and formal actors that are networking and communicating in every horizontal entrepreneurial stage [3]. For instance, it has been argued that economic activities are socially situated and cannot be explained by reference to individual motives alone; but rather on the robustness of the underlying social structures involving actors, related to each other in ongoing networks of inter-personal and inter-organizational relationships [5]. Thus, a better understanding of the entrepreneurial process in addition to how nascent entrepreneurs can achieve optimization at each stage of this process by making use of overbearing complex social network should lend fruitful insight for building theories in addition to serving as a guideline for practice among nascent entrepreneurs.

Though, the entrepreneurship literature have linked this process to several key stages, see for instance [6]: opportunity recognition and resource mobilization [7]: pre-founding stage, founding stage, and early development stage [8],: feasibility studies; assembling needed resources; and new business development [9,10]: opportunity identification, technology set up/organization creation and the exchange stages [11]: ideation, opportunity recognition, shaping the entrepreneurial intention, preparation, networking, entry, value creation, exit, and organization while some other studies have taken a more general approach in identifying the role of social network in some of the stages (cf. [3,12–15]). Nevertheless, a large chunk of these studies are centered on the early business establishment stages, and — on the impact of offline social networking on these stages despite the submission by (1) [16] that in doing social network analysis, makes it erroneous to only focus on business establishment stage with no regard for other phases which could be classified as involving the actual business operations and management; and (2) the observation by [17] that while globalization is spurring the need for adoption of technology in building business relationship, few studies have focused on how online social networking apparatus may aid in advancing and modifying business practices. Thus, we provide an antidote for this gap in knowledge by (1) highlighting the entrepreneurial process as encompassing opportunity recognition, resource mobilization, venture formation, value creation, and value exchange and (2) focusing on how nascent entrepreneurs can embrace the use of complex social network in an atmosphere of technological innovation at each stages of this process to achieve sustainable entrepreneurial outcome.

3 Entrepreneurial Process

In attempting to provide a conceptual view of the word 'entrepreneurial process'[18] align their view and proposed that it is a composition of activities that involves the discovery, evaluation and exploitation of opportunities to introduce new goals and services, ways of governing markets, processes, and raw materials through organizing efforts that previously had not existed. Consolidating on this, Al-Zoubi [3] described the process as encompassing how new business idea is discovered, evaluated, developed, and implemented for value creation and exchange purposes. In this regard, Chay [19] has used the entrepreneurial stage model to explain that since the act of entrepreneurship is a complex phenomenon which cannot be explained on the basis of individual alone, then it will make more sense by studying it as an outcome of some sorts of actions, activities, and interactions that occur between the entrepreneur and social networks. Put in another way, the entrepreneurial process has been highlighted as much desirable approach to understanding the why, what and how of entrepreneurial success.

Furthermore, Cornwall and Naughton [20] provided their own view on this topic by alluding to the fact that

> it is a course of action that involves all functions, activities and actions associated with identifying and evaluating perceived opportunities and the bringing together of resources necessary for the successful formation of a new firm to pursue and seize the said opportunities.

Reacting to this view, Kodithuwakku and Rosa [21] countered and suggested that this process does not end with assembling critically needed resources but also extends to include making strategic decisions regarding the allocation of scarce resources in pursuit of value adding and value exchange opportunities. Thus, in consistent with this view [22], that the entrepreneurial process is by no means an end in itself but consists of sequential chain of events which are interrelated. In their reasoning, while entrepreneurial idea generation may be the first step in this process, it transcends to idea screening, resource mobilization, financial commitment, value creation, and transfer of values to target users.

According to the entrepreneurial process literature, different approaches have been devised by authors in the classification of this process. While some have embraced the two-dimensional approach, others have hinged their classification on either three or four multi-dimensional orientation (cf. [6–10]). Nonetheless, of note among these classifications is the three-dimensional approach proposed by Bhave [8] which consists of opportunity stage, technology set-up/organization creation stage, and the exchange stage. According to Bhave [8], at the opportunity stage, the opportunity is recognized, a business concept is identified and the commitment to venture creation is made. In this regard, after opportunity is recognized, nascent entrepreneurs are expected to modify their business concept to the specific needs of users before making attempts towards any form of commitment to venture creation. Further, in the technology set-up and organization creation stage, human, financial and material resources are mobilized for the creation of the new venture while technology set-up, product development, and marketing activities are equally enhanced [9]. The last stage in this regard is the value exchange stage when products/services are transferred to target market in exchange for profitable outcomes. More specifically, typical activities in this stage would include advertisement, sales operations, strategic and operational feedback from customers, and the implementation of corrective measures by the organization. As such, within the framework of this study, we align our view with this model by proposing a classification that encompasses opportunity recognition, resource mobilization, venture formation, value creation and value exchange with a view to establish a link between the effective execution of the activities in each stage on one side, and the presence of a conducive platform for complex social networking on the other side. Depicted below in Figure 1 is a model showing the four stages under [8] classifications.

4 Social Network

Contrary to the wide held tradition that prevails in mid-twentieth century when mode of explanation of entities has been based primarily on individual attributes, this notion began to experience change at the later end of this century when researchers began to see an organization's environment as consisting of multiple individual players interacting separately with the focal organization [23]. From then on, the network perspective has been adopted by researchers and practitioners

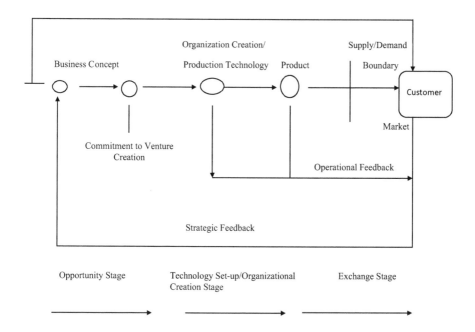

FIGURE 1: Process Model of Entrepreneurial Venture Creation (Source: Bhave, 1994)

in describing various political, economic, social and business outputs [24]. The network perspective views any system as a set of interrelated actors or nodes in which the actors can represent entities at various levels of collectivity, such as persons, firms, and countries [23]. Social networks on the other hand are nodes which may be in form of individuals, groups, organizations that are tied on a single or many types of interdependence [25]. This may be interpreted that it is made up of people who are brought together as a result of a common interest, shared value or aspirations with a view to foster information sharing or other mutual benefits. On the importance of this group of people [26], lamented that it has the ability of connecting individuals in order to enhance information flow among them in that 'most people we associate with also have other peoples who are significant others, and indirectly connected to us', additionally [14] alludes to the fact that a network is one of the most powerful assets that any individual can possess in that while it can serve as a source of access to information, opportunities, and power, it can also serve as a leeway to other networks that are brought together by social ties.

Granovetter [27] distinguishes between loose collections of ties and close-knitted ties. In the author's observation, these types of network ties may be characterized based on the frequency of contacts, the emotional intensity of the relationship, the degree of intimacy and reciprocal commitments between the actors involved. In close-knitted ties, the frequency of contact is relatively higher; the emotional commitment of actors is stronger, while parties tend to share more intimacy and reciprocal commitment. Although these may portend some critical advantages from a strategic stance [28], however, it is argued that it limits the range of diversified information that could be made available. In this regard, Burt [29] used the structural hole theory to explain that the presence of a bridge among nodes in a social network with loose ties would facilitate the sharing of diversified critical information, resources, ideas, and viewpoints from a wide range of sources, while the close-knitted ties would tend to manifest in arrays of redundant information [30]. By implying from this theory, it can be argued that the strength or size of social network may at times act as a deciding factor on the benefits acquirable from such network. However, the initial studies that were conducted on social network were primarily concerned with recognizing the character and resultant consequences of relationships exchange [31]. Nonetheless, as researches galvanized in this area, a new area of interest began to emerge making researchers to start focusing on the nature of network relationships as they pertain to the businesses environment, and have been labeled as study of 'organizational networks', 'inter-organizational networks' and 'intra-organizational networks' [32]. For instance, while relating this concept to the business domain, Carpenter et al. [33] pointed that since the entrepreneurial network approach assumes that people with whom entrepreneurs interact affect entrepreneurs' endeavors basically through the various resources that different relationships provide, then these individuals should be studied as socially embedded individual. Thus, in line with this contention, Baron [34] noted that at the core of any entrepreneurial process analysis, the network approach is attributable to clusters of social and economic relations between the entrepreneur and the informal and formal networks involved in all stages of the entrepreneurial process, and explains why and how they behave and under what circumstances. Thus, we extend on this line of thought by focusing on how the availability of an efficient complex social network platform might aid in advancing each of the stages in entrepreneurial process.

4.1   Complex Social Network and Opportunity Recognition

Opportunity recognition is defined as a process through which ideas for new business ventures are identified [35]. Furthermore, it is a discovery of an idea to create new businesses and the search for information regarding market and technological possibilities [36]. For [35], it is the cognitive process that imbibes individuals with the opinion that they have identified means of generating economic value (i.e., profit) that previously has not been exploited and is not currently being exploited by others. Consolidating on this, Schweizer et al. [37] pointed that one of the critical skill sets required of an entrepreneur is being able to recognize and select the right opportunities for new businesses in that having this recognition in a high-potential market can often lead to substantial gains in profit, growth and competitive positioning. Consistent with this view, Schweizer et al. [37] lamented that anyone can be an entrepreneur if they are alert in identifying and exploiting the market opportunities. Also Shane [38] has highlighted this act of recognition and described it as the most important element to drive the entrepreneurial process.

Bhave [8] recognized two major dimensions of opportunity recognition: externally stimulated and internally stimulated. In the former, which could be likened to the positivist orientation of opportunity recognition, it is assumed that entrepreneurial opportunities are formed by exogenous shocks to existing markets and it is there ready for entrepreneur to discover them [39]. Hence, studying the external environment and making inference from observations seem to be the key to recognizing opportunities here. In the later, it is suggested that opportunities are formed endogenously by the entrepreneurs themselves [40]. It follows the constructionist approach and posits that the existence of opportunity is based on individual's perception [37]. Here, instead of focusing on the environment, the nascent entrepreneur starts by identifying a particular problem/threat, which has the potential of obstructing his/her normal physical or social functioning [9]. As a result of this, he/she then engages in the search for relevant information or antidote that may aid in alleviating this problem while also taking efforts in identifying some other individuals who may be in need of the solution with the aim of commercializing it. Consider a potential entrepreneur who grew tired of trying to locate facial tissues while driving (problem), and thus came up with the idea of putting them into a cup-shaped container that would fit neatly into the cup-holders found in virtually all vehicles and then takes steps after this discovery to identify the potential customers who may be interested in the product before making attempt to commercialize it (entrepreneurial opportunity). Thus, a notable entrepreneur in this regard is Mark Zukerberg, the founder of Facebook.

Nonetheless, since it has been posited that no individual has perfect information, that is, they have limited ability in storing and processing information [18,41], then an exposure to varying social network platform should have a corresponding effect on their social boundary while also offering access to more knowledge and information that is required in exposing more potential venture opportunities [42]. In line with this view, the resource-based theory of entrepreneurship proposed by [43] highlighted social capital resources as crucial resources in opportunity-based entrepreneurship, and thus pointed that access to this type of resources enhances the individual's ability to detect and act upon discovered opportunities. In fact, prior research have made it known that individuals are more likely to recognize opportunities for ventures creation because they have superior access to information due to differentiated search behavior or social networks [44]. This may be unconnected with the reason why [45] inferred from previous research and concluded that both innovation and information are the two most crucial elements in any entrepreneurial process. Thus, information search for business opportunities could be described as a product of whole parts of a system rather than its individual parts [46].

Consider the externally stimulated recognition of business opportunity highlighted above: in this case, the ability of the nascent entrepreneurs in detecting this opportunity may not be optimally realized through his own sole effort but would be dependent on his/her connection or interaction with significant others who have critical information concerning the prevailing problems or what is needed in certain areas of the society that are out of his/her immediate reach. In this regard, many individuals have recognized the importance of weak social ties and the ability of an efficient social media platform in accessing information relating to business opportunities in areas encompassing wide geographical regions. Social networks, or social media sites, which are the major elements in social media platform, can be defined as online-based communities involving individuals who are related by common interest or activity, and having the means to facilitate effective communication among them [47]. Accordingly, Broughton et al. [48] described this platform as involving the use of an online platform or website for the facilitation of communication, through a variety of services, most of which are web-based and offer opportunities for people to interact over the Internet: via email and 'instant messaging' [49], via Facebook for social networking, via You Tube for video sharing, via Pinterest for picture sharing, via LinkedIn for professional networking, via Blogs for weblogs, via Foursquare for location-based social networking, and via Twitter as micro-blogging [50].

Take for example, a potential entrepreneur based in the United States of America, and interested in determining the prevalent needs/problems in the African markets, with a view of penetrating this market would need lots of market information, industry, technology and demographical situations, social values and other factors. Thus, in as much that visiting these countries and getting this information first hand would pose as an uphill task with unfavorable cost/benefit outcome, this entrepreneur may on the contrary choose to become part of technology-enhanced social network that encompasses members from different African countries thereby availing him/her the opportunity of acquiring these information with just a click of the button. Consistently, the social network theory advanced by Arnold [51] proclaimed that network ties provide access to resources and information that is critical to opportunity recognition and venture formation by connecting structural holes, linking lack of connection, easing information supply to facilitate innovation. It has been acclaimed that social media-enhanced market survey is inexpensive, faster, generate more honest response and are more versatile [52]. A typical email survey costs about half of what a conventional survey costs, and return rate can be as high as 50% [53]. Another estimate is that 75% to 80% of a survey-targeted response can be generated in 48 hours using online methods, as compared to a telephone survey that can take 70 days [54]. To obtain 150 interviews, people may be more open about their opinion when they can respond to a survey privately and not to another person who they feel might be judging them, especially on sensitive topics [55,56].

Various social media platforms: Facebook, Yahoo, Ebay, Tagged, Afro-introduction, Twitter, Facebook, and LinkedIn have been designed for buyers and vendors to exchange business information that may lead to the development of profitable opportunities. Also, various Universities and research institutes and development agencies among others have used this online platform in collaborating with partners from different parts of the world while this gesture has lead to the discovery of significant opportunity for profitable research exercise. In addition, individuals with variations in language background can now exchange business information with the aid of language translation-enhanced software which is usually built as a feature of these social platforms thereby eliminating the impediments that this has previously posed to business transaction in cross-cultural settings.

Furthermore, the process that produces an internally stimulated business opportunity may initially not require the need to engage in social networking as this form of recognition materializes as a result of individual perception [9,37]. Nevertheless, it can be succinctly stated that after the discovery of this opportunity, the need for information exchange in this regard should become crucial in the sense that the discovered opportunity can only become marketable by identifying the various markets that are potentially in need of this problem-solving technique. Consider the above-mentioned nascent entrepreneur with the problem of locating facial tissues while driving. While this entrepreneur may be given ample credit for finding the required solution to his lingering problem, his ability to enhance the commercialization of this problem-solving technique will require the inputs of significant others who are part of an interrelated nodes that comprise a varieties of individuals in urgent need of this problem-solving technique. Thus, in this regard, Mark Zukerberg was able to commercialize his ability for technology-enhanced social networking by disseminating information on this problem-solving technique among actors while these actors have served as a means of information sharing to billions of others from different parts of the world, thereby extending the popularity of this site beyond his/her University community. Thus, as of September, 2014, the site was reputed to be having about 864 million daily active users on average, 1.35 billion monthly active users, with approximately 82.2% of the daily active users outside the US and Canada [57] depicted below in fig 2 is a Diagram showing externally and internally stimulated entrepreneurial opportunity recognition as described by [8].

4.2 Complex Social Network and Resource Mobilization

Following the identification of an attractive entrepreneurial opportunity, nascent entrepreneurs must embark on the task of assembling a variety of resources which are vital to achieving the overall objectives of the new venture [12]. In this regard, Ayotte [58] noted that this process of acquisition is a vital, complex, and challenging entrepreneurial task. Accordingly, these crucial resources can be classified as follows: Technical know-how [59], Finance [60], Physical assets [61], and the human resource who are required to utilize their emotional and intellectual capabilities in actualizing those critical objectives that are needed for organizational success [21]. Indeed, while engaging in this acquisition, nascent entrepreneurs are often faced with challenges in numerous ways due to the uncertainty surrounding the likelihood of profitable exchange which may make resource holders to become reluctant in parting away with them [12]. Consolidating on this view, Santarelli et al. [62] noted that in the event that venture capitalists and

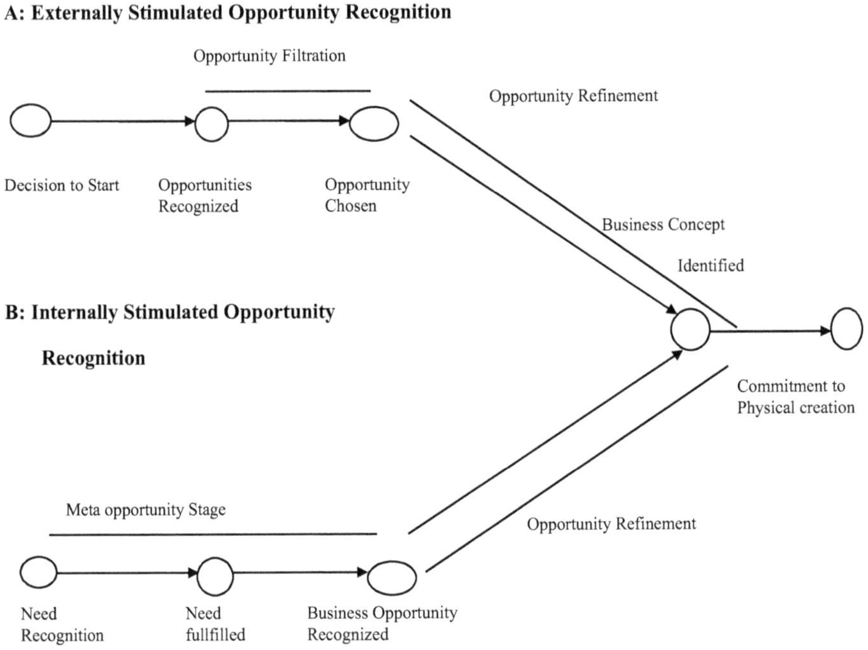

A: Externally Stimulated Opportunity Recognition

Opportunity Filtration

Opportunity Refinement

Decision to Start   Opportunities   Opportunity
                     Recognized   Chosen

Business Concept

Identified

B: Internally Stimulated Opportunity

  Recognition

Commitment to
Physical creation

Meta opportunity Stage

Opportunity Refinement

Need   Need   Business Opportunity
Recognition   fullfilled   Recognized

FIGURE 2: Diagram Showing Externally and Internally Stimulated Entrepreneurial Opportunity Recognition (Source; 8)

business angels are willing to invest in new ventures, they are more likely to commit their resources to those firms which they know one or more of the founders or which have the backing of reference from trusted sources in that this tends to alleviate informational asymmetry problems.

Thus, in combating these challenges, the presence of a rich social network has been identified. However, the closely bonded/strong network ties highlighted by [63] may be quite important at the early stage of venture creation as ties such as friends and family members who are in possession of these resources may, indeed, be less reluctant in making them available [28]. But this form of resource mobilization has been highlighted as having the capacity for imposing limitation on the entrepreneur's inclination to repay the funds and their commitment to the new venture [64]. And may limit the firm's capacity for expansion [65]. For instance, it has been argued that those startups with lack of existing radars or any previous relationship with potential investors run the risk of not receiving funding without an effective means of communications to sway the commitment of the investors [65]. Also, due to the fact that it may be nearly impossible for nascent entrepreneur to make provision for those information (assets and cash flows histories which are important to investors when evaluating firm's quality), this lack of knowledge on quality may impede their commitment in terms of human and financial resources [66,67].

Nevertheless, with the advent of globalization and the need to compete at global level while also extending business operations beyond the local shores, the need for an efficient social network platform that employs the use of technology in reaching out to individuals scattered across a wide geographical regions has become imperative for startup firms [17]. With efforts from previous studies mainly focused on this technologically enhanced platform as a marketing tool, a growing number of entrepreneurs have realized its diverse potential [68]. Also, evidences from researches have revealed that the tendency for a nascent entrepreneur to access critical business resources from investors increases with the degree of access to broader social network [69]. For instance, the potential influence of this platform in establishing contact with actors from diverse background and social settings to foster entrepreneurial activities is well documented in the literature. By using profile data involving 286 entrepreneurs, obtained from Facebook, Twitter and LinkedIn [17], was able to establish that entrepreneurs' networks are in fact networks of networks rather than a single network: while these entrepreneurs use all three online social networks – LinkedIn, Facebook and Twitter, their networks overlap at a range of between 19% (Twitter–Facebook), 21% (LinkedIn–Twitter) and 29% (Facebook–LinkedIn), in contrast to non-entrepreneurs, who use these networks separately with limited overlapping among them, at 2%, 2% and 8.4%, respectively. When firms manufacture a product, they select the lowest cost source, which may be Japan, for semi-conductor, Sri-Lanka for Textiles, Malaysia for simple electronics, and Europe for precision machinery [70]. Thus, one of the riskiest strategies for a domestic firm is to remain solely a domestic firm in an industry that is rapidly becoming global [71]. Hence, the need to utilize social media platform to get access to these crucial resources has become a crucial part of a firm strategy.

Nowadays, since many firms operate in an uncertain environment while at the same time facing the need for competition and survival, in order to minimize the dependence on this uncertain environment, they must seek resources from different providers and adapt to the changing environment at hand [72]. In consistent with this view, the resource dependence theory advanced by [73] provided an insight. It argued that while the survival of a firm lies in its ability to acquire resources and maintain resources from the environment, in an uncertain environment, however, these organizations must rely on different sources and providers from different environments. With the power of modern days technologically enhanced social media platform, nascent entrepreneurs are now equipped with the ability to mobilize for resources from divergent customers, stakeholders and investors. In their bid at lending support for this argument, Hong [65] uses social media activities on Twitter and venture financing data from Crunch-Base to determine the overall contribution of active social media presence, and strong Twitter influence: followers, mentions, impressions, and sentiment on firm's access to venture capital financing. From the analysis of these data, three basic findings were uncovered: startup firms active on social media have higher chances of getting funded, receive larger amounts of funding, and have a larger number of investors. Thus, in their conclusion, they noted that this platform enhances information communication which gives investors the ability to perform better firm evaluation and to discover potential investment opportunities through a reduction in search costs.

Accordingly, social entrepreneurial organizations such as OXFAM have been able to reach across to millions of potential donors from diverse parts of the world through social media platforms such as Yahoo, Facebook, and Twitter to convince them to donate to its numerous charitable projects. Also, numerous corporate organizations and non-governmental organizations took advantage of these network platforms to solicit and raised fund for the victims of Hurricane Tsunami and the recent one, among native Texans. Thus, with the advent of these platforms, members can now easily connect with each other, push through a business proposal and make funding-related applications based on the economic value of these proposals.

In terms of soliciting for the required human capital and the technical know-how required for actualizing organizational-based objectives, in addition to the fact that labor market is becoming more international–East Asian countries have become market leader in labor-intensive industries, Germany offers skilled labor [74]. Popular social media sites such as LinkedIn, Academia-edu, Research-Gate, Facebook and Twitter have now metamorphosed into a recruitment platform where job openings can be posted, and resume uploaded with the objective of attracting the attention of potential vendors. For instance, while searching for a human personnel with the potential of a product manager of UBER, Travis Kalanick, its founder, posted a message and a member of this online community with experience in web-based applications replied and have become the head of Global operations up till today [75]. From a survey on channels used by global talents to look for new jobs, O'Leary [76] found that 60% use online job boards, 56% use social professional networks while 50% use word-of-mouth which clearly demonstrates the power of social connectivity in talent sourcing activities. Also, it has been revealed that 'Over 75% of people who recently changed jobs used LinkedIn to inform their career decision', 'New employees sourced through LinkedIn are 40% less likely to leave the company within the first 6 months', 'LinkedIn influenced hires are 2x more likely to be high demand and above average hires', and that 'top recruiters are 60% more engaged with LinkedIn recruiting tools' [76].

Concerning the mobilization for, and acquisition of the intangible and physical assets, since firms are increasingly confronted with the need to source for raw material and other physical assets from location beyond their geographical boundary [77], for reasons that range from economy of scale, scope and core competencies, many nascent entrepreneurs are now focusing on online technologically enhanced platform to achieve these cardinal objectives. Though, the use of social media in the supply chain industry has been termed an emerging phenomenon [78]. However, (1) based on the fact that the knowledge of the circumstance that we are expected to make use of usually exists in dispersed bit of incomplete and frequently contradictory knowledge from separate individuals scattered about [79] and (2) consistent with the observation offered by [78] that supply chains can be quite large, including a number of vendors, distribution centers, who are in possession of numerous bits of information and knowledge that is required at different point in time along the chains, then an important tool that could aid in accessing these information and knowledge may be in form of a broad-based social media platform. In this regard, companies such as Best-Buy, Giant, Wall-Mart, Nivea, Adidas and Nike have established presence on social media platforms such as Facebook, Yahoo and Twitter with the view of attracting the attention of online participants while also influencing them to make recommendation of their product to their co-network members [80,81]. Other examples are the use of Twitter messages in indicating the arrival or departure of a shipment from a particular warehouse, and to establish transportation events that could influence delivery times and capabilities [78]. Others are its usage in channeling transaction information: companies involved, shipment number, date and time, etc. into different or multiple communication channels [82]. Concerning its ability for achieving effective delivery of ordered goods, it can also be used in this regard by indicating the customer and the specific order to which the goods corresponds [78]. Furthermore, companies such as E-bay and Amazon.com have provided a veritable platform that brings together vendors from different geographical locations with the aim of facilitating connectivity among buyers and sellers of firm-related assets or industrial raw materials.

4.3 Complex Social Network and Venture Formation

The ability to overcome those critical challenges associated with business registration procedure and other bureaucratic formalities could be determined by several factors among which may be classified as the level of acquaintance with the system, related regulations, tax laws, intellectuality, and fluency in native language [16]. In their opinion, a more serious challenge that may emanate from this factors is the dilemma of how to tackle them and whom to get in touch with concerning the information that may aid in dealing with them. Other activities in this stage may involve making attempts to identify and understand core operational problems and tweaking them to bring maximum output, identifying suitable management style and structure in addition to key variables for control and success [16]. Thus, in response to this highlighted business problems, Colleoni et al. [83] pointed that a social collaborative structure that lends supports to sharing of explicit and implicit knowledge and experiences can help in advancing the cause of the entrepreneur. For example, a potential entrepreneur who has intention of operating in a foreign market with no prior knowledge of the language or culture of this market may find it desirable to register as a member of a social networking platform that help in promoting the attributes of that culture, i.e., Afro-introduction for Africans, the multiracial platform of Tagged, etc. with the view of collaborating with these members, learning more about the cultural and country-level bureaucratic stipulations, and also using them as a conduit in facilitating his/her business registration process. Moreso, as many businesses are increasingly becoming aware of the benefits associated with the possession of an online presence, these businesses are doing so much to achieve much in this regard. For instance, businesses can nowadays register their domain name and web address within just a click of the button and even making use of their social media platform to achieve this end: this form of business registration is now available through social media platforms such as Twitter, Facebook, and Instagram.

Also, since it can be conveniently argued that the process involved in firm formation goes beyond the normal business registration rituals and may also include the creation of the awareness to achieve recognition and organizational legitimacy within the fold of relevant actors, then the social media as a mass self-communication, involving the production of knowledge that utilizes the capability of large number of users for the solution and prediction of challenge or problem [84] may serve as a useful tool in this regard. Through this platform, firms can establish contact with reference communities in order to access the network effect which encourages the creation of trust among users based on group similarities [85]. For instance, with the role of the social media as an institutional intermediary [84]. And since it has been highlighted as having the capacity for diverting mass attention towards certain firms and on specific issues, it can be argued that new firms can make use of this means to fuel the market place sentiment that is needed for building public place reputation, acceptability, and legitimacy, which are key parameters required for initiating business place transactions. In support of this notion, Lans et al. [86] used the agenda theory to argue that the media serves as a key in shifting people's perceptions and attitudes. While sharing the same view, Scuotto et al. [87] stressed that media platforms are indicators of social evaluation since it serves as a counteracting institution that reduces stakeholders' uncertainty about a firm's characteristics. Thus, new firm can now utilize this means for launching business operations in addition to gaining recognition and acceptability among a wide range of audience that spans different geographical locations.

4.4   Complex Social Network and Value Creation

Within the framework of this study, we define value creation as all the processes involved in the production of goods/services, and the innovative practices involved in bringing these process to reality. Amy and Poston [88] state that manufacturers are now on their toe to leverage on social media types of connections to enhance an easier access to needed expertise, business intelligence insights and new product ideas. Within this context, Hanna et al. [89] noted that in their active interaction with external actors, customers, public institutions, and other business organizations, they acquire and absorb external knowledge for the enhancement of innovative products and services, which gives them the impetus to compete favorably in the market-place. Accordingly, Garretson [90] stated that the strategic usage of social networking platform can accelerate and deepen enterprises' service innovation and growth by promoting specialization within customers, suppliers, and other businesses. Also, it can contribute significantly to fast-track product adoption, and lower product development cost for enterprises [89]. For instance, enterprises have taken to making use of sites such as Facebook for engaging with customers, to acquire information which may aid in personalizing products/services, in order to increase brand loyalty and reputation [91]. Since it has been noted by Kim [92] that consumers increasingly use digital media not just to research products and services, but to engage the enterprises they buy from, then it can be stated that this medium would give users a voice in bringing up a new innovative idea which will consequently aid in achieving the required decrease in costs of in-house research for innovation [89]. Consolidating on this, Bozz et al. [93] view the virtual environment as encompassing a wide range of activities such as creative adaptation or technological leapfrogging. In addition, it is a context that gives enterprises the avenue of meeting their global consumers in order to enhance an existing product beyond the original design parameter [94].

Furthermore, it has been lamented that the ongoing brain drain among engineering experts and the retirement time of older ones are fueling the need for some industrial companies to leverage on social media to connect their young scientists with those that are older and more experience for the purpose of facilitating mentorship. In 1993, there were a total of 11,000 students of petroleum engineering in 34 United States Universities; however, in 2006, the total number of students in this category in a total of 17 Universities has shrunken to just 1,700 [95], meaning a total reduction of about 64.6%. In Aramco, the state-owned national oil company of Saudi Arabia, half of the workforce is less than 30 years of age and more than 60% of its engineers have fewer than 10 years of experience, and hence the unavoidable need to groom these inexperience workforces by making use of social media to connect them to older more experienced mentors.

According to Peter Granger, Cisco's senior global market manager for the manufacturing industry, some manufacturers currently using socially enabling technology applications include Ford, Coca-Cola and Harley Davidson. In his statement, these companies are taking advantage of a converged IT/plant network to use IT apps in factory areas. Said in his word, 'for Ford, the company does this by bringing content to people, versus sending people to content, thereby creating an avenue for having town hall meetings with workers at plants scattered all over the globe'. In the area of product development in relation to firm versus customer interaction, Granger referenced Procter and Gamble and pointed that in 2000, about 15% of the company's product development ideas came from outside the company while that number has since risen to about 50% due to its outreach, and the monitoring of social media through its Connect and Develop Innovation Model (CDIM).

Similarly, Baker Highes, a Texas-based company, that provides reservoir consulting, drilling, pressure pumping, formation evaluation to global oil and gas industry, has used new connection technologies (Cisco-Pulse) as a social networking platform to seek for production-related expert opinions. Contrary to other expert locators that require manual updates, Cisco-Pulse includes tagging features, which enables it to automatically collect key terms and analyze business contents shared across a company's network. This system can dynamically rank users and the information they contribute for each tag, and even suggest updates for users' profiles in addition to linking information on someone in the system to social media sites, such as LinkedIn, to further enhance the data on that individual. In this regard, this technology provides a combination of human expertise identification, knowledge capture and locator services. For instance, users can share their backgrounds, highlight areas of experience, and provide contact information through their profiles. The system imports role and contact data from the corporate email database. To find an expert in the system, users can search by keywords to retrieve a list of relevant experts. These searches can also be refined by role, group, or location to see who is currently available to engage with on a particular issue. When integrated with Cisco's connection technologies such as Unified Communications, Tele-Presence or WebEx, those searching for experts can be directly connected to the relevant, available experts who turn up in their search results.

4.5 Complex Social Network and Value Exchange

In this study, we conceptualize the process of value exchange as all processes involved in the communication and delivery of product/services and for managing customer relationship among those vendors who act as users of these products and services. Social media marketing can be classified as an Internet marketing process that implements various social media networks in order to achieve marketing communication and branding goals [57]. It usually centers on efforts to create content that attracts attention and encourages readers to share it with their social networks, resulting in electronic word-of-mouth [96]. In today's atmosphere of technological innovation, retailers are increasingly adopting social networking sites to extend their marketing campaigns to a wider range of consumers [97]. Stated that as a result of the personal autonomy and freedom associated with this medium, people are actively using it as a means of establishing connection, and sharing experiences and opinions about tested products and services. And may even become more important than traditional advertising as a trusted source of information [47]. In this regard, Cheong and Morrison [98] pointed that 92% of consumers trust product recommendations from people they know which vastly exceeds any form of advertising or branded communication. Hence, retailers need to view marketing in a whole new way and include social media marketing as part and parcel of their business plan [99].

Recognizing the power of word-of-mouth, marketers have begun to reach out to influential consumers through the social media platform hoping that they can be used in convincing their peers more than traditional advertising would. By following this line of reasoning, we would like to refer to the famous work of Hoffman and Fodor [100] where evidence were obtained to prove that consumers hold more trust in product information created by other consumers than information generated from manufactures. From its traditional role as a platform for interacting with friends and family, it has metamorphosed into a place where consumers can learn more about their favorite companies and the products they sell [97]. Moreso, 'with the rise of technologically inclined powerful search engines, advanced mobile devices and interfaces, peer-to-peer communication vehicles, and online social networks, these mediums have extended marketers' ability to reach shoppers through new touch points'[101]. This is as a result of the fact that a positive rating of product/services by a consumer can spread virally very quickly throughout the various social media channels [57] thereby excising direct impact on consumer behavior. With the explosion of Internet-based messages transmitted through the social media, they are now a main factor in influencing many aspects of consumer behavior which could be in form of awareness, consideration, information gathering, opinions, attitudes, purchasing decisions and post-purchase evaluation [47]. Other benefits of this marketing strategy are brand exposure, targeted traffic, leads generation, market research, customer interaction, marketing effectiveness, and public relations.

Nowadays, most especially for all high involving purchases, buyers are finding it imperative to acquire information related to brand, product or service, and then making comparison with equivalent or competing brands before making purchase. Hence, while embarking on these processes, they make use of social media platform to interact with previous users of these brands, acquire brand-related information from them, and take decisions on either to initiate a purchase process or back out [47]. In line with this view, Hoffman and Fodor [100] noted that the repercussions of businesses-social media use cuts across issues such as value proposition segmentation, brand imaging, value messaging and sales. Thus, with the innovative capabilities of this online technology, some specific benefits may be in form of a football league promoting its image by sponsoring online games, a restaurant disseminating information about its services, and an online retailer making sales of his/her products [102]. Moreso, since social media sites such as Facebook, Qzone, Orkut and Netlog allow for the categorization of specialty groups according to interests, nationality, country of residency, and age of children through which people can create connections [103], then it may be reasonably argued that companies can make use of this technological innovation to realize the objective of market segmentation by ensuring that relevant products/services are used in targeting those chat groups or online communities that present the best business opportunities and economic returns consistently, Li and Hitt [97] reconciled with Eltantawy and Wiest [104] by highlighting two notable benefits: (1) it provides business growth for retailers due to the diversity of consumers patronizing it and (2) this diversity in consumer characteristics means that most target markets can be reached.

In a study on how social channels influenced sales conversions and to what extent, and how brands can use this information to optimize their media spend, Burt [105] employed the use of data from real-world third-party customer and some notable insights were provided: (1) social media provides significant impact on a customer's path to purchase and strongly influences their buying decisions and (2) social media is 87% much more likely than any other marketing channel to serve as a middle touch-point along the path to purchase, which is an important part of customer awareness and consideration of a product. Thus, realizing the overbearing influence of this channel, social media spending by e-marketers in the United States have been estimated to be around 6.6 billion dollars in 2014 alone. Although, there is a need for ample time to translate online relationship into desirable sales outcome, however, a significant number of marketers who indulge in this relationship find great results with more than half of marketers who've been using social media for at least three years reporting that it has helped them improve sales [57].

5 Theoretical Underpinning

To provide a robust theoretical basis for this research, the resource mobilization theory of social media advanced by Elfring and Hulsink [106] shall be adopted. As promoted by this theory, critical resources such as time, money, skills, expertise and certain social or political opportunities are very paramount in achieving desirable outcomes in any social or economic settings. However, as a result of the pronounced scarcity in the availability of these resources, it has become paramount for actors to extend search antennas to areas or environment, outside of their immediate reach [106], and hence the need to make use of technologically enhanced social media in achieving these vital objectives. For instance, while strong ties in comparison to weak ties may exhibit superiority in terms of frequency of contacts, emotional intensity of the relationship, the degree of intimacy and reciprocal commitments between the actors involved [14] weak ties, on the other hand, increase diversity both in contacts and in the range of socio-economic resources that may be accessible by members [107]. Thus, while a technologically enhanced social network platform may not necessarily provide the affective ties that foster loyalty and commitment as may be the case in strong-bonded ties, it, nevertheless, would render access to varieties of resources from numerous geographical locations at the different stages of the entrepreneurial process. On the basis of this, it is our assumption in this study that nascent entrepreneurs can optimize their search for opportunities, funding sources, skills and expertise, in addition to making improvement for organizational sales by creating a platform that encourages social connectivity in a technologically supported social media environment.

6 Conclusion

Gone are the days when entrepreneurship used to be viewed as a product of an individual entity with little or no regard for the role being played by interconnectivity of multiple players which tends to interact together with the view of achieving desirable outcome. Increasingly, the success rate of business venture is becoming hinged on the ability of owners to maximize the potentials that is inherent in a technologically driven social networking platform. As such, the entrepreneurial process, which may be termed as encompassing sub-components, including opportunity recognition, resource mobilization, venture formation, value creation and value exchange, is currently undergoing what could be termed as an information technological revolution, with an innate capability for re-writing the history of entrepreneurial practices, while also instituting a new order. Indeed, nascent entrepreneurs nowadays have the capability to tap into the resources inherent in divergent opportunity recognition sources as they can now widen their networking tentacles to involve vendors from various walks of life and geographical locations thereby enriching their-selves with varieties of business opportunities with a view aligning interest with the most profitable ones. Specifically, with just a click of the mouse, the socio-economic, psychological, physiological and demographical needs of markets in different parts of the world can now be learnt with a view of making provision for these needs, and exchanging them for profitable outcome.

With the recognition of an economically viable business opportunity, nascent entrepreneurs would need to pool necessary resources together to achieve the objective of what could be termed as value creation. These resources may be in form of financial, human, material and intellectual properties. However, since it has been revealed that the tendency to access these critical business resources increases with the degree of access to broader social network, then it may be broadly stated that the possession of efficient social media networking platform would contribute so much in achieving these cardinal objectives. For instance, this view has been succinctly shared by Hong [65] who noted that startup firms active on social media have higher chances of getting funded, receiving larger amounts of funding, and have a larger number of investors. Also, in the process of accessing the technical and operational expertise needed for the smooth running of their organization, nascent entrepreneurs nowadays have the capability of circulating information relating to various job specification and job description to the teeming contacts in their social media platform with the view of using them as conduit in accessing the services of those human potentials that are equipped with these expertise, but are, however, out of their immediate reach.

Furthermore, this technologically enhanced social media platform can now be employed to overcome the numerous socio, cultural and legal hurdles that emanate out of cross-border differences while making attempts to achieve the objective of firm registration and business formation. In this vein, nascent entrepreneurs are now equipped with the capability of learning the different cultures, languages, customs, traditions, bureaucracies and laws predominating in different geographical locations of the world with the view of using these acquired knowledge in ensuring that what is enshrined in their proposal for business registration/formation is in line with the specifications stated in the requirements obtained in their target country.

Also, it can be conclusively stated that nascent entrepreneurs would tend to derive maximum benefits if the capability of social media is put into cognizance while making attempts to execute the value creation stage of the entrepreneurial process. For instance, it was clearly shown in our literature review how firms are increasingly making use of this platform to enhance their manufacturing processes through the establishment of linkage with manufacturing experts across the world, and getting directives from them while carrying out manufacturing tasks. In addition, we showed how efficient social networking machinery can aid in addressing problems of brain drains in organizational settings by providing linkage between older more experienced mentors and the younger inexperienced mentees to ensure an adequate transfer of skills and knowledge in such a way that the absence of these mentors may become unnoticeable even after their retirement. Regarding the acts of exchanges that take place after the creation of these value-adding offerings, nascent entrepreneurs may either choose to employ this platform for disseminating products/services-related information, implementing sales strategies, executing actual sales and promotion of after sales activities such as positive word-of-mouth facilitation.

In conclusion, though, the fundamental assumption within most existing literature was that social capital primarily serves its purpose by contributing to the success of entrepreneurial venture at the establishment stage. However, this study counters such claims by suggesting that social capital not only helps entrepreneurs in the establishment phase of the business, but continues to be a big contributor to its success also in the latter stages of the business and may be optimally utilized by promoting its usage in a technologically enhanced atmosphere such as the current days online social media platforms.

7   Implications for Theory and Practice

Theoretically, this study lends credence to the structural hole theory advanced by [108] which argued that the presence of a bridge (occupied by entrepreneurs) among nodes in a social network with loose ties would facilitate the sharing of diversified critical information, resources, ideas, and viewpoints from a wide range of sources. For instance, while the stronger close-knitted ties in which individuals are closely bonded may portend higher measures of reliability and affective relations, this kind of ties has been noted to be limited in terms of size and scope [28]. And may not work effectively in the current era of globalization and inter-industry and inter-organizational competitiveness where there is an urgent need for business firms to extend their reach and tentacles to encompass individuals from diversified economic, political, social and cultural backgrounds. As such, it has become imperative to embrace the use of a technological platform that is capable of uniting vendors, who are loosely tied, and scattered across regions that transcend the immediate reach of business owners. With this innovative technology, firms can now foster the promotion of their business activities by aligning with significant others from various parts of the world without necessarily having any form of intimate or prior relationship with them. Similarly, the act of cooperation as against competition has been highlighted as being more productive in achieving profitable business outcome [108]. And are being used more: Lock-head team up with British Aerospace PLC to compete against Boeing company to develop modern fighter Jets, multi-national firms are becoming more globally cooperative, and increasingly, domestic firms are joining forces with competitive foreign firms to reap mutual benefits, then it may be reasonably suggested that firms occupying structural hole, with online capabilities for establishing connectivity with unrelated groups or individuals are likely to have better access to heterogeneous ideas and non-overlapping resources from arrays of organizations characterized by knowledge and material diversities.

In regards to practice, it is suggested that nascent entrepreneurs would achieve more by focusing on improving the size and scope of their networking at each stage of the entrepreneurial process. Also, nascent entrepreneurs must be aware that they can benefit more from social networking by creating an online presence which could serve as an aid in establishing links with individuals and groups that are in the strategic positions necessary for advancing business success. In addition, nascent entrepreneurs should take note of the power shift which now gives consumers the means to employ the use of social media in expressing their thoughts regarding products, services or advertisements to other consumers and producers of these goods and services. Hence, they must take advantage of these two-way communication to craft their products/services offerings in line with required specifications, aimed at eliciting optimum purchase behavior and word-of-mouth communications.

References

1 Antonio, F.F.M., Sergio-Rubio, C.M., & Pérez-Mayo, J. (2017): Academic entrepreneurial intention: the role of gender. In International Journal of Gender and Entrepreneurship, 9 (1), pp. 1–31.

2 Özarall, N., & Rivenburgh, N.K. (2016): Entrepreneurial intention: antecedents to entrepreneurial behavior in the U.S.A. and Turkey. In Journal of Global Entrepreneurship Research, 6, p. 3. DOI: 10.1186/s40497-016-0047

3 Al-Zoubi, M.O. (2016): The entrepreneurial process networks as a new theoretical framework for understanding and analyzing the practice of creating a new business venture. In Journal of Management Research, 8, p. 3.

4 Efring, T., & Hulsink, W. (2004): The strong versus weak tie effect on entrepreneurial processes: ICT-Start-ups in the Netherlands. Paper for 20th EGOS conference, Ljubljana, July 1-3, 2004 (draft version June 15th).

5 Pretorius, M., Nieman, G., & Vuuren, J. (2005): Critical evaluation of two models for entrepreneurial education: an improved model through integration. In International Journal of Educational Management, 19 (5), pp. 423–427.

Entrepreneurial Complexity

6 Gruber, J., & Emmanuel, S. (2002). The elasticity of taxable income: evidence and implications. In Journal of Public Economics, 84 (1), pp. 1–32.

7 Baron, R.A. (2004): OB and entrepreneurship: why both may benefit from closer links. In Research in organizational behavior, B.Staw, & R.Kramer (eds). JAI Press: Greenwich, CT.

8 Bhave, M.P. (1994): A process model of entrepreneurial venture creation. In Journal of Business Venturing, 9 (3), pp. 223–242. Retrieved 2010-04-08, from Science Direct Database.

9 Hisrich, R.D., & Peters, M.P. (2002): Entrepreneurship (5th ed.). McGraw-Hill: New York.

10 Salamzadeh, A., & Kirby, D.A. (2016): New venture creation: how start-ups grow? In AD-minister, 30, pp. 9–29.

11 Stuart, T.E., & Sorenson, O. (2005): Social networks and entrepreneurship. In International handbook series on entrepreneurship, Vol. 2, S.Alvarez, R.Agarwal, & O.Sorenson (eds). Springer: USA.

12 Anonio, F.F.M., Serg-Rubio, C.M., & Pér-Mayo, J. (2017): Academic the role of gender. In International Journal, 3 (4), pp. 1–31.

13 Matlala, T. (2012): The role of social capital, social networks and incubation in launching and growing a new venture. A research project submitted to the Gordon Institute of Business Science, University of Pretoria, in partial fulfillment of the requirements for the degree of Master of Business Administration.

14 Elfring, T., & Hulsink, W. (2003): Networks in entrepreneurship: the case of high technology firms. In Small Business Economic, 21, pp. 409–422.

15 Huse, M. (2014): The role of networks in the entrepreneurial process: a case study of three Norwegian craft breweries. A project submitted to the Centre for Technology, Innovation and Culture (TIK) University of Oslo Faculty of social science.

16 Dowla, A.U. (2011): How entrepreneurs use social networks in their business. Master Thesis, Swedish University of Agricultural Sciences Faculty of Natural Resources and Agricultural Sciences Department of Economics.

17 Song, Y. (2015): From offline social networks to online social networks: changes in entrepreneurship. In Informatics Economică, 19 (2). pp. 34–42.

18 Venkataraman, S. (2003): Preface. In A general theory of entrepreneurship. The individual–opportunity nexus, S.A.Shane (eds). Edward Elgar Publishing, Inc.: Massachusetts.

19 Chay, Y. (1993): Social support, individual differences and well-being. In Journal of Occupational and Organizational Psychology, 4, pp. 286–303.

20 Cornwall, R.J., & Naughton, J.M. (2003): Who is the good entrepreneur? An exploration within the Catholic social tradition. In Journal of Business Ethics, 44 (1). 11th symposium on ethics, business and society. Ethical challenges in the age of globalization 61–75. [Online] available: www.jstor.org/stable/25075016 (October 27, 2013).

21 Kodithuwakku, S.S., & Rosa, P. (2002): The entrepreneurial process and economic success in a constrained environment. In Journal of Business Venturing, 17 (5), pp. 431–465.

22 Brockner, J., Higgins, E.T., & Low, M.B. (2004): Regulatory focus theory and the entrepreneurial process. In Journal of Business Venturing, 19, pp. 203–220.

23 Borggatti, S.P., & Li, X. (2009): On social network analysis in a supply chain context. In Journal of Supply Chain Management, 21 (4), pp. 103–126.

24 Jackson, M.O. (2010): An overview of social networks and economic applications. In Handbook of social economic. ed Jess Benhabib, Alberto Bisin, and Matthew O. Jackson, forthcoming, Elsevier Press.

25 Ogunnaike, O.O., & Kehinde, O.J. (2013): Social networking and business performance: the case of selected entrepreneurs in Ota, Nigeria. In Journal of Business Administration and Management Sciences Research, 2 (5), pp. 116–122. Accessed from www.apexjournal.org/ JBAMSR.

26 Van-Geenhuizen, M. (2008): Knowledge networks of young innovators in the urban economy: biotechnology as a case study. In Entrepreneurship and Regional Development, 20, pp. 161–183.

27 Granovetter, M. (1985): Economic action and social structure: the problem of embeddedness. In American Journal of Sociology, 91 (3), pp. 481–510.

28 Adams, M., Makramalla, M., & Miron, W. (2014): Down the Rabbit hole: how structural holes in entrepreneurs' social networks impact early venture growth. In Technology Innovation Management Review, 31 (4), pp. 45–57.

29 Burt, R.S. (2002): The social capital of structural holes. In The new economic sociology, M.F.Guillen, R.Collins, P.England, & M.Meyer (eds). pp. 148–189. Russell Sage Foundation: New York.

30 Abou-Moghli, A.A. & Al-Kasasbeh, M.M. (2012): Social network and the success of business start-up. In International Journal of Business and Management, 7 (9), pp. 14–25.

31 Raider, H., & Krackhardt, D. (2002): Intra-organizational networks. In The Blackwell companion to organizations. pp. 58–74.

32 Klyver, K., & Hindle, K. (in press): Influence of social network structure on entrepreneurship participation: gender differences studied across 47 countries. In International Entrepreneurship and Management Journal 4(3), pp. 331–347 DOI: 10.1007/s11365-007-0053-0.

33 Carpenter, D.P., Esterling, K.M., & Lazer, D.M.J. (1998): The strength of strong ties: a model of contact-making in policy networks with evidence from US health politics. In Journal of Theoretical Politics, 10 (4), pp. 417–444.

34 Baron, R.A. (2006): Opportunity recognition as the detection of meaningful patterns: evidence from comparisons of novice and experienced entrepreneurs. In Management Science, 52 (9), pp. 1331–1344.

35 Ozgen, E. (2003): Entrepreneurial opportunity recognition: information flow, social and cognitive perspectives. n.p.

36 Lim, W.L., & Xavier, S.R. (2015): Opportunity recognition framework: exploring the technology entrepreneurs. In American Journal of Economics, 5 (2), pp. 105–111. DOI: 10.5923/c.economics.201501.10.

37 Schweizer, R., Vahlne, J.-E., & Johanson, J. (2010): Internationalization as an entrepreneurial process. In Journal of International Entrepreneurship, 8 (4), pp. 343–370. DOI: 10.1007/s10843-010-0064-8.

38 Shane, S. (2000): Prior knowledge and the discovery of entrepreneurial opportunities. In Organizational Sciences, 11 (4), pp. 448–469.

39 Alvarez, A.S., Barney, J.B., & Young, S.L. (2007): Debates in entrepreneurship: opportunity formation and implications for the field of entrepreneurship. Springer Science Business Media, LLC USA.

40 Sharma, A., & Salwan, P. (2016): Role of social ties in opportunity recognition and moderation effect of SE. Conference paper in Academy of Management Annual Meeting Proceedings. DOI: 10.5465/AMBPP.17314.

41 Kontinen, T., & Ojala, A. (2011): International opportunity recognition among small and medium sized family firms. In Journal of Small Business Management, 49 (3), pp. 490–514.

42 Davidsson, P., & Honig, B. (2003): The role of social and human capital among nascent entrepreneurs. In Journal of Business Venturing, 18 (3), pp. 301–331.

43 Dyer, J.H., Gregersen, H.B., & Christensen, C. (2008): Entrepreneur behaviors, opportunity recognition, and the origins of innovative ventures. In Strategic Entrepreneurship Journal, 2, pp. 317–338.

44 Egbert, H. (2009): Business success through social networks? A comment on social networks and business success. In American Journal of Economics & Sociology, 68 (3), pp. 665–677. DOI: 10.1111/j.1536-7150.2009.00643.x.

45 Rapport, A. (1986): General system theory: essential concepts & applications. Abacus Press: Cambridge, MA.

46 Arca, C. (2012): Social media marketing benefits for businesses: why and how should every business create and develop its social media sites?Thesis submitted in partial fulfillment of Master of International Marketing, Alborg University: Denmark.

47 Stoka, O.S., & Tomski, P. (2015): Internet social media and international entrepreneurial intentions. The 2015 WEI International Academic Conference Proceedings Vienna, Austria.

48 Broughton, A., Foley, B., Ledermaier, S., & Cox, A. (2013): The use of social media in the recruitment process, Research Paper, Institute for Employment Studies Sovereign House: Brighton. p. 1.

49 Fischer, E., & Reuber, A.R. (2011): Social interaction via new social media: (How) can interactions on Twitter affect effectual thinking and behavior?In Journal of Business Venturing, 26, pp. 1–18.

50 Butler, J., & HansenG. (1991): Network evolution, entrepreneurial success, and regional development. In Entrepreneurship and Regional Development, 3 (1). DOI: 10.1080/08985629100000001.

51 Arnold, C. (2004): Not done net: "new opportunities still exists in online research". In Marketing News, p. 17.

52 Nima, M.R., & Sharon, W.T. (2003): Contributing factors: several issues affects e-research validity. In Marketing News, p. 50.

53 Dysart, J. (2004): Cutting market research cost with on-site surveys. *The Secured Lender.* pp. 64–67.

54 Miles, L. (2004): Online on tap. In Marketing, pp. 39–40.

55 Oyza, I., & Edwin, A. (2015): Effectiveness of social media networks as a strategic tool for organizational marketing management. In Journal of Internet Banking, 2, pp. 6.

56 Brett, E., Kleinert, V., & Karamatova, L. (2010): The new venture creation process in cooperation with science park Jönköping. Bachelor Thesis, Jön-Köping international business school.

57 Rwigema, H., & Venter, R. (2004): Advanced entrepreneurship. Oxford University Press: Southern Africa.

58 Ayotte, K. (2007): Bankruptcy and entrepreneurship: the value of a fresh start. In The Journal of Law, Economics, & Organization, 23 (1), pp. 161–185.

59 Mc-Mahon, R.G.P. (2001): 'Development orientation and business growth and performance among Australian manufacturing SMEs', Accessed 22 July, 2008, from www.sbaer.uca.edu/research/icsb/1999/16.pdf.

60 Shane, S., & Cable, D. (2002): Network ties, reputation, and the financing of new ventures. In Management Science, 48 (3), pp. 364–381.

61 Granovetter, M. (1973): Strength of weak ties. In American Journal of Sociology, 78 (6), pp. 1360–1380.

62 Santarelli, E., & Tran, H.T. (2012): The interplay of human and social capital in shaping entrepreneurial performance: the case of Vietnam. In Small Business Economics, 40 (2), pp. 435–458.

63 Jin, F., Wu, A., & Hitt, L. (2017): Social is the new financial: how startup social media activity influences funding outcomes. In Management Science, 57 (9), pp. 1623–1639.

64 Aldrich, H.E., & Fiol, C.M. (1994): Fools rush in? The institutional context of industry creation. In Academy of Management Review, 19 (4), pp. 645–670.

65 Hong, N. (2013): If you look good on Twitter, VCs may take notice. In The Wall Street Journal. Accessed 21 March, 2014, fromhttp://online.wsj.com/news/articles/SB10001424127887324659404578997919605.

66 Clark, M.& Melancon, J. (2013): The influence of social media investment on relational outcomes: a relationship marketing perspective. In International Journal of Marketing Studies, 5 (4), pp. 132–142.

67 Baron, R.A., & Markman, G.D.(2003): Beyond social capital: the role of entrepreneurs' social competence in their financial success. In Journal of Business Venturing, 18 (1), pp. 41–60.

68 David, F. (2009): Strategic management concepts and cases. Pearson education Inc: Upper Saddle River, NJ. Person Prentice Hall.

69 Lamons, B. (2001): Eureka! Future of B to B research is online. In *Marketing News*, pp. 9–10.

70 Desa, G. (2008): Mobilizing resources in constrained environments: a study of technology social ventures. A dissertation submitted in partial fulfillment of the requirements for the degree of Doctor of Philosophy, University of Washington.

71 Pfeffer, J., & Salancik, G.R. (1978): The external control of organizations: a resource dependence perspective. Harper & Row: New York.

72 Kotler, P., Keller, K.L., Ang, S.H., Leoung, S.M., & Tan, C.T. (2009): Marketing management: an Asian perspective. Pearson education: South Asia, Singapore.

73 Business insider. (2016): The top 5 digital trends for 2016. BI Intelligence.

74 Global Talent Trends. (2015): Linkedin talent solution.

75 Weil, H.B. (2012): Turning Innovation into value. In Systemic management for intelligent organizationsS.Grösser & R.Zeier (eds). Springer-Verlag Berlin Heidelberg: New York, NY.

76 O'Leary, D.E. (2011): The use of social media in the supply chain: survey and extensions. In Intelligent Systems in Accounting, Finance and Management, 18, pp. 121–144.

77 Hayek, F.A. (1945): The use of knowledge in society. In American Economic Review, 35 (4), pp. 519–530.

78 Surowiecki, J. (2004): The wisdom of crowds. Random House: New York.

79 Ashcroft, J. (2010): Social media in the supply chain. Aberdeen Group Presentation, 13April. http://summits.aberdeen.com/1/Day1-%20Jeff%20Ashcroft.pdf.

80 O'Leary, D.E. (2000): Reengineering merge-in-transit for electronic commerce. In Information System Frontiers, 1 (4), pp. 379–387.

81 Anderson, A.R.& Jack, S.L. (2002): The articulation of social capital in entrepreneurial networks: a glue or a lubricant?In Entrepreneurship & Regional Development, 14 (3), pp. 193–210.

82 Bria, F. (2015): Social media and their impact on organizations: building firm celebrity and organizational legitimacy through social media. Doctor of Philosophy thesis submitted to imperial college business school, London.

83 Colleoni, E., Arvidsson, A., Hansen, L.K., & Marchesini, M. (2011): Measuring corporate reputation using sentiment analysis. In *The 15th International Conference on Corporate Reputation*.

84 Scheufele, D.A., & Tewksbury, D. (2007): Framing, agenda setting, and priming: the evolution of three media effects models. In Journal of Communication, 57 (1), pp. 9–20.

85 Deephouse, D.L. (2000): Media reputation as a strategic resource: integration of mass communication and resource-based theories. In Journal of Management, 26 (6), pp. 1091–1112.

86 Lans, T., Blok, V., & Gulikers, J. (2015): Show me your network and I'll tell you who you are: social competence and social capital of early-stage entrepreneurs. In Entrepreneurship & Regional Development, 27, pp. 7–8.

87 Scuotto, V., Guidice, M.D., & Carayannis, E.G. (2017): The effect of social networking sites and absorptive capacity on SMES' innovation performance. In Journal of Technology Transfer, 42, pp. 409–424. DOI: 10.1007/s10961-016-9517-0

88 Amy, K., & Poston, B. (2013): Social media and product—Early adopters reaping benefits amidst challenge and uncertainty. Kalypso white paper. Accessed fromhttp://kalypso.com/downloads/insights/Kalypso_Social_Media_and_Product_Innovation_1.pdf.

89 Hanna, R., Rohm, A., & Crittenden, V.L. (2011): We're all connected: the power of the social media ecosystem. In Business Horizons, 54, pp. 265–273.

90 Garretson, R. (2008): Future tense: the global CMO, [online] Accessed 12 October, 2014, fromhttp://graphics.eiu.com/upload/Google%20Text.pdf.

91 Hobday, M. (1995): East Asian latecomer firms: learning the technology of electronics. In World Development, 23 (7), pp. 1171–1193.

92 KimW.-S. (2004): Effects of a trust mechanism on complex adaptive supply networks: an agent-based social simulation study. In Journal of Artificial Societies and Social Simulation, 12, p. 4.

93 Bozz, Allen, & Hamilton. (2008): New product management for the 1980s. New York.

94 Kietzmann, J.C. (2013): Bittersweet! Understanding and managing electronic word of mouth. In Journal of Public Affairs, 13, pp. 146–159.

95 Paquette, H. (2013): Social media as a marketing tool: a literature review. Major papers by University of Rhodes Highland Master of Science Students. Paper 2. Accessed fromhttp://digitalcommons.uri.edu/tmd_major_papers/2.

96 Amaldoss, W.C.H. (2010): Product variety, informative advertising, and price competition. In Journal of Marketing Research, 47 (1), pp. 146–156.

97 Li, X.& Hitt, L.M. (2008): Self-selection and information role of online product reviews. In Information Systems Research, 19 (4), pp. 456–474.

98 Cheong, H.J., & Morrison, M.A. (2008): Consumers' reliance on product information and recommendations found in UGC. In Journal of Interactive Advertising, 8 (2), pp. 1–30.

99 Shankar, V., Inman, J., Mantrala, M., Kelley, E., & Rizley, R. (2011): Innovations in shopper marketing: current insights and future research issues. In Journal of Retailing, p. 87. DOI: 10.1016/j.jretai.2011.04.007.

100 Hoffman, D.L., & Fodor, M. (2010): Can you measure the ROI of your social media marketing?In MIT Sloan Management Review, 52 (1), pp. 41–49.

101 Arreolla, M.F. (2016): The emergence of the social media entrepreneur. ESSCA School of Management 56 Quai Alphonse Le Gallo 92513 Boulogne-Billancourt: France.

102 Cha, J. (2009): Shopping on social networking web sites attitudes toward real versus virtual items. In Journal of Interactive Advertising, 10 (1), pp. 77–93.

103 AOLPlatform. (2014): Myth-busting social media advertising: do ads on social Web sites work? Multi-touch attribution makes it possible to separate the facts from fiction. In Convertro Cross-Client Attribution Data, Q1, p. 2014.

104 Eltantawy, N., & Wiest, J.B. (2011): Social media in the Egyptian revolution: reconsidering resource mobilization theory. In International Journal of Communication, 5, pp. 1207–1224.

105 Burt, R.S. (1992): Structural holes: the social structure of competition. Harvard University Press: Cambridge, MA.

106 Elfring, T., & Hulsink, W. (2002): Entrepreneurs, innovation and high-technology firms: the network effect. In Journal of Management Research, 1 (5), pp. 22–44. DOI:10.1023/A:1026180418357.

107 Andrew, K. (2007): Cooperation between cooperation and environmental groups: a transaction cost perspective. In Academy of Management Perspective, 32 (3), p. 889.

108 Aarstad, J. (2012): Do structural holes and network connectivity really affect entrepreneurial performance? In Journal of Entrepreneurship, 21 (2), pp. 253–268. DOI:10.1177/0971355712449788.

Chapter 4

Sustainable Entrepreneurial Activity within Complex Economic Systems

Panagiotis E. Petrakis and Kyriaki I. Kafka

1   Introduction

The functioning of economies is perceived as a complex system of economic and social relations and actions. Such relations in this complex system are especially compound.

The economic system's complexity does not leave entrepreneurial activity untouched. The increase in the degree of complexity in the past decades since the new conditions that have been observed, stemming from the constantly changing environment (due to economic and political events, globalization, as well as disruptive technologies, etc.), raises questions concerning the factors that form entrepreneurial evolution in the global competitive markets.

Due to this increased degree of complexity, the environment where enterprises operate is usually characterized by a high degree of uncertainty, which affects decision-making in firms. In this context of complex relationships, enterprises lay their strategic planning on foundations with sociological, psychological, and economic elements both individually and at corporate level.

This chapter aims at first to present and analyze the concept of economic complexity within the context of economic theory and then to describe the effect of economic complexity upon entrepreneurial activity. To this end, five hypotheses are formed concerning the relation of complexity with entrepreneurial activity and are tested whether they can be confirmed or not. Accordingly, data from 93 economies across the world from 2001 to 2016 are used to shed light on the effects of complexity upon entrepreneurial activity: the interconnection of complexity with the utilization of entrepreneurial opportunities, the skills and knowledge required for starting up a new firm, entrepreneurial failure, early-stage entrepreneurial activity, and the motives of entrepreneurial action.

The chapter is structured as follows: Section 2 presents the concept of complexity and describes it within the context of economic theory; Section 3 shows the theoretic interconnection between economic complexity and entrepreneurial activity, whereas, at the same time, our hypotheses are developed and then tested; Section 4 describes the relation between the index of economic complexity and several variables that represent entrepreneurial activity to ascertain whether these hypotheses are confirmed or not; lastly, the Section 5 presents the conclusions.

2   The Concept of Complexity within Economic Theory

The economic system's complexity is linked with an economy's ability to reach the point of equilibrium. In a complex economic system, it is difficult to reach equilibrium since economic agents constantly change their strategies and behaviors.

Thus, the economy is a complex system comprised by elements that interact in multiple ways. Similar complex systems are found in biology, physics, chemistry, etc. A system as such describes how relations among several components form collective and individual behaviors as well as how interactive relations with the economic and social environment are developed.

Definitions that may be attributed to a complex system vary. However, a definition made by Herbert Simon [1, p. 267] is dominant: *Roughly, by a complex system I mean one made up of a large number of parts that interact in a non-simple way. In such systems, the whole is more than the sum of the parts, not in an ultimate, metaphysical sense, but in the important pragmatic sense that, given the properties of the parts and the laws of their interaction, it is not a trivial matter to infer the properties of the whole. In the face of complexity, an in-principle reductionist may be at the same time a pragmatic holist.*

The concept of complexity is not a new approach in economic theory. It rather offers a different perspective on how the economy is perceived [2–4] focusing on the process of changes and creation.

'*It is very important to understand that the world with which we are concerned is continually changing*' [5]. Our world is non-ergodic,[1] we live and learn in uncertainty, knowledge and prediction are limited, always founded on representations and images from the past, while at the same time, we are unable to develop perfect strategies. Thus, however, collective knowing becomes the main evolutionary force that connects and sets the rules of the game in the market systems of which quality changes over time. Therefore, complexity is described as a 'messy cognitive evolution' in which people change beliefs and behaviors.

Durlauf and Young [9] form a similar logic. By using the term 'new social economics', they describe economy as a socio-economic system comprised by heterogeneous individuals that interact among themselves, such as for instance the prices through markets. Individuals and other stakeholders in the economy are connected through networks that considerably affect the economy's evolution. Thus, interactions among consumers, firms, and institutions would constantly evolve and no automatic tendency to equilibrium would exist in the sense in which this term is used in economics [10].

Along with the concept of complexity, the concept of time is also introduced adding the creation of new structures. Neoclassical economics handles time poorly [11,12] equating the economy with a simple system. At the point of equilibrium, the outcome is simply maintained and the concept of time is absent [13] or, in dynamic models, a parameter may keep changing in order to denote the current outcome [14]. In a complex system, time adds a special character to the economy where non-repeatable events lead to new outcomes, new structures, new technology, new institutions, and ultimately to a new future path.

The economic system's complexity raises questions on governance and the effectiveness of policies applied. Adam Smith was one of the first who tried to approach and express this phenomenon in a clear manner. The effort made by Pareto [15,16] to demarcate the forces that determine income distribution was one of the first attempts to explain phenomena where equilibrium is absent as well as complex situations. The weakness of economics to include complex systems in its analysis may be one of the most important reasons behind the fact that economic theory has not advanced in the past years compared to other sciences [17].

Generally, since 'The Wealth of Nations', economics have dealt more with resource allocation rather than economic evolution and the time path between equilibrium points. However, an equilibrium path signifies multiple levels of decisions and implies macroevolution, which is not only the progression of microevolution [18]. Then, through general equilibrium models that were developed, an attempt was made to resolve the problem of resource allocation using mathematical models.

Neoclassical economics were greatly influenced by the principles of physical science in the late nineteenth century and especially the idea that a great number of interacting identical elements could be objectively analyzed via simple mathematical equations [19]. Over time it became common wisdom that the core of economic theory could be captured via simple mathematical expressions. This led to an oversimplification of economic theory that neglected complexity. This happened because the mathematization of economics ignored important parameters such as politics, society, uncertainty, and expectations. Thus, the neoclassical economists saw the economy as a simple system with predetermined relations between the homogeneous economic agents and their behaviors.

Historically, economist and philosopher Friedrich Hayek can be characterized as one of the founders of the complex systems phenomenon analysis in economics. His main contribution is that complex economic phenomena should expand towards biology, psychology, etc. with humans as protagonists in order to construct models with limited predictive capacity.

According to Schumpeter, markets do not function mechanically reaching equilibrium in homogeneous goods markets by providing profit maximization to producers and utility maximization to consumers. He notes that what matters are the system's inflows and outflows. The phrase he used to describe this was 'creative destruction', which identifies with the perspective of complexity science [20].

According to the evolutionists [21,22], it is impossible to interpret this complex world with a simple theoretic conception that includes a set of processes, such as production, prices, and profit maximization within the framework of the theory of the firm, as well as individual utility maximization behavior in a constantly changing equilibrium. Evolutionary thinking includes behaviors, practices, routines, and technologies that keep changing in line with innovative developments and are transmitted between successive actors and firms via the cultural background platform over time.

The change in one element of the system, which may come from an external or internal shock, makes the system deviate from equilibrium.

Studying a complex system includes examining how a system's structural elements that are hierarchically low interact and phenomena emerge that may ultimately affect stability and create distortions.

A complex system is characterized by both self-organization and having its own rules. Thus, one may claim that it is adaptive [23]. Beinhocker [24], in the book titled *The Origins of Wealth: Evolution, Complexity, and the Radical Remaking of Economics* trying to explain how the economy works, elucidates the concept of 'adaptivity'. The adjective 'adaptive' is used to stress the fact that the economy follows an evolutionary dynamic that is never in equilibrium. On the contrary, it is always vulnerable to endogenous or exogenous shock.

The differences between neoclassical theory and the supporters of the idea that the economy is a complex system are outlined as follows [24]: a) in system dynamics (in the sense that a complex economy is far from a point of equilibrium since it has dynamic characteristics that always keep it at distance contrary to the Walrasian general equilibrium); b) in the role of economic agents (individuals' knowledge and information are limited while their processing incurs high costs; thus, they develop heuristic rules in contrast with the neoclassical model where information is perfect and costless); c) in the process of evolution (the evolutionary process provides the system with the elements of differentiation and innovation so that it augments); in the Walrasian model, no mechanisms can be developed that would create new structural elements or maximize complexity and the relations among the economic agents.

The relations developed cannot be explained by the assumption that the economic system's stakeholders develop behaviors as that of a representative agent. On the contrary, the systems consist of heterogeneous individuals that form totally different behaviors with varying responses to similar situations they have to deal with. In a complex system, such as the economy, the approach of the representative agent is quite weak and simplifying. Ideally, this would be realistic if all stakeholders had access to the same information and knew the others' reactions. Consequently, a deeper problem in the foundations of economic theory is created, pertinent to the view that the economy is a compound and self-regulated system. This problem is no other than the fact that all information is dispersed among individuals, something which Hayek [25] had overtly stressed.

Although the Walrasian general equilibrium model focuses on the agents' exchanges and the markets that form the prices, it is unable to take into account the 'externalities' that play a key role in the behaviors and preferences of the individuals that deviate from the rationality axiom and the assumption for any tendency to equilibrium. This is where the basic difference of the general equilibrium model and the economy as a complex system approach lies.

Another important parameter of the complex system is the fact that individuals have limited intellectual abilities to handle and process the amount of available information. It would also be realistic to assume that their rationality is bounded [26] and that they experience informational limitations [10]. Such restrictions lead people to make decisions based on heuristic rules rather than the rationality assumption. Investment choices are driven by psychology. This results to a weakened relation between information and the tendency of the market to become devitalized. Behavioral economics attempt to cover the chasm between theory and praxis regarding imperfect information and the behavior of individuals by incorporating elements of psychology. Some economic phenomena may be better understood if we assume that investors are not completely rational. 'Herd behavior' is a typical example where individuals mimic other people's actions assuming that the latter have inside information which they are unaware of [27,28].

3 Complexity and Entrepreneurial Activity

This section analyzes the relationship between complexity and entrepreneurship in the context of five aspects: a) the utilization of entrepreneurial opportunities, b) the requirements concerning skills and knowledge to start up a new firm, c) entrepreneurial failure, d) early-stage entrepreneurial activity and e) the motives of entrepreneurial activity.

3.1 Utilization of Entrepreneurial Opportunities and Complexity

In literature, the concept of 'entrepreneurial opportunity' has been approached and analyzed variedly. It concerns the activity that includes the discovery, evaluation, and utilization of entrepreneurial capabilities, the introduction of new products and services, the organizational method, new markets, new processes, and raw materials [29,30].

There are two general positions concerning the types and sources of entrepreneurial opportunities: a) Schumpeter's entrepreneurial opportunities [31], according to whom entrepreneurial opportunities are related to a society's individuals who have the responsibility to create innovative entrepreneurial forms and may be found in technological changes, political/regulatory changes, but also socio-demographic changes, and b) Kirzner's [32], according to whom an entrepreneur is the person who will discover the opportunities, which are found in the environment and emerge due to the market disequilibrium. Entrepreneurial opportunities may be found anytime and anywhere since they will come up due a market disequilibrium caused by errors or oversights.

However, the most reliable and complete discussion on entrepreneurial opportunity is considered to be that of Shane and Venkataraman [29] because they correlate it with entrepreneurship. Hence, the real dimensions of both concepts are described. In particular, Shane and Venkataraman's approach [29] focuses on the entrepreneurial opportunities through three fundamental questions: 1) When, how, and why opportunities emerge creating new goods and services; 2) when, how, and why certain people – and not others – discover and make use of these opportunities; 3) when, how, and why different methods of action are employed for the utilization of entrepreneurial opportunities.

In order to formulate a complete definition on the concept of entrepreneurship, who the entrepreneur is but also what he or she does, an approach is needed to research creative opportunities, acumen, the ability to perceive opportunities and the limits of action. It is, thus, especially important to understand how individuals: a) use already existing knowledge and experience to discover and make use of entrepreneurial opportunities, b) develop strategies to get higher returns than the cost of resources needed to make use of an entrepreneurial opportunity, and c) discover and create competitive advantages in an uncertain and competitive environment.

Complexity's role in all three concerns is deemed important; it is expected to affect how individuals use already existing knowledge and experience and how easily they may develop strategies and discover and create competitive advantages.

For instance, in the past years, a reduction of small entrepreneurial activity is observed in the USA [33–35]. It mostly concerns a decrease in startups given that firm startup rates decreased from about 13% in the early 1980s to 10% before the Great Recession and eventually to 8% by 2012 [36]. This seems to be owed to the effects of globalization and foreign competition against US businesses which is probably more serious than what was previously believed [37–39] leading to the creation of technological giants that absorb these new ideas. This results to the disappearance of entrepreneurial opportunities [40] and it happens mostly in globalized and developed economies where the degree of complexity is high.

This is how Hypothesis 1 is formulated, according to which the high degree of complexity is negatively linked with the utilization of entrepreneurial opportunities.

Hypothesis 1: The high degree of economic complexity is negatively linked with the utilization of entrepreneurial opportunities.

3.2 Requirements for Skills and Knowledge and Complexity

The new conditions, stemming from the constantly changing environment, globalization, the changing economic and political structures, new technologies, specialized customer requirements, and the emphasis on product and service quality, have led economies to appreciate the especially important role of skills and knowledge in the persistently more and more competitive global markets.

Skills and knowledge are mostly acquired through exchanges and communication with other individuals as well as through information via reading and observing. The concepts and management of skills and knowledge are subjects of systematic research in the attempt to find the reasons for the development of firms [41–45]. If skills and knowledge are properly used and capitalized, they create a comparative advantage for firms to be created or so that already existing firms become more sustainable, competitive and innovative [46].

Skills and knowledge as an internal instrument to strengthen competition [47] are basic instruments especially for smaller firms so that they catch up with the rapid expansion of markets [48]. The weakness of small- and medium-sized firms lies on the fact that they are all entrepreneur-driven and most have very weak knowledge in management practices. The challenge for firms is to be able to capture knowledge and to leverage it through their functioning. Consequently, the development of small- and medium-sized firms seems to depend at an important extent on the provision of education to workers and the official training of lead entrepreneurs [49].

However, Hershbein and Kahn [50] using microdata from nearly 100 million electronic job postings in the United States that span the Great Recession (between 2007 and 2015) conclude that skill requirements in job vacancy postings differentially increased in firms that were hit hard by the Great Recession, compared to less hard-hit firms. This means that the conditions of crisis and uncertainty lead to higher requirements for skills and knowledge. We should therefore expect that also in conditions of a high degree of economic complexity, the requirements for skills and knowledge for starting up new entrepreneurial activities to increase. Therefore, those who believe that they have the skills and knowledge required to start up a business will be less.

Thus, Hypothesis 2 is formed due to the fact that countries with a high number of small-and medium-sized firms are usually less developed that are related to a decreased degree of complexity and because complexity conditions and in general uncertain situations lead to higher requirements for skills and knowledge.

Hypothesis 2: The high degree of economic complexity is negatively linked with the number of individuals who believe that they meet the appropriate requirements for skills and knowledge in order to be in position to start up an entrepreneurial activity.

3.3 Entrepreneurial Failure and Complexity

The literature includes various views concerning the definition and the causality of entrepreneurial failure. In general, it is deemed that it is related either to the discontinuity of a firm's operation or its bankruptcy. Some researchers believe that entrepreneurial failure exists only when a business goes bankrupt [51]. Others maintain that there are many forms of entrepreneurial failure, such as mergers with other companies or buy-outs. There are, lastly, also those who state that entrepreneurial failure takes place when the firm is not able to meet its obligations towards its stakeholders (employees, suppliers, customers and owners).

Simplified definitions of entrepreneurial failure, such as the discontinuance of ownership or business and bankruptcy, are not satisfying. Due to the problems brought about by these simple definitions, researchers have formed more sophisticated definitions of entrepreneurial failure.

Ulmer and Nielsen [52] defined failure as follows: *'firms that were disposed of (sold or liquidated) with losses to prevent further losses'*. This definition, although satisfying, since it includes both bankrupt companies and those that are conclusively on the way to go bankrupt and have been sold to avoid it, it does not include the firms that are sold for profit. Bruno and Ledecker [53] include in their definition of failure the firms that are liquidated without declaring bankruptcy, the firms that are minimized to a proportion of their actual size, the firms wishing to merge due to financial difficulties, the firms that cannot pay off their debts and the firms that are insolvent and inefficient in fulfilling their obligations.

As to the main factors responsible for the failure of a firm, they are differentiated into exogenous and endogenous.

Exogenous factors include: a) state policy and the general economic environment (tax rates, the increase in money supply and the reduction of interest rates, uncertainty, bureaucratic procedures, etc.), b) the impact of the business cycle on the failure rates of firms [54], and c) natural disasters and extreme events since it is possible that they psychologically affect individuals and their economic behavior, they have assets of firms destroyed and they disrupt the economy and competition. Furthermore, they may create new entrepreneurial opportunities since they influence the population's perceptions [55] and consequently its habits, etc.

Factors of entrepreneurial failure which are usually considered as endogenous are: a) stagnation given that small firms fail when they fail to grasp new action methods and trust only one method that at some point stops being functional while at the same time the firm's existing structure may be harming to productivity and corporate entrepreneurship, b) the lack of funds or the erroneous evaluation of needs in capital, c) bad management and the entrepreneur's traits, the most commonly mentioned factor of entrepreneurial failure [56] and d) the wrongful handling of competition and the market. Gaskill et al. [57] stress the importance of a firm's ability to compete when successful. They mention the importance of high-quality services and goods as an ingredient for successful firms.

By using data drawn from a panel of 37 countries over a period of nine years (2006–2014), García-Ramos et al. [58] found that the greater the regulatory complexity, the higher the rate of entrepreneurial failure. Entrepreneurial activity is also negatively affected when regulation is too complex and there are too many administrative requirements, due to the fact that individuals' preferences change [59–62]. Regulatory complexity and the bureaucracy associated with entrepreneurial creation may also affect entrepreneurial failure [63].

Thus, a significant impact of complexity on the risk of entrepreneurial failure should be expected, since complexity directly concerns the external environment of a firm and is perhaps one of the most important exogenous factors that lead to entrepreneurial failure. Thus, Hypothesis 3 is formed which correlates economic complexity with the risk of entrepreneurial failure.

Hypothesis 3: The high degree of economic complexity is positively linked with the risk of entrepreneurial failure.

3.4 Early-Stage Entrepreneurial Activity and Complexity

Countries with a low per capita income, which are at the phase of development, usually reach higher levels of early-stage entrepreneurship, mainly due to their great number of small businesses which is quite typical to them. However, development and in particular industrialization and scale economies require larger and established firms that can meet the increasing demand. Therefore, the decrease in early-stage entrepreneurship in countries with low incomes may be a sign of development and transition to higher living standards. Nonetheless, a period of a long process of development allows the search for new entrepreneurial opportunities given that established firms play an important and increasing role.

Complexity is directly interconnected to the level of the observed bureaucracy.[2] Sorensen [64] argues that bureaucracy's impact is twofold: a) it may reduce the ability of individuals to perceive certain entrepreneurial opportunities, and b) it may increase the value of the available entrepreneurial opportunities, making firms leave innovations unexploited. For instance, Saxenian [65] examines the difference between markets in terms of firm size and bureaucracy. She concludes that markets, such as the one at Boston's Route 128, dominated by bureaucratic firms means that employees in these firms are overly insulated from entrepreneurial experiences and opportunities, in contrast with markets such as in Silicon Valley where the extent of bureaucracy is smaller.

There are four main channels through which bureaucracy impacts on entrepreneurial activity [64]: a) bureaucracies may influence the attitudes and mental dispositions of their employees in ways that make them less likely to enter entrepreneurship [66–68]; b) work in bureaucracies may limit the development of the skills necessary for successful entrepreneurship, and may therefore lower the expected value of entrepreneurial opportunities [69,70]; c) an employer's level of bureaucratization may shape the exposure of employees to entrepreneurial opportunities and activities [65,71,72]; d) bureaucracies create job stability and internal routes of advancement, thereby increasing the opportunity costs of leaving paid employment to find a new venture [73,74].

On the above grounds, we should expect that the high degree of economic complexity that mainly characterizes developed economies is linked with lower rates of early-stage entrepreneurial activity.

Hypothesis 4: The high degree of economic complexity is linked with lower rates of early stage entrepreneurial activity.

3.5   Entrepreneurial Action Motives and Complexity

Depending on the individual's motive in order to enter the business world, entrepreneurship is differentiated into necessity-motivated entrepreneurship and improvement-driven opportunity entrepreneurship.

In improvement-driven opportunity entrepreneurship, the motive is to utilize an entrepreneurial opportunity that is found by the aspiring entrepreneur. This entrepreneurial opportunity is evaluated in the context of the economic environment of the individual and is considered to be adequate to either lead to an income increase or offer professional independence or cover some other internal need.

Respectively, necessity-motivated entrepreneurship refers to the case when individuals resort to entrepreneurial activity because they have no other option for work, they feel discontent with their jobs, they fear of getting fired in the near future or because they aim at preserving their income which they may be expecting that it will keep decreasing in the future.

The division between necessity-motivated entrepreneurship and improvement-driven opportunity entrepreneurship is directly linked with the level of each country's per capita income [75]; the highest the per capita income (usually in developed countries), the greater the percentage of new entrepreneurs motivated by their desire to take advantage of an opportunity than for livelihood [76]. In developing countries, the phenomenon of necessity-motivated entrepreneurship is more blatant since opportunities to find salaried employment are relatively limited.

On the above grounds and given that most developed economies seem to have a high degree of complexity [77], we should expect that the higher the degree of complexity, the greater the rate of new entrepreneurship characterized as improvement-driven opportunity entrepreneurship rather than necessity-motivated entrepreneurship and this is how Hypothesis 5 is formulated.

Hypothesis 5: The high degree of economic complexity is positively linked with improvement-driven opportunity motivated entrepreneurship and negatively with necessity-motivated entrepreneurship.

4   Hypothesis Testing: Complexity and Entrepreneurial Activity

Economic complexity is estimated by how composite is a country's base of production and reflects the structures emerging to maintain and combine knowledge [77]. Increased economic complexity is necessary for a society so that it may maintain and use a greater amount of productive knowledge and we may measure it via the mix of the products that countries are in position to produce.

The Economic Complexity Index (ECI) as calculated[3] in the Atlas of Economic Complexity of the Center of International Development of Harvard University is a measure of a society's productive knowledge and illustrates the complexity of economies on the basis of the quantity and complexity of exported products, as well as the frequency of exports from 128 countries. The networks of industries, the mutual utilization, and development of their products, as well as the increase in their complexity, may substantially contribute to social prosperity. Therefore, knowledge and utilization of common knowledge are of crucial importance for a society. The countries with low ECI export a limited number of products exported by countries that may not be very different, showing that there are countries with low variation and that their exported products are not very advanced.

The below scatter plots show the relation among ECI values with variables that indicate entrepreneurial activity as they are calculated by the Global Entrepreneurship Monitor (GEM), the world's foremost study of entrepreneurship. The analysis includes data from 93 countries – across the world – for the period spanning from 2001 to 2016, while not all data are equally available for all countries. Also, the analysis is limited to economies and the years for which there are data in the Atlas of Economic Complexity and the Global Entrepreneurship Monitor.

Figure 1 shows the relation between economic complexity and the perceived entrepreneurial opportunities. Perceived opportunities express the percentage of the population aged 18–64 years who see good opportunities to start up a business in their area. Hypothesis 1 is confirmed, since it seems that the higher the degree of economic complexity, the smaller the percentage of individuals aged 18–64 years who see good opportunities to start up a business in their area. This is an expected relation and shows the fact that in economies characterized by an increased complexity degree, this presents difficulties for economic agents initially to trace and then to make use of any entrepreneurial opportunity existing in their area, since they do not use in a satisfying manner already existing knowledge and experience and cannot adequately and effectively develop strategies and discover and create competitive advantages.

Figure 2 shows the relation between economic complexity and perceived capabilities. Perceived capabilities are expressed as the percentage of the population aged 18–64 years who believe that they have the skills and knowledge required to start up a business. Again, as in the case of perceived opportunities, the greater the degree of complexity, the smaller the percentage of the population who think that they have the skills and knowledge required to start up a business. This is linked with a) the fact that developing and less developed economies,

Entrepreneurial Complexity

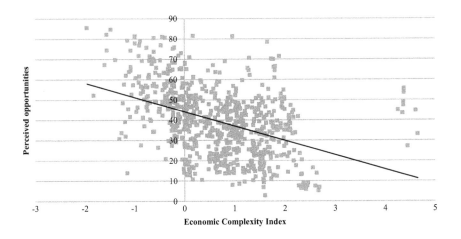

FIGURE 1: Economic complexity and perceived opportunities

Note: The diagram was based on 734 observations made in respect with the available data for the two variables.

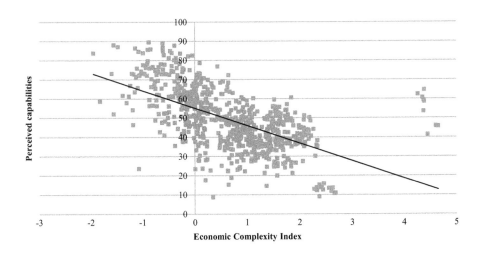

FIGURE 2: Economic complexity and perceived capabilities

Note: The diagram was based on 734 observations made in respect with the available data for the two variables.

characterized by a great number of small and medium sized firms, mostly rely on skills and knowledge and that large economies are characterized by a high degree of complexity and b) the fact that increased complexity is pertinent to stricter requirements for skills and knowledge so that someone is in a position to start up a business, given that the economic system's complexity requires higher management costs and abilities so that a new business is created and survives in the market. Thus, these individuals do not think that they meet these requirements and Hypothesis 2 is confirmed.

Figure 3 shows the relation between economic complexity and the rate of fear of failure. The fear of failure rate is the percentage of the population aged 18–64 years perceiving good opportunities but indicating that fear of failure would prevent them from starting up a business. While confirming hypothesis 3, the positive relation between the two measures is obvious. This means that the more economic complexity increases, the greater becomes the percentage of the population aged 18–64 years perceiving good opportunities but indicating that fear of failure would prevent them from starting up a business.

Figure 4 shows the relation between economic complexity and total early-stage entrepreneurial activity (TEA). TEA is the percentage of the adult population aged 18–64 years who are in the process of starting up a business (a nascent entrepreneur) or had started up a business in less than 42 months before the survey took place (owner-manager of a new business). It is rather an overall indicator of entrepreneurial activity and Figure 4 clearly shows it is negatively linked with economic complexity, confirming thus Hypothesis 4: the greater the degree of economic complexity, the lower the percentage of individuals who have started up

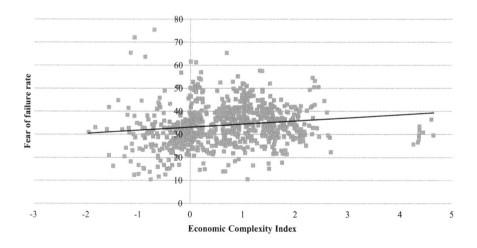

FIGURE 3: Economic complexity and fear of failure rate

Note: The diagram was based on 734 observations made in respect with the available data for the two variables.

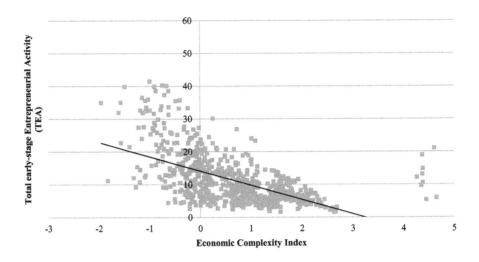

FIGURE 4: Economic complexity and total early-stage entrepreneurial activity
Note: The diagram was based on 734 observations made in respect with the available data for the two variables.

some entrepreneurial activity in the past 42 months or who are thinking of starting up one now.

Figure 5 shows the relation between economic complexity and the motivational index. This index expresses the percentage of those involved in TEA that are improvement-driven opportunity motivated, divided by the percentage of TEA that is necessity-motivated. The relative prevalence of an opportunity-owned business versus necessity-motivated (no other options for work) entrepreneurial activity provides useful insights into the quality of early stage entrepreneurial activity in any given economy. The positive relation shown in Figure 5 means that the greater the degree of economic complexity, the greater the percentage of those involved in TEA who are improvement-driven opportunity motivated than those who are necessity-motivated. This was an expected relation that confirmed Hypothesis 5 given that necessity-motivated entrepreneurship is observed at a great extent in economies with a low level of development and low degree of orientation to exports and of product variety, something which is linked with a lower degree of complexity.

5   Conclusions

In the contemporary globalized world, economic complexity is one of the basic features of how mostly developed economies function since it concerns

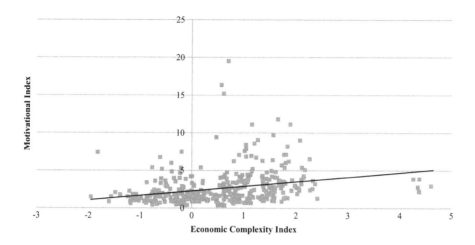

FIGURE 5: Economic complexity and motivational index

Note: The diagram was based on 445 observations made in respect with the available data for the two variables.

how complex an economy's base of production is and reflects the structures emerging to maintain and combine knowledge. The effects of complexity vary. However, this chapter focuses on the effects of complexity on entrepreneurial activity.

The previous analysis makes the impact of complexity on entrepreneurial activity obvious. Economies that are characterized by a high degree of complexity are usually economies that accomplish high performance and high levels of innovation and are able to produce adequately differentiated and innovative products that make them competitive within the market.

However, complexity is negatively interconnected with entrepreneurial activity. The analysis shows that all five hypotheses are confirmed since by using data from 93 countries for the period from 2001 to 2016, the following observations were made in countries with a high degree of complexity: 1) economic agents were faced with difficulties at first to trace and then to make use of any entrepreneurial opportunities existing in their area; 2) the percentage of the population who thinks that has the skills and knowledge required to start up a business is smaller; 3) the percentage of the population aged 18–64 years perceiving good opportunities but indicating that fear of failure would prevent them from starting up a business is higher; 4) the percentage of individuals who have started up an entrepreneurial activity in the past 42 months or who are thinking of starting up one now is smaller; 5) the percentage of those involved in TEA that are improvement-driven opportunity motivated rather than necessity-motivated is greater.

In order, thus, for a firm to be sustainable, it should be in a position to effectively manage high complexity and to predict the expected developments in the economy and society. The extent to which an entrepreneur is in position to manage complexity and to accept risk and uncertainty depends on his or her cognitive biases, which in their turn affect the decision-making process.

Notes

1 *"In a non-ergodic world, the future is unknown due to the existence of uncertainty. In general, the ergodic axiom assumes the economic future is already predetermined. The economy is governed by an existing ergodic stochastic process. One merely has to calculate probability distributions regarding future prices and output to draw significant and reliable statistical inferences (information) about the future. Once self-interested decision-makers have reliable information about the future, their actions on free markets will optimally allocate resources into those activities that will have the highest possible future returns thereby assuring global prosperity"* [6]. *"In a non-ergodic world, one can never expect whatever data set exists today to provide a reliable guide to future outcomes. In such a world, markets cannot be efficient"* [7]. *"In a world where observations are drawn from a non-ergodic stochastic environment, past data cannot provide any reliable information about future probability distributions. Agents in a non-ergodic environment 'know' they cannot reliably know future outcomes"* [8].

2 Bureaucracy is defined as a specific form of organization defined by complexity, division of labor, permanence, professional management, hierarchical coordination and control, strict chain of command, and legal authority (Encyclopedia Britannica). Thus it may be seen as an indication of complexity in economies.

3 The ECI is defined in terms of an eigenvector of a matrix connecting countries to countries, which is a projection of the matrix connecting countries to the products they export. Since the ECI considers information on the diversity of countries and the ubiquity of products, it is able to produce a measure of economic complexity containing information about both the diversity of a country's export and their sophistication [77].

References

1 Simon, H.A. (1969): The sciences of the artificial. Cambridge, MA: MIT Press.
2 Arthur, W.B. (1999): Complexity and the economy. In Science, 284, pp. 107–109.
3 Arthur, W.B. (2006): Out-of-equilibrium economics and agent-based modeling. In L. Tesfatsion and K. Judd, (op. cit. below).
4 Fontana, M. (2010): Can neoclassical economics handle complexity? The fallacy of the oil spot dynamic. In Journal of Economic Behavior & Organization, 76, pp. 584–596.
5 North, D. (1990): Institutions, institutional change and economic performance. Cambridge: Cambridge University Press.
6 Davidson, P. (2012): Is economics a science? Should economics be rigorous? Real-world economics, Review no 59, March 12, pp. 58–66.
7 Davidson, P. (2002): Financial markets money and the real world. Cheltenham: Elgar.
8 Davidson, P. (2006): Keynes and Money. In P. Arestis and M. Sawyer (eds.), A handbook of alternative monetary economics, Cheltenham, UK and Northampton, MA: Edward Elgar, pp. 139–153.

9 Durlauf, Steven N. and H. Peyton Young. (2001): The New Social Economics. In Steven N. Durlauf and H. Peyton Young (eds.), Social dynamics, Washington, DC: Brookings Institution Press, Cambridge, MA and London: MIT Press, pp. 1–14.

10 Kirman, A. (2016): Complexity and economic policy: a paradigm shift or a change in perspective? A review essay on David Colander and Roland Kupers's complexity and the art of public policy. In Journal of Economic Literature, 54(2), pp. 534–572.

11 Smolin, L. (February 2009): Time and symmetry in models of economic markets. Mss.

12 Smolin, L. (2013): Time reborn. Harcourt, NY: Houghton, Mifflin.

13 Arthur, W.B. (2013): Complexity and the economy: a different framework for economic thought. SFI Working Paper: 2013-04-012, 2013-04-012.

14 Harris, D.J. (2003): Joan Robinson on 'History versus equilibrium', J. Robinson Centennial Conference, Burlington, VT.

15 Pareto, V. (1895): La Legge della Domanda. In Giornale Degli Economisti, 10(6), pp. 59–68.

16 Pareto, V. (1896): La Courbe de la Reparti-tion de la Richesse. In G. Busino (ed.), Oevres Completes de Vilfredo Pareto, 3,1-15 Ecrits sur la Corbe de la Repartition de la Richesse, Geneva: Librairie Droz, 1965. Originally published in 1896.

17 Farmer, J.D. (2012): Economics needs to treat the economy as a complex system. CRISIS publications working paper.

18 van Den Bergh Jeroen, C.J.M. and John M. Gowdy. (2003): The microfoundations of macroeconomics: an evolutionary perspective. In Cambridge Journal of Economics, Oxford University Press, 27(1), pp. 65–84, January.

19 Arthur, B. (2014): Complexity and the economy. New York: Oxford University Press, October 2014.

20 Allen, P.M. (2014): Evolution: complexity, uncertainty and innovation. In Journal of Evolutionary Economics, 24(2), pp. 265–289.

21 Nelson, Richard R. and Sidney G. Winter. (1974): Neoclassical vs. evolutionary theories of economic growth: critique and prospectus. In Economic Journal, December, 84(336), pp. 886–905.

22 Nelson, Richard R. and Sidney G. Winter. (1982): An evolutionary theory of economic change. Cambridge, MA: Harvard University Press.

23 Allen, P.M. (1990): Why the future is not what it was. In Futures, 22, pp. 554–570.

24 Beinhocker, E.D. (2006): The origin of wealth: evolution, complexity, and the radical remaking of economics. Boston: Harvard Business School Press.

25 Hayek, F. (1945): The use of knowledge in society. In The American Economic Review, 35(4), pp. 519–530.

26 Simon, Herbert A. (1947): Administrative behavior: a study of decision-making processes in administrative organizations. New York: Simon and Schuster, Free Press.

27 Banerjee, A.V. (1992): A simple model of herd behavior. In Quarterly Journal of Economics, 107(3), pp. 797–817.

28 Chamley, C.P. (2004): Rational herds: economic models of social learning. Cambridge and New York: Cambridge University Press.

29 Shane, S. and S. Venkataraman. (2000): The promise of entrepreneurship as a field of research. In Academy of Management Review, 25(1), pp. 217–226.

30 Venkataraman, S. (1997): The Distinctive Domain of Entrepreneurship Research: An Editor's Perspective. In J. Katz and R. Brockhaus (eds.), Advances in entrepreneurship, firm emergence, and growth, Vol. 3. Greenwich, CT: JAI Press, pp. 119–138.

31 Schumpeter, J.A. (1934 [1911]): The theory of economic development. New York: Oxford University Press.

32 Kirzner, I.M. (1973): Competition and entrepreneurship. Chicago: University of Chicago Press.
33 Ayyagari, M. and V. Maksimovic. (2018): The decline in quality of manufacturing entrepreneurship in the US. VoxEu.org, 25March
34 Decker, R.A., J. Haltiwanger, R.S. Jarmin, and J. Miranda. (2016): Declining dynamism, what we know and the way forward. In American Economic Review, 106(5), pp. 203–207.
35 Pugsley, B., P. Sedláček, and V. Sterk. (2018): Disappearing gazelles: new evidence from administrative data. VoxEu.org, 11May
36 Pugsley, B.W. and A. Sahin. (2015): Grown-up business cycles. US Census Bureau, Center for Economic Studies Paper No CES-WP- 15-33.
37 Acemoglu, D., D.H. Autor, D. Dorn, G.H. Hanson and B. Price. (2016): Import competition and the great US Employment Sag of the 2000s. In Journal of Labor Economics, 34 (S1), pp. S141–S198.
38 Autor, D., D. Dorn, and G.H. Hanson. (2013): The china syndrome: local labor market effects of import competition in the United States. In American Economic Review, 103(6), pp. 2121–2168.
39 Pierce, J.R. and P.K. Schott. (2016): The surprisingly swift decline of us manufacturing employment. In American Economic Review, 106(7), pp. 1632–1662.
40 Ohyama, A. (2017): Industry growth through spinoffs and start-ups. VoxEu.org, 14December
41 Dalmaris, P., E. Tsui, W.P. Hall, and B. Smith. (2007): A framework for the improvement of knowledge-intensive business processes. In Business Process Management, 13(2), pp. 279–305.
42 Nonaka, I. (1994): A dynamic theory of organizational knowledge creation. In Organization Science, 5(1), pp. 14–37.
43 Randeree, E. (2006): Knowledge management: securing the future. In Journal of Knowledge Management, 10(4), pp. 145–156.
44 Smith, A. (2002): Tutorial on principal components analysis. Available at: http://www.cs.otago.ac.nz/cosc453/student_tutorials/principal_components.pdf
45 Von Krogh, G., K. Ichijo, and I. Nonaka. (2000): Enabling knowledge creation. New York: Oxford University Press Inc.
46 Petrakis, P.E. and P.C. Kostis. (2015): The role of knowledge and trust in SMEs. In Journal of the Knowledge Economy, March 2015, 6(1), pp. 105–124.
47 Desouza, K.C. and Y. Awazu. (2006): Knowledge management at SMEs: five peculiarities. In Journal of Knowledge Management, 10(1), pp. 32–43.
48 Teese, D.J. (2003): Knowledge and Competence as Strategic Assets. In C.W. Holsapple (ed.), Handbook of knowledge management, Heidelberg: Springer, pp. 129–152.
49 Smith, A. and B.K. Temple. (2007): The impacts of knowledge transfer from educational programmes on individuals and SME business development, Management of International Business and Economic Systems (MIBES). Larissa, Greece, September.
50 Hershbein, B. and L.B. Kahn. (2018): Do recessions accelerate routine-biased technological change? evidence from vacancy postings. In American Economic Review, 108(7), pp. 1737–1772.
51 Cahill, E. (1980): Company failure and the vigilant accountant. In Accountancy, 19(1045), pp. 63–65(September).
52 Ulmer, M. and A. Nielsen. (1947): Business turn-over and causes of failure. In Survey of Current Business, (April), pp. 10–16.
53 Bruno, A.V. and J.K. Leidecker. (1988): Causes of new venture failure: 1960's vs. 1980's. In Business Horizons, 31(6), pp. 51–57.

54 Gaskill, L., H. Van Auken, and R. Manning. (1993): A factor analytic study of the perceived causes of small business failure. In Journal of Small Business Management, 31(4), pp. 18–31.

55 Brück, T., W.A. Naudé, and P. Verwimp. (2011): Small business, entrepreneurship and violent conflict in developing countries. In Journal of Small Business and Entrepreneurship, 24(2), pp. 161–178.

56 Siropolis, N. (1990): Small business management. 4th edition. Boston: Houghton Mifflin Company.

57 Gaskill, L.R., H.E. Van Auken, and R.A. Manning. (1993): A factor analytic study of the perceived causes of small business failure. In Journal of Small Business Management, 34 (4), pp. 18–31.

58 García-Ramos, C., N. Gonzalez-Alvarez, and M. Nieto. (2017): Institutional framework and entrepreneurial failure. In Journal of Small Business and Enterprise Development, 24 (4), pp. 716–732.

59 Begley, T.M., W.L. Tan, and H. Schoch. (2005): Politico-economic factors associated with interest in starting a business: a multi-country study. In Entrepreneurship: Theory and Practice, 29(1), pp. 35–55.

60 Bowen, H.P. and D. De Clercq. (2008): Institutional context and the allocation of entrepreneurial effort. In Journal of International Business Studies, 39(4), pp. 747–767.

61 Djankov, S., R. La Porta, F. Lopez-de-Silanes, and A. Shleifer. (2002): The regulation of entry. In Quarterly Journal of Economics, 117(1), pp. 1–37.

62 Klapper, L., L. Laeven, and R. Rajan. (2006): Entry regulation as a barrier to entrepreneurship. In Journal of Financial Economics, 82(3), pp. 591–629.

63 Grilo, I. and R. Thurik. (2005): Latent and actual entrepreneurship in Europe and the US: some recent developments. In International Entrepreneurship and Management Journal, 1 (4), pp. 441–459.

64 Sorensen, J.B. (2007): Bureaucracy and entrepreneurship. In *Administrative Science Quarterly* 52, pp. 387–412.

65 Saxenian, A. (1994): Regional advantage: culture and competition in Silicon Valley and Route 128. Cambridge, MA: Harvard University Press.

66 Merton, R.K. (1968): Bureaucratic Structure and Personality. In R.K. Merton (Ed.), Social theory and social structure, 2nd edition. New York: The Free Press, pp. 249–260.

67 Spenner, K.I. (1988): Social stratification, work and personality. In Annual Review of Sociology, 14, pp. 69–97.

68 Whyte, W. (1956): The organization man. New York: Doubleday.

69 Dunn, T. and D. Holtz-Eakin. (2000): Financial capital, human capital, and the transition to self-employment: evidence from intergenerational links. In Journal of Labor Economics, 18, pp. 282–305.

70 Lazear, E.P. (2005): Entrepreneurship. In Journal of Labor Economics, 23, pp. 649–680.

71 Gompers, P., J. Lerner, and D.S. Scharfstein. (2005): Entrepreneurial spawning: public corporations and the genesis of new ventures, 1986 to 1999. In Journal of Finance, 60, pp. 577–614.

72 Sorenson, O., and P.G. Audia. (2000): The social structure of entrepreneurial activity: geographic concentration of footwear production in the United States, 1940–1989. In American Journal of Sociology, 106, pp. 424–462.

73 Briscoe, F. (2007): From iron cage to iron shield? How bureaucracy enables temporal flexibility for professional service workers. In Organization Science, 18(2), pp. 297–314.

74 Doeringer, P.B. and M.J. Piore. (1971): Internal labor markets and manpower analysis. Lexington, MA: D.C. Heath.

75 Petrakis, P.E. (2011): The Greek economy and the crisis. Challenges and responses. New York and Heidelberg: Springer, ISBN 978-3-642-21174-4.

76 Global Entrepreneurship Monitor. (2017): Global report 2017–2018.

77 Hausmann, R., C.A. Hidalgo, S. Bustos, M. Coscia, S. Chung, J. Jímenez, A. Simoes, and Muhammed A. Yildirim. (2014): The atlas of economic complexity: mapping paths to prosperity. Cambridge, MA: MIT Press.

Chapter 5

Integration Opportunities of Stability-Oriented Processes for Real Estate Transaction Entities

Linda Kauškale and Ineta Geipele

1 Introduction

Real estate market has a number of functions and tasks, and the entrepreneurial activity in the real estate business has its own characteristics. The main contribution of the chapter is discussion and findings related to stability-oriented processes for real estate transaction entities, and their integration opportunities to management of enterprise. It is especially related to planning activities and includes economic analysis. Authors define that *Real Estate Transaction Entity* is an organization (such as a business or governmental unit) that has an identity separate from those of its members, and which that economic activity (in a form of transaction) is related with real estate. The article is focused on analysis of implementation opportunities for the entrepreneurs at Real Estate Market. Entity and Transaction separate definitions are as follows [1]:

'Entity' [Def.3, 1] – organization (such as business or governmental unit) that has an identity separate from those of its members

'Transaction' [Def.1a–2b, 1]:

1a: something transacted; especially, exchange or transfer of goods, services, or funds

 b: transactions plural: frequently published record of the meetings of the society or association

2a: act, process, or instance of transacting
 b: communicative action or activity involving two parties or things that reciprocally affect or influence each other.

The necessity of integration of stability-oriented processes to companies can be based on many factors. As it was found previously, there are many problems to be resolved in the development of the economy in the country and of the real estate market [2]. In practice, the construction companies, as well as other companies operating in the real estate market, are facing a number of challenges – both in internal and external environments, and a number of risks exist at the stage of taking any investment decision and construction process – both at the determination of the economic viability of the project, and at the determination of the best conditions of the project realization and its practical implementation.

Stoner and Freeman direct/indirect action environment model is shown in Figure 1.

Real estate transaction entities are being influenced by a variety of direct and indirect influences on the organization, and often should adapt to the external situation.

---

2   Direct and Indirect Influences on Real Estate Transaction Entities (Economic Focus)

For the analysis of direct and indirect influences on real estate transaction entities, real estate market participants could use the following criteria that are described in Tables 1 and 2, and in related models (Figures 2 and 3).

FIGURE 1: Direct/Indirect Action Environment Model [3, p. 32]

TABLE 1: Ratings Related to Real Estate Market and Its Analysis [4, pp. 541–545] (developed by the authors)

Rating types	Object rating	Product rating
Market and location rating	Assessment of the development	Valuation of real estate products, such
Assessment of the development of the property	potential of an individual property	as closed or open real estate funds,
market at the location of the property, assessment	Application areas are:	which receives:
of potential and risk		
Application areas are:	– Credit analysis in the granting	– Investment decisions
	of real estate loans	– Risk analysis of investment
– Investments and divestments for real estate	– Risk analysis of portfolios	products
at the site	– Investment and disinvestment	– Comparison between different
– Market value calculation	decisions	plant alternatives for selling
– Risk analysis of real estate portfolios	– Portfolio analysis and control	– Checklist for the concept of
– Portfolio analysis and control	– 'Internal Ratings Advanced	funds
– Real estate asset allocation	Approach' according to Basel	
	II.	Measure of the attractiveness
FERI property market rating, based on the regional		includes:
and real estate market forecast. In which selected and	Market value calculation according to	
prognosticated economic indicators include growth	IAS* /IFRS**	– Macro site (supply, demand,
and employment, employment by sector, rental rates,		value development
purchase prices, income, income distribution,		– Micro site (location quality,
households & population – then benchmark and then		transport infrastructure,
the rating indicator (0–100) classification into 10		supply infrastructure)
evaluation classes (AAA-E) calculated with adoption		– Object quality (building
of Feri Rating Algorithm, which real estate is		quality, land quality)
analyzed, receives scaling, weighting, and summation		

*   IAS, International Accounting Standards
** IFRS, International Financial Reporting Standards

TABLE 2: Ratings for Real Estate Market Analysis (developed by the authors)

Ratings

Schäfer and Conzen [4]:	S&P Dow Jones Indices [5], and includes:	The BCIS [8]:
• Ratings related to real estate and its analysis	• Dow Jones U.S. Select Real Estate Securities Index	• BCIS cost indices;
• FERI real estate funds rating	• Dow Jones U.S. Select REIT Index	• BCIS tender price indices;
• REIT (real estate investment trust) and global tendencies analysis; for example, S&P Dow Jones Global index	• Dow Jones Global ex-U.S. Select Real Estate Securities Index (also available is a USD-hedged version of this index)	• BCIS regional price indices;
• Power fields	• Dow Jones Global ex-U.S. Select REIT Index	• BCIS output indices;
• Sector analysis	• Dow Jones Global Select Real Estate Securities Index	• BCIS trade indices;
• Real estate cycle analysis	• Dow Jones Global Select REIT Index	• Construction new orders;
• Preventive activities	• Dow Jones Americas Select Real Estate Securities Index	• Construction output;
• Optimal use of resources in the entrepreneurial process	• Dow Jones Americas Select REIT Index	• House prices;
	• Dow Jones Asia/Pacific Select Real Estate Securities Index	• Housing starts and completions;
	• Dow Jones Asia/Pacific Select REIT Index	• Resource indices;
	• Dow Jones Europe Developed Markets Select Real Estate Securities Index	• Retail prices.
	• Dow Jones Europe Developed Markets Select REIT Index	
	• Dow Jones Europe Select Real Estate Securities Index	
	• Dow Jones Europe Select REIT Index	
	• Dow Jones Middle East & Africa Select Real Estate Securities Index	
	• Dow Jones Middle East & Africa Select REIT Index	

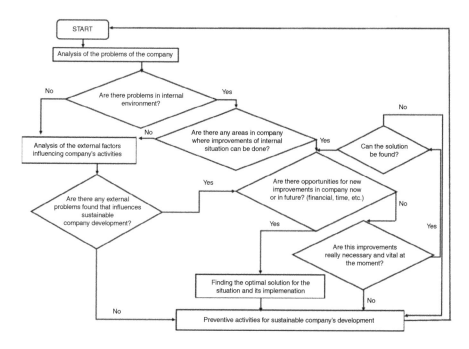

FIGURE 2: Systematic Problem Analysis Algorithm for Integration of Sustainability Aspects for Real Estate Transaction Entities (developed by the authors).

FIGURE 3: Stability-Oriented Process Integration for Real Estate Transaction Entities (developed by the authors).

There are different types of indexes used for evaluation. For example, Dow Jones U.S. real estate index is designed to track the performance of real estate investment trusts (REITs) and other companies that invest directly or indirectly in real estate through development, management, or ownership, including property agencies [5]. FERI EuroRating Services AG operates a rating agency that provides research, ratings, and selection of investment markets [6]. Indices related to REITs are Real Time Index Returns, Daily US Returns, Daily Global Returns, PureProperty® Index, Historical REIT Returns, and Top 20 Global Constituents [7], and other indices analysis can also be necessary for entrepreneurs. The RICS (Institution of Chartered Surveyors) and BCIS (Building Cost Information Service of RICS) offer advice and guidance for market participants and offer statistical information on indices in the relevant analysis and constructions sectors. The BCIS is subdivided into several indices that are used to determinate the cost involved with building various schemes [8], and that can be used also by real estate transaction entities, which can be found in Table 2.

For real estate transaction entities, it is preferable also to analyze indexes and indicators mentioned in Table 2.

Index analysis is a part of integrated sustainable development of real estate market analysis.

3   Integration of Stability-Oriented Aspects for Real Estate Transaction Entities

Adaptation of company situation to the influencing external factors can be done after analysis of cyclical development, real estate market, and other indicators, as well by including company's internal factors into account. For successful implementation of stability-oriented aspects in real estate transaction entities, a systematic problem analysis algorithm for integration of sustainability aspects for real estate transaction entities was developed and is shown in Figure 2.

The integration of sustainability aspects to real estate companies becomes crucial and vital for sustainable development in general. According to McKinsey & Company Global Survey results [9], more and more companies are addressing sustainability to align with their business goals, from which top three reasons are alignment, reputation, and cost cutting.

Stability-oriented process integration for real estate transaction entities is shown in Figure 3.

Implementation system for the sustainable processes at real estate market should be implemented in all sectors of real estate market. Sector analysis is important and necessary because it is being influenced by supply and demand shocks and economic fluctuations, and different tendencies within different sectors of real estate market can be observed.

4   Sector Analysis

Sectors of real estate are as follows [10]:

- *Apartments:* number of households, age of persons in households, size of household incomes, interest rates, home ownership, affordability, apartment rents, housing prices

- *Office space:* categories of employment with very high proportions of office use include service and professional employment, including lawyers, accountants, engineers, insurance, real estate brokerages and related activity, banking, financial services, consultants, medical–dental, pharmaceutical, etc.
- *Warehouse space:* categories of employment with high concentrations in warehouse use including wholesaling, trucking, distribution, assembly, manufacturing, sales/service, etc.
- *Retail space:* demand indications include household incomes, age, gender, population, size, and taste/preferences.

From a property perspective, industrial property is a property (land and buildings) that can be used for a variety of purposes, with the following being the most common uses [11]:

- production;
- manufacture;
- storage;
- distribution;
- energy production;
- waste disposal;
- industrial land, e.g., mining/quarrying.

In the analysis of real estate market, the skyscraper development and its correlation with economic development can be analyzed as well. 'In the sense that skyscrapers seem to mark a very large economic boom that typically ends in large recession. And they tend to be associated with bigger economic cycles' [11, p.43].

Regular analysis of mentioned criteria is necessary for construction companies and real estate transaction entities. Industrial sector analysis is also important for the analysis of real estate market, and for analysis of sustainable development in general, as may produce significant emissions.

---

5 Conclusion

The overall economic and real estate market development affects the level of real estate prices and economic results of entrepreneurial activities. These are the reasons why the integration of stability-oriented processes is so important in real estate and construction companies worldwide. This chapter provided an overview of integration opportunities of stability-oriented processes for real estate transaction entities. The additional research direction, that is crucial for analysis of this issue, is an integration of stability-oriented processes to real estate market.

References

1 MW – Merriam-Webster Dictionary. Definitions. [accessed on 28 November 2017] Available at: www.merriam-webster.com/dictionary/leg.

2 Kauškale, L., Geipele, I. (2016): Economic problems of real estate market and its influence on the development of business environment. In: Proceedings of the 2016 International Conference "Economic Science for Rural Development". No. 43, Latvia, Jelgava, 21–22 April, 2016. Jelgava. pp. 39–48. ISBN 978-9984-48-225-5.ISSN 1691-3078. ISI WoS, WOS:000391253200004.

3 Stoner, J.A.F., Freeman, R.E. (1989): Management. 4th edition. Englewood Cliffs, NJ: Prentice-Hall. 796 p.

4 Schäfer, J., Conzen, G. (2016). Praxishandbuch Immobilien-Investitionen [Practice manual real estate investments]. 3rd edition. München: C.H. BECK Immobilienrecht [C. H. BECK Property Rights]. 721 p.

5 S&P Dow Jones Indices. (2017) [online]. Dow Jones U.S. Real Estate Index [accessed on 6 June 2018]. Available at: https://us.spindices.com/indices/equity/dow-jones-us-real-estate-index.

6 Company Overview of FERI EuroRating Services AG. (2017): [online]. Bloomberg L.P. webpage [accessed on 5 November 2017]. Available at: www.bloomberg.com/research/stocks/private/snapshot.asp?privcapId=253506848.

7 REIT Indices. (2017): [online]. NAREIT (the National Association of Real Estate Investment Trusts) [accessed on 22 August 2017]. Available at: www.reit.com/data-research/reit-indexes.

8 Capper, G., Gledson, B., Humphrey, R., Johansen, E., Jowsey, E., Kirk, M., Hatcher, C., Weirs, J. (2015): Construction real estate concepts: a handbook. In Jowsey, E. (Ed.): With contributions from staff at Northumbria University pp. 97–119. New York: Routledge. 494 p.

9 McKinsey & Company. (2008): Enduring ideas: the GE–McKinsey Nine-box Matrix [online]. The McKinsey Quarterly, September [accessed on 15 March 2016]. Available at: www.mckinseyquarterly.com/Enduring_ideas_The_GE-McKinsey_nine-box _matrix_2198.

10 Brueggeman, W.B., Fisher, J.D. (2011): Real estate finance and investments. 14th international edition. New York: McGraw-Hill Irwin. 760 p.

11 Dunhill, A., Fearon, D., Holmes, J., Thomson, B. (2015): Commercial property. Real estate concepts: a handbook. In Jowsey, E. (Ed.): With contributions from staff at Northumbria University, pp. 79–96. New York: Routledge. 494 p.

12 Lawrence, A. (2012): Talking tall – The Skyscraper Index [online]. Council on Tall Buildings and Urban Habitat. [accessed on 20 October 2016]. Available at: www.ctbuh.org/LinkClick.aspx?fileticket=uXxzolM8loU%3D&language=en-GB.

Chapter 6

Entrepreneurial Dispositions Personality Inventory

Development and Validation

Konrad Janowski, Marcin Waldemar Staniewski and Katarzyna Awruk

1   Introduction

The level of entrepreneurship is viewed in modern societies to be a key factor in the stimulation and growth of national and global economies as well as a contributor to socio-economic prosperity [1]. In particular, the creation and development of small- and medium-sized businesses, usually founded and run by individual entrepreneurs or families, have gained recognition as the main components affecting multiple facets of the economy, including the generation of employment opportunities, innovation, productivity, and growth [2]. Therefore, the stimulation of indigenous entrepreneurship and entrepreneurial behaviours among citizens has become the goal of national economic policies in many countries worldwide [3].

The role of personality characteristics in entrepreneurial behaviour has been the subject of research and scientific debate for a long time. Research has focused mainly on the identification of personality traits related to entrepreneurial behaviour and on the predictive power of these traits in terms of explaining variance in indices of entrepreneurial behaviours, such as the generation of business ideas [4], entrepreneurial intention [5], and the foundation and success of new businesses [6]. Some researchers have suggested that the findings on the predictive role of personality in entrepreneurial behaviour were disappointing and that personality traits might play little or no role in the creation or success of new businesses [7,8]. However, findings from more recent meta-analyses have indicated that the relationships between personality characteristics and entrepreneurial behaviour do exist and can be demonstrated if more precise research methodology is applied [9].

One facet of research in this field is connected with the choice of instruments designed to measure personality traits relevant to entrepreneurship. In many studies, standard personality questionnaires are used to measure one (e.g., locus of control) or more such traits (e.g., the 'Big Five' personality traits). Such an approach is particularly useful if the researcher wishes to identify which of the personality characteristics are relevant for entrepreneurship. On the other hand, there are also questionnaires that have been designed to measure only those personality traits that have already been demonstrated to be positively linked to entrepreneurship, and this approach is useful if the researcher wants to assess the level of personality traits predisposing toward desirable entrepreneurial behaviour. The repertoire of the traits usually included into such measurement instruments may differ, depending on the aim of the study or the purpose of the application of the instrument.

In Central and Eastern European countries, which underwent transformations from communist centrally governed economies into free market economies in the 1990s, the development of entrepreneurship has been a challenge of particular significance for the last 25 years [10,11]. Cultural factors taking the form of social mentalities inherited from the communist system implied important obstacles in the transition of these countries toward economies based on the citizens' entrepreneurship [12,13]. Therefore, numerous education and economic policies have been implemented in an attempt to change the mentality and increase the level of entrepreneurship evidenced by the citizens of these countries. This effort is based on the assumption that entrepreneurial behaviours, such as business creation and its successful continuation, are to some extent dependent on individual psychological characteristics and that these characteristics can be enhanced. However, the whole field of study on entrepreneurship in these countries is at a very early stage of development because the entrepreneurial reality emerged on a greater scale no earlier than 25 years ago. The field of study on entrepreneurship has also been impeded by a relative deficit of measurement instruments that could be reliably used in research or for practical applications.

This paper presents the results of studies that have been part of a more extensive research project aimed at identification of predictors of entrepreneurial success in people starting new businesses in Poland. The objective of this paper is to present a questionnaire instrument, the Entrepreneurial Dispositions Personality Inventory, which was developed to measure personality characteristics relevant to entrepreneurship in a Polish population. We wanted to develop an instrument that would cover a wide range of personality predictors of entrepreneurship as having these predictors measured on the same measurement scale would facilitate intra-profile analyses. Three studies are reported here, and their aims were: 1) to test the initial version of the instrument and, where possible, to improve its psychometric properties, 2) to test the convergent validity of the instrument, and 3) to test the criterion validity of the instrument.

2 Study 1 – Development of the EDPI

The aim of this study was to develop a multidimensional questionnaire measuring the psychological dispositions of entrepreneurs. In particular, this study focused on an evaluation of the psychometric properties of the items used in the initial version of the EDPI. Based on this evaluation, the final decisions were made for a given item about its inclusion in the final version of the questionnaire.

2.1 Participants and Methods

2.1.1 The Initial Version of the EDPI

The relevant literature has been abundant in suggestions regarding which personality characteristics are linked to entrepreneurship. On the basis of our literature review, we chose 14 personality characteristics that had been found most frequently to be related to entrepreneurship in previous research. The following characteristics were included: risk-taking propensity, autonomy, disagreeableness (the negative pole of agreeableness), openness to experience, emotional stability (the positive pole of neuroticism), conscientiousness, need for achievement, innovativeness, extroversion, self-efficacy, resistance to stress, internal locus of control, passion, and authoritative parenting [cf.6,9]. As some of these characteristics cannot be arguably called 'traits' in a strict sense, we decided to term these characteristics personality dispositions. They are conceptualized as 'predisposing' to or increasing the likelihood of entrepreneurial behaviour.

The initial version of the EDPI consisted of 131 items that had been generated to cover the identified psychological entrepreneurial dispositions. The contents of the items were created by the authors of this article based on psychological descriptions of each entrepreneurial predisposition available in the relevant literature. Each predisposition was represented by between 8 and 11 items.

2.1.2 Participants

Two-hundred and eleven participants took part in the study. The participants were recruited through announcements on the Internet. The sample consisted of 102 women (48.3%) and 109 men (51.7%). The mean age in the sample was M=38.73 (SD=14.80). Eighty-four percent of the sample reported that they had never had their own business, 7% reported that they had their own business in the past, and 9% reported that they currently ran their own business. The majority of the sample (73%) reported living in a major city, 19% reported living in a small town, and 8% reported living in rural areas. All participants were given a link to the web page with the initial version of the EDPI, and they completed the questionnaire via the Internet.

2.2   Results

2.2.1 Analysis of the Properties of the Items

The first step in the analyses was to evaluate the psychometric properties of the individual items in relation to the subscale to which they had been initially assigned. Therefore, reliability coefficients (Cronbach's alpha) were calculated for each subscale. The corrected item-total correlations were computed for each item within the subscale and the alpha values for the subscale if the item had been deleted. These data served as the criteria for maintaining or deleting items from the subscale; if the item had contributed to the subscale's lower reliability, it was deleted and the whole process was reiterated. Table 1 presents values of the Cronbach's alpha for the initial version of the EDPI and after items with inadequate contribution to reliabilities of subscales had been deleted.

2.2.2 Distribution of the Scores in the Subscales

Table 2 presents the properties of distribution of the scores obtained on the resultant subscales after items with inadequate psychometric properties were

TABLE 1:   The number of items and reliabilities (the Cronbach's alpha) for the subscales of the initial version of the EDPI and after items with inadequate psychometric properties had been deleted.

Subscale	Initial version of the EDPI		The EDPI after item deletion	
	No. of items	Cronbach's alpha	No. of items	Cronbach's alpha
Risk-Taking Propensity	9	0.70	6	0.72
Autonomy	11	0.72	6	0.74
Disagreeableness	10	0.67	6	0.71
Openness to Experience	9	0.52	6	0.55
Emotional Stability	9	0.85	6	0.86
Conscientiousness	10	0.69	7	0.73
Need for Achievement	11	0.77	6	0.77
Innovativeness	10	0.77	6	0.78
Extraversion	9	0.71	7	0.72
Self-efficacy	8	0.78	6	0.78
Resistance to Stress	8	0.67	7	0.68
Internal Locus of Control	9	0.49	6	0.48
Passion	9	0.68	6	0.79
Authoritative Parenting	9	0.81	5	0.87

deleted. For all of the subscales, the scores cover almost the whole range of possible scores. Skewness and kurtosis were all within the range above -1.0 and below 1.0.

The final version of the questionnaire accepted for further research consisted of 86 items constituting 14 subscales.

3   Study 2 – Convergent Validity of the EDPI

In Study 2, the convergent validity of the EDPI was tested by assessing associations between the scores on the EDPI and similar constructs related to entrepreneurial personality dispositions, as measured by independent instruments. To this end, the correlations were calculated between scores for the EDPI subscales and scores obtained with such measures as the NEO-FFI, Rotter's Locus of Control Scale, the State-Trait Anxiety Inventory, the Generalized Self-Efficacy Scale, the Questionnaire of Achievement Motivation, the Questionnaire of Parenting Styles in a Family, and the Test of Risky Behaviours.

TABLE 2:   Descriptive statistics for the subscales of the EDPI after items with inadequate psychometric properties were deleted.

	Min	Max	M	SD	Skewness	Kurtosis
Risk-Taking Propensity	8	30	19.41	4.16	0.09	−0.06
Autonomy	11	30	22.36	4.13	−0.12	−0.49
Disagreeableness	11	30	19.64	4.09	0.08	−0.27
Openness to Experience	7	29	20.12	3.76	−0.18	0.11
Emotional Stability	6	30	19.04	5.58	−0.22	−0.49
Conscientiousness	11	35	24.75	4.50	−0.06	−0.19
Need for Achievement	11	30	21.55	4.25	−0.23	−0.34
Innovativeness	13	30	22.84	3.50	−0.17	0.18
Extraversion	12	35	25.69	4.39	−0.01	−0.03
Self–efficacy	9	30	22.97	3.59	−0.26	0.35
Resistance to Stress	11	34	23.92	4.48	−0.27	−0.03
Internal Locus of Control	7	30	18.34	3.53	0.06	0.51
Passion	12	30	20.30	3.90	0.03	−0.53
Authoritative Parenting	7	25	16.21	4.16	−0.04	−0.55

3.1   Participants and Methods

3.1.1   Participants

The study was conducted with 724 people aged between 18 and 60 years (M=24.46, SD=6.57), who had been selected at random from the general population. The sample included 559 women and 165 men. The majority of the participants came from large cities with over 100,000 residents (47.24%) and had received   secondary education (53.59%). The proportion of the respondents who declared that they had owned their own business in the past amounted to 31.91%, whereas 30.94% were currently running a business. Socio-demographic data for the sample under analysis are provided in Table 3.

For the purposes of the study, the participants were divided into 4 groups. Group 1 (N=327 respondents) completed the set composed of the EDPI and the NEO-FFI. Group 2 (N=100) was asked to complete the set consisting of the EDPI, the Test of Risky Behaviours, and the State-Trait Anxiety Inventory. Group 3 (N=190) completed the EDPI, the Questionnaire of Parenting Styles in a Family, the Questionnaire of Achievement Motivation, and the Generalized Self-Efficacy Scale (GSES). Finally, group 4 (N=107) was presented with the set consisting of the EDPI and Rotter's Locus of Control Scale.

Informed consent for participation in the study was obtained from all of the subjects.

3.1.2   Methods

The Entrepreneurial Dispositions Personality Inventory (EDPI) – as developed in Study 1.

TABLE 3: Socio-demographic data for the sample under examination.

		N	%
Sex	Female	559	77.21
	Male	165	22.79
Education	Primary	1	0.14
	Secondary	140	19.34
	Vocational	58	8.00
	General secondary	388	53.59
	Higher/Bachelor's Degree	71	9.81
	Higher/Master's Degree	66	9.12
Place of residence	Rural	196	27.07
	Small town up to	186	25.69
	100 thousand residents	342	47.24
	Large city with over		
	100 thousand residents		
The respondent has conducted business activity in the past	Yes	231	31.91
	No	493	68.09
The respondent is running a business now	Yes	224	30.94
	No	500	69.06

The NEO-FFI – is a 60-item tool of self-report developed by Costa and McCrae [14] and adapted into Polish by Zawadzki, Strelau, Szczepaniak, and Śliwińska [15]. The tool measures 5 personality dimensions corresponding to the 'Big Five' personality traits, i.e., neuroticism, extraversion, openness to experience, agreeableness, and conscientiousness. The score for each of the 5 scales is calculated by summing the points for answers consistent with the answer key. The reliability of the questionnaire was assessed on the basis of internal consistency using Cronbach's α and amounted to 0.68 for the *Openness to Experience* subscale, 0.68 for the *Agreeableness* subscale, 0.77 for the *Extraversion* subscale, 0.88 for the *Neuroticism* subscale, and 0.82 for the *Conscientiousness* subscale [15].

The Test of Risky Behaviours, developed by Studenski [16], is a self-report tool composed of 25 test items concerning risky activity or the motives for undertaking risky activity. The task of the person under examination is to select one of the following answer choices: *very frequently, frequently, sometimes, rarely, very rarely, or never*. The responses are awarded points on a 5-degree scale ranging between 0 (very rarely or never) and 4 (very frequently). The reliability of the questionnaire estimated with the Cronbach's α amounted to 0.93 [16].

The State-Trait Anxiety Inventory (STAI) is a tool authored by Spielberg, Strelau, Tysarczyk, and Wrześniewski [17]. It serves to measure state anxiety and trait anxiety. The reliability of the STAI estimated with the Cronbach's α in this study was 0.94 for the state anxiety subscale and 0.91 for the trait anxiety subscale.

The Questionnaire of Parenting Styles in a Family is a 68-item tool developed by Ryś [18], in which the respondent is to retrospectively assess the behaviour of their mother and father exhibited toward them in childhood (up to the age of approximately 12 years). Test items form 4 subscales altogether, which correspond to parenting styles (democratic, authoritative, liberal-loving, liberal-non-loving) of the parents together, followed by the mother and the father separately. The results are calculated separately for each subscale/parenting style by way of summing the scores recorded for each test item. The responses are awarded between 0 (*definitely not*) and 3 (*definitely yes*) points. The reliability of the questionnaire estimated on the basis of the *Cronbach's* α in the present study amounted to 0.93 for the *Mother-democratic style* subscale, 0.90 for the *Mother-authoritative style* subscale, 0.64 for the *Mother-liberal-loving style* subscale, 0.91 for the *Mother-liberal-non-loving style* subscale, 0.92 for the *Father-democratic style* subscale, 0.91 for the *Father-authoritative style* subscale, 0.65 for the *Father-liberal-loving style* subscale, and 0.89 for the *Father-liberal-non-loving style* subscale.

The Questionnaire of Achievement Motivation, developed by Widerszal-Bazyl [19], is a 20-item self-report tool serving to measure achievement motivation, also known as the need for achievement. The task of the person under examination is to answer questions regarding their inclinations, beliefs, and preferences in various circumstances. The total score is calculated by summing the points scored for particular test items, and scores range between 20 and 100 points. The higher the score, the greater the respondent's need for achievement. In the present study, the reliability measured with the Cronbach's α was 0.49.

The Generalized Self-Efficacy Scale is a 10-item tool developed by Schwarzer [20] which serves to measure the depth of individuals' convictions about their self-efficacy of dealing with difficult circumstances and obstacles. The respondent is asked to take an attitude towards the statements that they are presented with by selecting one of the possible answers: 1 – *no*, 2 – *rather not*, 3 – *rather yes*, 4 – *yes*. The general score, which indicates self-efficacy, is estimated by summing all of the points obtained in the questionnaire. Scores range from 10 to 40 points, with the higher the score, the greater the sense of self-efficacy. The estimated reliability of the questionnaire, based on the Cronbach's α, was 0.85, and the reliability estimated with the test–retest method (with a 5-week deferral) was 0.78 [21].

Rotter's Locus of Control Scale is a 29-item self-report tool authored by Rotter [22], which was adapted to Polish by Drwal [23]. Each test item contains two statements: one points to an internal source of control, and the second points to an external one. The respondent is to choose one out of two statements. The score is calculated by summing the points obtained for the diagnostic answers pointing to an internal source of control. A higher score achieved in the questionnaire indicates that control originates from internal sources, and a lower score indicates that control originates from external sources. The reliability of the questionnaire was satisfactory in this study and amounted to 0.75.

3.2   Statistical Analyses

Statistical analyses were carried out with the use of the statistical package SPSS (version 21.0) for Windows. Distributions of the results were verified with descriptive statistics, i.e., arithmetic mean, standard deviation, minimum, maximum, skewness, and kurtosis. Correlations between the variables under analysis were tested with the Pearson's r coefficient of correlation or Spearman's rho (if the distribution of the scores was significantly different from the normal distribution). The threshold of statistical significance was set to $P \leq 0.05$.

3.3   Results

3.3.1   Relationships between the Scores on the EDPI Subscales and the 'Big Five' Personality Traits

It was expected that the EDPI subscales measuring *Emotional Stability, Extroversion, Openness to Experience, Disagreeableness*, and *Conscientiousness* should be significantly correlated with the scales measuring analogous traits on the NEO-FFI. Because *Emotional Stability* and *Disagreeableness* are scored in the opposite direction in the EDPI than in the NEO-FFI, the correlations between these subscales and their counterparts in the NEO-FFI (i.e., *Neuroticism* and *Agreeableness*) were expected to be negative.

As expected, the scores on the EDPI subscales (*Extraversion, Openness to Experience, Conscientiousness, Emotional stability*, and *Disagreeableness*) were significantly correlated with all the dimensions of the 'Big Five'.Table 4 presents the Pearson's *r* coefficients of correlation for the variables under analysis.

It is also worth noting that the results in other subscales of the EDPI were positively correlated with three dimensions of the NEO-FFI. i.e., *Extraversion, Openness to Experience*, and *Conscientiousness*. Significant negative correlations were found between the subscales of the EDPI and the scores on two NEO-FFI subscales: *Emotional stability* and *Nonconformity*. However, no significant correlation was discovered between the scores on the EDPI subscale *Authoritative parenting* and personality dimensions measured with the NEO-FFI.

3.3.2   Relationships between the Scores on the EDPI Subscales and Rotter's Locus of Control Scale

It was expected that the EDPI *Internal Locus of Control* should correlate positively with Rotter's LOC Scale.

As expected, the scores on the *Locus of control* subscale of the EDPI were positively correlated with the scores obtained in Rotter's Locus of Control Scale. Positive correlations were also found between the scores on two EDPI subscales *Emotional stability* and *Need for achievement* and the source of control. The correlations in question are presented in Table 4.

TABLE 4: The Pearson's r coefficients of correlation between scores on the subscales of the EDPI and the subscales of the NEO-FFI and Rotter's Locus of Control Scale.

EDPI	NEO-FFI (N=327)					Rotter's Locus of Control Scale (N=107)
	Extraversion	Neuroticism	Openness to experience	Agreeableness	Conscientiousness	Locus of control
Risk-Taking Propensity	0.38**	−0.39**	0.24**	−0.15**	0.18**	
Autonomy	0.33**	−0.23**	0.24**	−0.18**	0.28**	
Disagreeableness	0.22**	−0.19**	0.14*	**−0.52****	0.19**	
Openness to Experience	0.31**	−0.30**	**0.45****		0.22**	
Emotional Stability	0.43**	**−0.86****			0.40**	0.24*
Conscientiousness	0.23**	−0.28**		−0.20**	**0.75****	
Need for Achievement	0.45**	−0.48**	0.16**		0.74**	0.19*
Innovativeness	0.44**	−0.32**	0.34**		0.39**	
Extraversion	0.88**	−0.38**	0.13*	0.13*	0.35**	
Self-efficacy	0.49**	−0.68**	0.33**		0.43**	
Resistance to Stress	0.25**	−0.62**			0.23**	
Internal Locus of Control	0.30**	−0.24**	0.19*	0.19**	0.24**	**0.55****
Passion	0.42**	−0.15**	0.21**		0.46**	
Authoritative Parenting						

* $P \leq 0.05$.
** $P \leq 0.001$.

The Pearson's r coefficients of correlation indicating the level of theoretical validity of the EDPI are bolded.

3.3.3 Relationships between the Scores on the EDPI Subscales and the Scores on the Test of Risky Behaviours and STAI

The following was hypothesized:

1) The EDPI *Risk-Taking Propensity* would correlate positively with the scores obtained in the *Test of Risky Behaviours*

2) The EDPI *Risk-Taking Propensity* would correlate negatively with the scores obtained in the *STAI*

3) The EDPI *Resistance to Stress* would correlate positively with the scores achieved in the *Test of Risky Behaviours*

4) The EDPI *Resistance to Stress* would correlate negatively with anxiety levels as measured by the *STAI*, in particular with trait anxiety.

In line with the expectations, the scores on the EDPI subscale *Risk-Taking Propensity* were positively correlated with the total score in the *Test of Risky Behaviours*. Negative correlations were also found between the scores on the EDPI subscale *Risk-Taking Propensity* and state anxiety as well as trait anxiety. Moreover, significant positive correlations were discovered between the results on the EDPI *Resistance to stress* and the general score obtained in the *Test of Risky Behaviours*. Negative correlations were observed between *Resistance to stress* and state anxiety as well as trait anxiety. The correlations described above are provided in Table 5, along with other statistically significant data.

3.3.4 Correlations between the EDPI Scores and Generalized Self-Efficacy and Achievement Motivation

The following relationships were expected:

1) the EDPI *Self-efficacy* and *Need for Achievement* should correlate positively with *generalized self-efficacy* and *achievement motivation* as measured by the GSES and the Questionnaire of Achievement Motivation, respectively.

2) the EDPI scores for *Passion* should correlate positively with *generalized self-efficacy* and *achievement motivation* as measured by the GSES and the Questionnaire of Achievement Motivation, respectively.

Scores on the EDPI *Self-efficacy* were positively correlated with self-efficacy, measured with the GSES, and achievement motivation. Positive correlations were found between *Self-efficacy*, measured with the GSES, and all of the other EDPI subscales, excluding *Authoritative Parenting* (due to lack of significant correlation).

The need for achievement measured with the EDPI was positively correlated with achievement motivation assessed with the *Questionnaire of Achievement Motivation* and self-efficacy measured with the GSES. Furthermore, positive correlations were

TABLE 5: Spearman's rho coefficients of correlation between the scores on the EDPI and the *Test of Risky Behaviours, STAI, Achievement Motivation Questionnaire, and Generalized Self-Efficacy Scale*

EDPI	Test of Risky Behaviours (N=100)	STAI (N=100)		Questionnaire of Achievement Motivation (N=190)	GSES (N=190)
	Test of Risky Behaviours	State-anxiety	Trait-anxiety	Achievement Motivation	Self-efficacy
Risk-Taking Propensity	**0.49****	−0.30**	−0.46**	0.36**	0.48**
Autonomy	0.36**		−0.35**	0.24**	0.50**
Disagreeableness	0.47**		−0.32**	0.22**	0.40**
Openness to Experience	0.44**	−0.32**	−0.48**	0.24**	0.46**
Emotional Stability	0.30**	−0.58**	−0.79**	0.28**	0.53**
Conscientiousness	0.35**		−0.28**	0.30**	0.47**
Need for Achievement		−0.40**	−0.46**	**0.58****	0.58**
Innovativeness	0.26**	−0.29**	−0.46**	0.38**	0.62**
Extraversion		−0.31**	−0.23*	0.38**	0.38**
Self-efficacy	0.32**	−0.43**	−0.58**	0.40**	**0.77****
Resistance to Stress	**0.29****	−0.37**	−0.64**	0.21**	0.56**
Internal Locus of Control		−0.22*	−0.25*	0.20**	0.22**
Passion	0.20*	−0.42**	−0.33**	**0.29****	**0.40****
Authoritative Parenting	0.49**				

* $P \leq 0.05$.
** $P \leq 0.001$.

The Spearman's rho coefficients of correlation indicating the level of theoretical validity of the EDPI are bolded.

found between achievement motivation and all of the other EDPI subscales, excluding *Authoritative Parenting* (due to lack of significant correlation).

Passion measured with the EDPI showed the expected positive correlations with both achievement motivation and generalized self-efficacy. The above-mentioned correlations and the remaining statistically significant relationships are presented in Table 5.

3.3.5 Correlations between the Scores on the EDPI and Parenting Styles

The following relationships were expected:

1) the EDPI *Authoritative Parenting* should correlate positively with the mother's and the father's authoritative parenting styles.

2) the EDPI *Authoritative Parenting* should correlate negatively with the mother's and the father's liberal and democratic parenting styles.

Positive correlations were discovered between the scores on the *Authoritative Parenting* subscale of the EDPI and the scores on the subscales *Mother-authoritative style* and *Father-authoritative style*. Negative correlations were found between the scores on the EDPI subscale *Authoritative Parenting* and the scores on the subscale *Father-liberal-non-loving style*. No significant correlations were revealed between the EDPI *Authoritative Parenting* and either parent's democratic style or the mother's liberal style (Table 6).

---

4 Study 3 – Criterion Validity of the EDPI

Study 3 was primarily designed to verify the criterion validity of the Entrepreneurial Dispositions Personality Inventory. To demonstrate the validity of the EDPI, the mean scores obtained by the entrepreneurs and the non-entrepreneurs on the EDPI were compared. It was expected that the subjects who were running their own business would score higher on the EDPI subscales than would the subjects who did not have their own business.

4.1 Participants and Methods

4.1.1 Participants

In the present study, data were gathered from 192 participants. The sample consisted of 92 entrepreneurs who had their own businesses at the time of the study and 100 non-entrepreneurs, defined as participants who had never had their own business.

TABLE 6: Spearman's rho coefficients of correlation between the scores on the EDPI and the results obtained in the *Questionnaire of Parenting Styles in a Family* (N=190).

EDPI	Mother's parenting styles				Father's parenting styles			
	Democratic	Authoritative	Liberal Loving	Liberal-non-loving	Democratic	Authoritative	Liberal Loving	Liberal-non-loving
Risk-Taking Propensity	0.20**	−0.19**	0.18*	−0.18*				
Autonomy	0.16*	−0.14*	0.15*					
Disagreeableness								
Openness to Experience	0.15*				0.15*		0.15*	
Emotional Stability					0.22**	−0.21**	0.20**	−0.19**
Conscientiousness	0.32**	−0.24**	0.26**	−0.28**	0.20**			−0.18**
Need for Achievement	0.31**	−0.21**	0.19**	−0.31**	0.14*			
Innovativeness	0.28**	−0.14*	0.21**	−0.18*				
Extraversion	0.23**			−0.23**				
Self-efficacy	0.26**	−0.25**	0.23**	−0.23**	0.15*	−0.17*	0.15*	
Resistance to Stress	0.17*	−0.19*	0.21**	−0.15*			0.16*	
Internal Locus of Control	0.16*	−0.15*						
Passion	0.22**			−0.16**		**0.15***		
Authoritative Parenting		**0.28***						−0.15*

* $P \leq 0.05$.
** $P \leq 0.001$.

The Spearman's rho coefficients of correlation indicating the level of theoretical validity of the EDPI are bolded.

The entrepreneurs in the sample were aged between 23 and 66 (M=36.12, SD=9.00). Men slightly prevailed (64.1%) among the respondents, and the most frequently reported educational level was higher education, a master's degree (43.5%). The participants mostly came from large cities with over 100,000 residents (47.8%). Their companies usually operated locally (45.7%) and were situated in the Mazowieckie Province (56.5%). The majority reported being able to maintain liquidity (paying current bills) (85.9%) and being the sole founder of the company (91.3%). Most of the respondents self-assessed the level of their companies' competitiveness and innovation to be average (56.5% and 64.1%, respectively). They assessed the prospects for the development of their own businesses (52.2%) and their branches (55.4%) to be moderate. Most of the respondents declared that they had not participated in specialized trainings or courses (57.6%), and most reported they did not have valuable knowledge (67.4%). A proportion of the respondents (56.5%) also reported that they had a family member who could be considered a successful entrepreneur.

The control group consisted of 100 people, aged between 19 and 37 years (M = 23.28, SD = 2.48), who had not had their own business. The control group was recruited from the general population. The majority were women (85%) with secondary education (73%) who came from large cities with over 100,000 residents (43%). Detailed information on the study sample and data on the characteristics of the companies are provided in Tables 7 and 8, respectively.

4.1.2 Methods

All participants completed the EDPI as developed in Study 1. The entrepreneurs also completed a short questionnaire gathering data on the characteristics of their companies, such as the date the company was started, the number of employees, the range of the company's activity, and self-assessments of the company's competitiveness or innovativeness. Basic socio-demographic data concerning the sex, age, educational level, and place of residence of the participants were also collected.

Informed consent for participation in the study was obtained from all the subjects.

4.1.3 Statistical Analyses

Statistical analyses were performed using SPSS (version 21.0) for Windows. Significance differences between the group of entrepreneurs and the control group were tested by Student's t-tests for independent samples. The level of statistical significance was set to $P \leq 0.05$.

---

5 Results

Comparisons of the scores on the EDPI between the entrepreneurs and the control group revealed significant differences for the majority of the EDPI subscales. As expected, the entrepreneurs scored statistically significantly higher than the control

TABLE 7: Data on the participants in the study (group of entrepreneurs and control group).

Group of entrepreneurs		N	%
Sex	Female	33	35.87
	Male	59	64.13
Place of residence	Rural	22	23.9
	Small town (up to 1000,000 residents)	26	28.3
	Large city (above 1000,000 residents)	44	47.8
Educational level	Doctor's degree	1	1.09
	Master's degree	40	43.48
	Bachelor's degree	16	17.39
	Engineer's degree	1	1.09
	General secondary education	17	18.47
	Secondary vocational education	13	14.13
	Basic vocational education	4	4.35
Status before setting up a business	Unemployed	25	27.17
	Graduate	6	6.53
	Employed on the basis of civil law contracts	23	25
	Employed as a salary-earning employee	32	34.78
	Conducting other business activity	6	6.52
Age when starting a business	Up to 23 years old	9	9.79
	24–29	33	35.87
	30–39	35	38.04
	40–49	10	10.87
	50+	5	5.43
The entrepreneur is the sole founder of the business	Yes	84	91.30
	No	8	8.70
Having experience in managing a company	Yes	61	66.30
	No	31	33.70

(*Continued*)

TABLE 7: (Cont.)

Group of entrepreneurs		N	%
Completed trainings	Yes	39	42.39
	No	53	57.61
Having valuable knowledge	Yes	30	32.61
	No	62	67.39
Having experience in running one's own company	Yes	20	21.74
	No	72	78.26
Having contact with clients	Yes	69	75
	No	23	25
Efficient entrepreneur in the family	Yes	52	56.52
	No	40	43.48
Control group			
Sex	Female	85	85
	Male	15	15
Education	General secondary	73	73
	Bachelor's degree	20	20
	Master's degree	7	7
The respondent has conducted business activity before	No	100	100
The respondent is currently running a business	No	100	100

group of non-entrepreneurs on *Risk-Taking Propensity, Autonomy, Openness to Experience, Emotional Stability, Conscientiousness, Innovativeness, Extraversion, Self-efficacy, Need for Achievement, Resistance to stress,* and *Passion.* However, three of the EDPI subscales (*Disagreeableness, Internal Locus of Control,* and *Authoritative Parenting*) did not demonstrate the expected significant differences. The results of this analysis are presented in Table 9.

6 Discussion

The aim of the analyses presented in this paper was to develop and test the psychometric properties of the EDPI, a questionnaire measure of 14 entrepreneurial personality dispositions as described in the relevant literature. Such a measure had been lacking in Poland, where this research was conducted. In Study 1, we tested the initial (pilot) version of the EDPI in regard of the psychometric

TABLE 8:   Data on business activity.

		N	%
The range	Local	42	45.65
	Regional	22	23.91
	Poland-wide	20	21.74
	International	8	8.70
The size of initial capital	Up to PLN 4,000	31	33.70
	PLN 40,001–10,000	9	9.78
	PLN 10,001–20,000	14	15.22
	PLN 20,001–50,000	19	20.65
	PLN 50,001–100,000	14	15.22
	PLN 100,001–500,000	5	5.43
Company's annual turnover	0–3% growth	16	17.39
	7–10% growth	25	27.17
	0–3% loss	4	4.35
	4–6% loss	3	3.26
	7–10% loss	21	22.83
	Loss of over 10%	8	8.70
	I do not know; I have no such information	15	16.30
Assessment of the prospects for the development of the business	Bright	23	25
	Average	48	52.17
	Poor	21	22.83
Assessment of the prospects for the development of the sector	Bright	27	29.35
	Average	51	55.43
	Poor	14	15.22
Assessment of the level of innovativeness of one's own business	Very high	5	5.43
	High	24	26.09
	Average	59	64.13
	Low	3	3.26
	Very low	1	1.09

TABLE 9:   Differences between the entrepreneurs and non-entrepreneurs in terms of average scores achieved on the EDPI subscales.

	Entrepreneurs (N=92)		Control group (N=100)		Student's t-test	
	M	**SD**	**M**	**SD**	**t**	**P**
Risk-Taking Propensity	19.56	3.95	17.58	4.04	3.42	0.001
Autonomy	23.42	3.56	21.62	4.74	2.98	0.003
Disagreeableness	19.03	5.14	18.98	4.23	.08	0.940
Openness to Experience	20.73	3.24	19.41	3.36	2.76	0.006
Emotional Stability	21.16	4.44	16.38	5.96	6.34	0.000
Conscientiousness	25.88	4.28	24.45	4.99	2.12	0.036
Need for Achievement	25.47	5.04	23.40	3.35	3.37	0.001
Innovativeness	23.89	2.71	20.99	4.37	5.58	0.000
Extraversion	25.67	4.03	21.82	3.98	6.64	0.000
Self-efficacy	24.47	3.09	22.57	3.23	4.13	0.000
Resistance to Stress	26.39	3.88	22.26	4.48	6.80	0.000
Internal Locus of Control	18.27	3.33	17.55	4.09	1.33	0.184
Passion	22.68	3.62	21.20	4.21	2.59	0.010
Authoritative Parenting	15.76	4.81	16.61	4.80	−1.21	0.229

properties of its items and subscales. The initial pool of 131 items was reduced to 86 in the final version of the EDPI. This step led to a significant decrease in the length of the instrument and made it more economical in use. The internal consistency (Cronbach's alpha) coefficients estimated for the subscales after item deletions ranged from 0.48 to 0.87 and were acceptable, except probably for the *Internal Locus of Control* subscale, whose reliability was found to be fall below 0.50. Such a result suggests that almost all of the EDPI subscales showed satisfactory reliability.

In Study 2, we made an effort to test the convergent validity of the EDPI subscales. Primarily, we intended to test whether the particular EDPI subscales showed expected correlational relationships with other independent instruments measuring similar or the same constructs. Because the number of items (from numerous methods) filled in by one participant for the purpose of this study would be enormous, we decided to divide our study sample into four subsamples, each with a different set of instruments against which we wanted to validate the EDPI subscales. This methodological design decreased the overload caused by too many methods that the respondents would otherwise have experienced.

The findings from Study 2 were mostly in accordance with our hypotheses about the relationships between the constructs. The 'Big Five' personality dimensions, as operationalized in the EDPI (*Extraversion, Emotional Stability, Openness to Experience, Disagreeableness*, and *Conscientiousness*), were found to correlate significantly with their analogous traits as measured by the NEO-FFI. It is notable that each 'Big Five' trait in the EDPI showed the highest correlation coefficient precisely for its counterpart from the NEO-FFI. Apart from this aspect of convergent validity, it could be observed that the majority of the remaining EDPI subscales also showed the pattern of correlations that could have been expected on the basis of data from previous research. So, we observed that the EDPI subscales revealed positive correlations with the NEO-FFI *Extroversion, Conscientiousness*, and *Openness to Experience* but negative correlations with the NEO-FFI *Neuroticism* and *Agreeableness*. Notably, as demonstrated by other studies, low scores on neuroticism and agreeableness and high scores on extraversion, conscientiousness, and openness to experience constitute what could be called 'the entrepreneurial personality profile' or 'enterprising personality' [9,24].

We were also able to demonstrate that the EDPI subscales reflecting the efficacy of regulation of stress and anxiety (*Resistance to Stress* and *Risk-Taking Propensity*) correlated with independent measures of risk taking and anxiety in the expected way. Again, if the remaining EDPI subscales revealed significant correlations with theses independent measures, these correlations were positive for risk taking and negative for anxiety. Previous research also indicated that entrepreneurship was positively related to risk taking and negatively related to anxiety [1,25].

The findings from Study 2 showed that the EDPI subscales reflecting self-related beliefs (i.e., *Self-efficacy* and *Internal Locus of Control*)and achievement-related attitudes (*Need for Achievement* and *Passion*) also revealed the expected pattern of correlations with similar constructs measured by separate instruments, obtaining the highest correlation values for the analogous measures. It is also of note that almost all of the subscales of the EDPI (except for *Authoritative Parenting*) showed positive correlations with independent measures of self-efficacy and achievement motivation, which were among the first and probably most frequently studied personality predictors of entrepreneurship [26,27].

The findings from Study 2, however, did not confirm the validity of the *Authoritative Parenting* subscale of the EDPI. This subscale showed only weak correlations with the authoritative parenting style in an independent measure, and it did not show negative correlations with the democratic or liberal parenting styles. This result could be explained somewhat by the differences in conceptualising these parenting styles on the EDPI and the measure of parenting styles. However, a probably more serious concern was that the EDPI *Authoritative Parenting* subscale did not demonstrate a consistent correlational pattern with other measures, whereas other EDPI subscales did. This result may suggest that the *Authoritative Parenting* subscale is not a valid measure of the concept or that it is not a valid predictor of entrepreneurship. Some researchers, however, have indicated that authoritative parenting is a factor that predisposes the human being toward successful entrepreneurship in the early stage of development [28]. Anyway, the concern about the EDPI with respect to the

Authoritative Parenting subscale informs us that either this subscale should probably be abandoned from the future versions of the EDPI or it should not be scored and taken into account in interpretation of the EDPI results.

Study 3 aimed at testing the criterion validity of the EDPI by comparing the scores achieved in the EDPI subscales between individuals who were actual entrepreneurs and those who had never had their own business. It must be mentioned that this criterion is obviously a very robust yardstick against which such an instrument can be validated. Many factors other than personality dispositions may affect a person's decision to establish a business, which may cause the non-entrepreneur sample to include people with personality predispositions for entrepreneurship that have never been actualized through business foundation. On the other hand, there might be people among the entrepreneurs who have decided to set up a business but have no personality characteristics of entrepreneurs. This methodological limitation must be taken into account when interpreting the results of Study 3. Despite the robustness of the discriminative criterion, the majority of the EDPI subscales demonstrated the expected differences, with entrepreneurs revealing statistically significantly higher scores on the EDPI than non-entrepreneurs. The following three EDPI subscales failed to demonstrate such differences: *Disagreeableness, Internal Locus of Control*, and *Authoritative Parenting. Authoritative Parenting* has already aroused some doubts as to its validity, and this analysis adds to the concern. *Locus of control* and *Agreeableness*, however, were found to relate to entrepreneurship in previous research [e.g. 29,30]. Interpretation of our findings with respect to these EDPI subscales may require more data to be obtained in future research.

In conclusion, the data presented in this paper generally support the reliability and the convergent and criterion validity of a new questionnaire designed to measure the personality dispositions of entrepreneurs. Nevertheless, some limitations to the use of this instrument should be borne in mind. The EDPI may prove a useful research instrument in a country where such measures are still scant. Future research on this instrument may prove its predictive power as to different facets of actual entrepreneurial behaviour.

Acknowledgements

This study was conducted as part of a research project of the National Science Centre (No. UMO-2011/03/B/HS4/04038) entitled 'Organizational and Psychological Predictors of Success in Business' carried out between February and August, 2013.

References

1 Singh, S. (1989): Personality characteristics, work values, and life styles of fast- and slow-progressing small-scale industrial entrepreneurs. In Journal of Social Psychology, 129(6), p.801.
2 Van Praag, C. M., & Versloot, P. (2007): What is the value of entrepreneurship: A review of recent research. In Small Business Economics, 29, pp.351–382.

3 Thurik, A. R. (2009): Entreprenomics: Entrepreneurship, economic growth and policy. In: Z. J.Acs, D. B.Audretsch and R.Strom(eds) *Entrepreneurship, Growth and Public Policy*, Cambridge, UK: Cambridge University Press, pp.219–249.

4 Obschonka, M., Silbereisen, R. K., & Schmitt-Rodermund, E. (2012): Explaining entrepreneurial behavior: Dispositional personality traits, growth of personal entrepreneurial resources, and business idea generation. In Career Development Quarterly, 60(2), pp.178–190.

5 Cismariu, L. (2014): The entrepreneurial intention between personality and values. In Annals of the University of Oradea, Economic Science Series, 23(1), pp.292–301.

6 Rauch, A., & Frese, M. (2007): Let's put the person back into entrepreneurship research: A meta-analysis on the relationship between business owners' personality traits, business creation, and success. In European Journal of Work and Organizational Psychology, 16(4), pp.353–385.

7 Gartner, W. B. (1985): A conceptual framework for describing the phenomenon of new venture creation. In Academy of Management Review, 10(4), pp.696–706.

8 Gartner, W. B. (1989): "Who is an entrepreneur?" Is the wrong question. In Entrepreneurship Theory and Practice, 12(2), pp.47–68.

9 Brandstätter, H. (2011): Personality aspects of entrepreneurship: A look at five meta-analyses. In Personality and Individual Differences, 51(3), pp.222–230.

10 Fogel, G., & ZapalskaA. (2001): A comparison of small and medium-size enterprise development in Central and Eastern Europe. In Comparative Economic Studies, 43(3), pp.35–68.

11 Kshetri, N. (2009): Entrepreneurship in post-socialist economies: A typology and institutional contexts for market entrepreneurship. In Journal of International Entrepreneurship, 7(3), pp.236–259.

12 Korzhov, G. (1999): Historical and cultural factors of entrepreneurship re-emergence in post-socialist Ukraine. In Polish Sociological Review, 128, pp.503–532.

13 Runst, P. (2013): Post-socialist culture and entrepreneurship post-socialist culture and entrepreneurship. In American Journal of Economics & Sociology, 72(3), pp.593–626.

14 Costa, P. T., & McCrae, R. R. (1989): *NEO Five-Factor Inventory (NEO-FFI)*. Odessa, FL: Psychological Assessment Resources.

15 Zawadzki, B., Strelau, J., Szczepaniak, P., & Śliwińska, M. (1998): *Inwentarz osobowości NEO-FFI Costy i McCrae. Adaptacja polska.* Podręcznik [Personality Inventory – NEO-FFI by Costa and McCrae. Polish Adaptation. Textbook]. Warszawa: PTP.

16 Studenski, R. (2007): Autodestrukcyjna motywacja do zachowań ryzykownych [Auto-destructive motivation for risky behaviour]. In Kolokwia Psychologiczne, 16, pp. 176–195.

17 Wrześniewski,K., Sosnowski,T., Jaworowska,A., & Fecenec,D. (2006): *Inwentarz Stanu Cechy Lęku STAI, Polska adaptacja STAI* [State-Trait Anxiety Inventory – STAI, Polish adaptation of the STAI]. Warszawa: Pracownia Testów Psychologicznych PTP.

18 Ryś, M. (2001): *Systemy rodzinne. Metody badań struktury rodziny pochodzenia i rodziny własnej* [Family Systems. Measurement Tools to Assess the Structure of the Family of Origin and One's Own Family]. Warszawa: Centrum Metodyczne Pomocy Psychologiczno-Pedagogicznej MEN.

19 Widerszal-Bazyl, M.(1978): Kwestionariusz do mierzenia motywu osiągnięć [The questionnaire measuring motivation of achievement]. In Przegląd Psychologiczny, 21(2), pp.355–368.

20 Schwarzer, R. (1993): *Measurement of Perceived Self-efficacy: Psychometric Scales for Cross-cultural Research*. Berlin: Freie Universität Berlin, Institut für Psychologie.

21 Juczyński, Z. (2001): *Narzędzia pomiaru w promocji i psychologii zdrowia* [Measuremet and Promotion Tools in Health Psychology]. Warszawa: Pracownia Testów Psychologicznych Polskiego Towarzystwa Psychologiczne.

22 Rotter, J. B.(1975): Some problems and misconceptions related to the construct of internal versus external control of reinforcement. In Journal of Consulting and Clinical Psychology, 43, pp.56–67.

23 Drwal, R. Ł.(1995): *Adaptacja kwestionariuszy osobowości* [Adaptation of Personality Questionnaires]. Warszawa: Wydawnictwo PWN.

24 Leutner, F., Ahmetoglu, G., Akhtar, R., & Chamorro-Premuzic, T. (2014): The relationship between the entrepreneurial personality and the big five personality traits. In Personality and Individual Differences, 63, pp.58–63.

25 Macko, A., & Tyszka, T. (2009): Entrepreneurship and risk taking. In Applied Psychology: An International Review, 58(3), pp.469–487.

26 Collins, C. J., Hanges, P. J., & Locke, E. A. (2004): The relationship of achievement motivation to entrepreneurial behavior: A meta-analysis. In Human Performance, 17(1), pp.95–117.

27 Culbertson, S. S., Smith, M. R., & Leiva, P. I. (2011): Enhancing entrepreneurship: The role of goal orientation and self-efficacy. In Journal of Career Assessment, 19(2), pp.115–129.

28 Schmitt-Rodermund, E. (2004): Pathways to successful entrepreneurship: Parenting, personality, early entrepreneurial competence, and interests. In Journal of Vocational Behavior, 65(3), pp.498–518.

29 Hansemark, O. C. (2003): Need for achievement, locus of control and the prediction of business start-ups: A longitudinal study. In Journal of Economic Psychology, 24(3), pp.301–319.

30 Nga, J. K. H., & Shamuganathan, G. (2010): The influence of personality traits and demographic factors on social entrepreneurship start up intentions. In Journal of Business Ethics, 95(2), pp.259–282.

Chapter 7

Mapping the Entrepreneurship from a Gender Perspective[1]

Magdalena Suárez-Ortega, María del Rocío Gálvez-García and María Fe Sánchez-García

1   Introduction

In this chapter, we focus on describing and analyzing exploratoryly the situation of entrepreneurship in the Spanish context, identifying some gender keys that allow us to understand, re-think and act accordingly to alleviate some barriers that condition the professional/vital paths entrepreneurs, especially of many women entrepreneurs who will be represented in our protagonists (women participating in this study).

Considering the scientific literature on the subject, and focusing on the motivations that drive entrepreneurial activity, we find three essential reasons that can explain entrepreneurial behavior, with the first two being more clear and relevant [1–3]: a) When entrepreneurship is the result of a previously identified business opportunity, or arises from the entrepreneurial vocation of the person [4]; b) When the venture arises as a need, or is a forced decision, usually in the face of difficulties in accessing employment for others; c) When the enterprise is given for other more diversified reasons that have less weight in the whole of the citizenship. We find that, in many cases, the Spanish entrepreneurship is taking place by business opportunity or by necessity (approximately 66.1% vs. 27.1%, respectively), that entrepreneurs by necessity grow in the last decade by investing the balance when it comes to entrepreneurship by vocation, and that the index of consolidated entrepreneurs is higher when undertaken by opportunity [3–5]. However, although the statistical data are relevant to draw the general picture, the understanding of them comes from personal experiences and discourses. Consequently, to understand the situation under study, we need to establish a link with the characteristics of one's professional/work and personal trajectory, as well as with the socio-labor dynamics that drive trends and actions in the citizenship.

Many authors agree on the importance of entrepreneurship for the economic and social development of a country (for example, [1,6–10]). In economic terms, an entrepreneur is the one who starts an economic project that has to become a company, which is the driving force of a value-generating idea [11]. Spain is one of the countries in the European Union with the highest growth rate [12]; during 2017, the number of active companies in Spain amounted to 3,279,120 according to the Central Companies Directory (DIRCE), of which 99.9%, classified as small and medium enterprises, generate 66.4% of employment [13], which is one of the most relevant social indicators at an economic and social level [1].

In recent years, women entrepreneurs have been steadily increasing, thus reducing the existing gender gap, although at present the entrepreneurial profile remains predominantly masculine [14]. Studies devoted to female entrepreneurship have also increased [15], but there is still a great lack of knowledge about female entrepreneurship [16] and about the reasons that cause the gender gap in the entrepreneurial field [17]. And, it is that, few studies connect entrepreneurship with their own career considered in a holistic way where multiple variables interact.

When we inquire into the reality of women entrepreneurs [4], we find that there are more women entrepreneurs than those listed in the official data, appearing in 'satellite' situations that support male entrepreneurship. In the same way, many women have an essential role in the maintenance of business, as well as in life, which, in turn, makes them possible. This is when we need to have some specific data that tell us about the characteristics of the women they undertake, considering their trajectories (age, educational level, number of children, motivation to undertake, working conditions, availability for employment, background to entrepreneurship, etc.). These types of variables are those that can explain the intention and entrepreneurial development, and make evident some gender gaps that cause imbalances between the career paths of women, also affecting men.

In this chapter, we try to approach the national entrepreneurial reality, considering social and labor indicators that allow us to draw, in an exploratory way, the entrepreneurial panorama, at the same time as analyzing testimonials from entrepreneurial women, that allow us to glimpse some keys for the professional guidance intervention in entrepreneurship. Therefore, results are presented on the figures of entrepreneurship, as well as the entities that support entrepreneurs, on motivations that drive entrepreneurship, deepening in some constraints and barriers of female entrepreneurship from the voices of the participating women themselves.

From the data set considered, some keys for female entrepreneurship are identified. These can become starting points for the establishment of proposals and formative and guiding actions that can boost the entrepreneurial ecosystem by integrating a gender perspective.

2 Background to the Study and Objectives

The increase of women in the labor market and specifically in the business world has been reflected in multiple levels, for example, in the academic world where the study of women as entrepreneurs has been gaining relevance [10,18,19]. The studies carried out so far confirm gender differences [20,21], and this gender inequality is evident at any stage of women's career [22] not only in the initial phase [23]. For example, in the scientific field, the development of the professional career has the form of 'scissors' where the research staff in the initial predoctoral stage as a researcher in training is predominantly female; however, in the next postdoctoral phase, the majority of men occupy these positions, increasing the difference in the following stages, where only 25% are women in the highest category according to data from the Higher Council for Scientific Research (CSIC) [24]. The study [22] tries to understand why women abandon their professional careers, and in this pretense they look at variables that have to do with personal decisions and family and with the care and support of life in general.

As for wages, women in Europe charge an average of 18% less per hour than men [20]; although it is true that it has been decreasing in recent years, there is still a great inequality in this regard. Gender differences in wages are seen in all countries of the European Union. In Spain, the salary gap is below the European average, with 16.2% in the economy in general and 17.7% in the scientific field. These salary differences can be a demotivating element to follow and develop a professional career [25]. As regards the representation of women in management positions in the largest companies in Europe, it is much smaller than that of men. Only 25.3% are women; Spain is 2.5 points below with 22%, France is the most equitable country with 43.4% female representation in the main companies, and Estonia, with a female representation so only 7.4% and it is the least egalitarian country [26]. Inequalities in the professional career remain in the business world; the data speak for themselves: there are more men than women entrepreneurs and when they start, they do it differently [3]. In Spain, female entrepreneurship accounts for almost 35%, while in Europe women entrepreneurs are 31%.

With respect to entrepreneurship orientation [27], in their study of the influence of gender stereotypes in entrepreneurship, they conclude that for women to define themselves with a clear entrepreneurial orientation in their life, they have to assume socially considered masculine roles. This reflects, in our opinion, what imaginary people have about the profile of the entrepreneur, and the values and attributes that this person must put into play in the development and management of their work.

Among the main obstacles to creating a company is the high risk and lack of capital, women stand out compared to men because they have a greater fear of business failure, consider that they do not have the appropriate knowledge and experience, and doubt their entrepreneurial capacity to a greater extent than men [10,18,19]. Lack of confidence [19] and greater aversion to risk [28] are characteristics of female entrepreneurial behavior that act as important limitations when developing an entrepreneurial career.

Regarding the main reasons to create a company are personal independence and business opportunity; from a gender perspective, women value more than men economic independence and the motivation of necessity for not finding an adequate job [18]. Another motivation more typical of female entrepreneurs is time flexibility [19], which can relate the complication when it comes to reconciling work and family life. And, it is that, work and family conciliation is one of the main points of conflict, assumed as constraints and barriers to entrepreneurship (employment in general) for women.

Although it is true that it is an aspect that affects both women and men as different roles are combined in the life plan, it seems that the weight of the family or the renunciation of the development of a professional career is more usual in women [29], there is still a cultural and generational pressure, even valued as feminine symbolic, which means that there are not enough social facilities available for women to live their professional development equally. We see it especially when fewer women continue their professional career, when this transit (or another related to the world of work, for example promoting or accepting decision-making positions) coincides with the moment of forming a family. A clear example is research, since 44% of women are married with children, while in men they are 70% [22], but we also see this decline in the business world [30].

On the other hand, according to the study [25], it should be noted that the majority of women, 60%, have never interrupted work to do other activities. Of the percentage of women who have interrupted their professional career, 62.5% have been to conciliate and take care of the family. And, according to a study carried out on the professional career of women [31], women give higher priority to the family (67%) than to work (32%), while the priority of men is more equitable (family 51% and work 40%). Perhaps because they have help or support that allows this reconciliation, which is presupposed including personal, free and leisure time.

Although entrepreneurship is favored, and actions are taken to promote equal opportunities, in general, we obtain that the majority profile of the person who undertakes is: self-employed in the services sector, without salaried employees, with only one activity, male, between 40 and 50 years old, Spanish, who has been in business for 5 years or more and who is quoted at the minimum contribution base [4,12,14,18]. However, if we compare with other countries of the European Union, we find that Spain is above the average in terms of female entrepreneurship, approximately 31.5% [20,32]. It is for all of this that in this work we set out as a goal the specific knowledge of the female reality in the general entrepreneurial framework, in order to identify specific barriers that allow to show gender gaps on which to intervene.

It can be seen how there is research that defends that the differences between male and female entrepreneurship are due to external and discriminatory barriers of access to opportunities under equal conditions, as well as difficulties in obtaining financing from women [33,34] and other barriers that cause women to decide not to undertake [35], including disadvantages in access to education they receive [23]. Studies devoted to the institutional and social context [36] have also been prepared, although to a lesser extent, where policies to support entrepreneurship are studied [37]. But most studies are based on differences in entrepreneurial behavior between men and women, investigating differences in motivation between men and women [33], entrepreneurial skills and abilities [38] and entrepreneurial intention [39]. At this point, the work we present takes the witness and aims to analyze and interpret the female professional and business profile inscribed in the Spanish reality.

Specifically, we set ourselves the following objectives:

1) Describe the general situation in entrepreneurship, specifically considering the female reality.

2) Know and explain possible motivations and decisions that promote female entrepreneurship, identifying gender gaps.

3) Evidence constraints and barriers felt by women in their entrepreneurial professional development.

4) In light of the above, we propose some formative and guiding recommendations integrating a gender perspective in the entrepreneurial professional development.

With the intention of responding to the objectives formulated, next we propose the following methodological design, combining techniques of quantitative and qualitative character with an exploratory character.

3 Methodological Approach

The study has been carried out following a mixed method. On the one hand, the analysis of a compendium of social indicators, statistics and documentary sources has been carried out (other studies, mainly, [2,3,5]). Fundamentally, variables [4] have been taken into account, such as: a) The Entrepreneurial Activity Rate (ASR) represented by the percentage of the population aged 18–64 surveyed that indicates that they have created a company that has not yet reached 3; 5 years. This is the sum of the nascent entrepreneur (less than 3 months) and new entrepreneur (between 3 months and 3.5 years); b) the profile of a consolidated entrepreneur considered according to [2] as those entrepreneurs whose business initiative is more than 3.5 years old; and, c) the profile of entrepreneur in transition, considered as nascent or new entrepreneurs, are those whose entrepreneurial initiatives are not older than 3 years [2,4].

These data, of a quantitative nature, have been contrasted with other qualitative data, coming from interviews carried out with women entrepreneurs in different stages of their professional career. Specifically, the sample consisted of 12 women, who were interviewed in depth (with an exploratory character and as a basis prior to the realization of life histories, the subject of another work). The participants were selected intentionally according to the following criteria: a) Moment of their entrepreneurial career (initial or in development/consolidated); b) Context and characteristic (autonomy/origin, urban/rural); personal/family situation (especially number of dependent children/dependents). Below we describe their profiles grossomodo (Table 1):

As a central technique, therefore, we use the open interview, in order to explore the general situation of women entrepreneurs, know their motivations and key decisions that drive entrepreneurship and entrepreneurial career management, and identify possible conditions and barriers of gender felt by the women who are at the base of this process and professional entrepreneurial behavior.

Consequently, and taking into account the objectives served by this technique, the script used was composed of the following dimensions: a) Description of the general entrepreneurial situation; b) Characterization of female entrepreneurship; c) Motivations and decisions that drive female entrepreneurship; d) Transitions to the enterprise (initial, development, consolidation); e) Determinants and barriers felt by women; f) Gender gaps in the female entrepreneurial reality.

TABLE 1:   Profiles of the participating women

Women	Moment of the entrepreneurial career	Context	Personal/family situation
María	Consolidated/development	Madrid	Mother of 2 children
Gema	Consolidated/development	Madrid	Mother of 2 children
Elena	In transition	Andalucía	Mother of 1 child
Julia	In transition	Bilbao	Mother of 2 children
Luisa	In transition	Madrid	No children
Vanesa	Consolidated/development	Andalucía	Mother of 2 children
Mónica	Consolidated/development	Andalucía	Mother of 3 children
Irene	Consolidated/development	Andalucía	Primeramaternidad
Esther	In transition	Andalucía	No children
Lidia	Consolidated/development	Andalucía	Mother of 1 child
Silvia	In transition	Bilbao	Mother of 2 children
Carmen	In transition	Barcelona	No children, 1 dependent person in charge

Source: Prepared by the authors.

Given that we treat mixed data, quantitative data from social indicators fundamentally, and qualitative data derived from the open interviews applied, the analysis procedure required this methodological and analytical integration through triangulation. Specifically, we proceeded to the interpretation of statistics from scientific reports and documents, together with the analysis of content derived from the discourses provided by the women in the interviews. This content analysis was carried out after coding and categorization of the information, elaborating a mixed category system, attending fundamentally in this work to the categories of analysis mentioned in the script, and in coherence with the objectives to which we try to respond. The most significant results of this study are shown below.

4 Results

The results were organized in coherence with the objectives set and with the main dimensions studied. Thus, in the first place we stop to present the general reality of entrepreneurship in Spain, emphasizing the female situation; second, we present results on the motivations and decisions that characterize entrepreneurial behavior in women entrepreneurs, to focus on the main conditions and barriers to female entrepreneurship. It has been tried that the data triangulation is present in the course of the whole section, thus showing the results in an integrated way as far as possible. We finish with the identification of a series of felt needs that provide some relevant keys in terms of training and guidance for female entrepreneurship.

4.1 Entrepreneurship in Spain in Figures

We draw the entrepreneurial panorama according to the data provided by the report 'The profile of the self-employed worker' prepared by [14] where, as of December 31, 2017, a total of 3,231,279 self-employed members were registered in the Security Social, of which 1,962,774 are self-employed, this means that they are natural persons who are not integrated into mercantile societies, cooperatives and other corporate entities, nor are they family collaborators or registered as part of any special group of workers. Figure 1 reflects a small recovery in the number of self-employed workers since reaching the minimum in this period in 2012.

In Figure 2, we see the weight that each Autonomous Community has on the total of self-employed workers in Spain during 2017. Almost half of this group is concentrated in 3 communities: Andalusia (17.5%), Catalonia (16.5%), and Madrid (12%). Referring to the importance of employment, it is interesting to note that only 21.60% of the self-employed in Spain have salaried employees. Ceuta is the Community with the highest percentage of self-employed workers and Navarra the community with the least.

Entrepreneurial Complexity

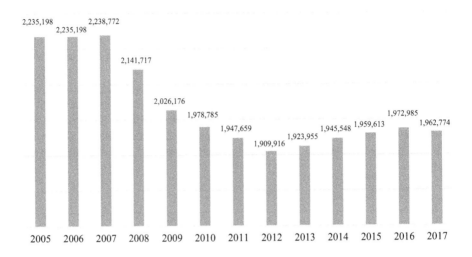

FIGURE 1: Evolution of the number of self-employed workers in Spain during the period 2005–2017

Source: Prepared by the authors based on data from [14].

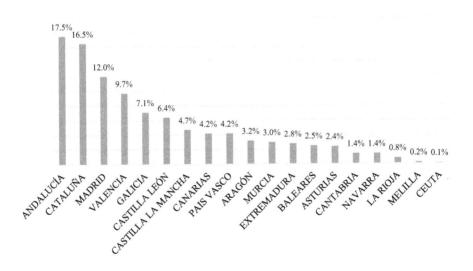

FIGURE 2: Percentage distribution of self-employed workers by communities as of December 31, 2017.

Source: Prepared by the authors based on data from [14].

The Services Sector is the sector that collects the largest number of companies, 73%, a trend that is followed in all Autonomous Communities, followed by Agriculture, Construction and Industry. It is interesting to note that the Sector where there are fewer women is Construction with 3.5% women and the sector with the highest female representation in the Services Sector with 41.4% of women. Regarding nationality, 8% of self-employed workers are immigrants, of which 64.3% are men and 35.7% are women, with Melilla being the autonomous community with the most self-employed foreigners, followed by the Balearic Islands and Canary Islands. On the other hand, Extremadura and Galicia are the Communities with less foreign affiliates on their own account in Social Security.

Considering the gender distinction, of the 1,962,774 self-employed registered in 2017, 65.2% are men and 34.8% are women. The gap between men and women is greater in Melilla, with only 27.9% of women, while the most equitable communities are Galicia with 42.2% of autonomous women and Asturias with 40.8%. Figure 3 represents the evolution of the number of self-employed workers in Spain according to gender, where we can see a constant and progressive reduction in the gap between men and women.

The average age of self-employed workers is 46.2% in the 40–54 age brackets. By comparing age according to sex according to Figure 4, autonomous women are younger than men, since the majority age group of men is 55 years of age or older and the majority age group of women is younger than men, between 25 and 39 years. In this issue, we can identify a different trend in terms of the moment in which the entrepreneurial decision emerges mainly, which could explain transitions in the entrepreneurial, initial, development and decline career, associated with gender factors.

With these data, we can define the autonomous majority profile is a male Spanish, between 40 and 54 years (although with a significant presence between 25 and 39 years), which operates in the services sector, which has no employees at his expense, which carries 5 years or more in your business, and which is quoted by the minimum contribution base [14].

	2005	2006	2007	2008	2009	2010	2011	2012	2013	2014	2015	2016	2017
Hombre	68.60%	68.60%	68.90%	68.30%	67.50%	67.10%	66.80%	66.50%	66.10%	65.50%	65.40%	65.20%	65.10%
Mujer	31.40%	31.40%	31.10%	31.70%	32.50%	32.90%	33.20%	33.50%	33.90%	34.50%	34.60%	34.80%	34.90%

FIGURE 3: Distribution by sex of the number of self-employed during the period 2005–2017.

Source: Prepared by the authors based on data from [14].

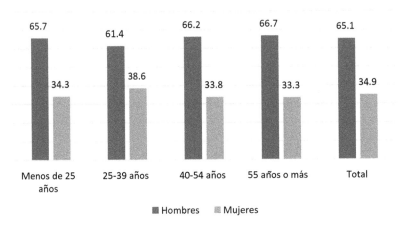

FIGURE 4: Distribution of self-employed workers according to sex by age.
Source: Prepared by the authors based on data from [14].

Other interesting profiles that help us to complete the map of entrepreneurship in Spain are those described by the Global Entrepreneurship Monitor: it is about the profile of potential entrepreneurs, the profile of the entrepreneurs in the initial phase and the profile of the consolidated entrepreneur [28]. Entrepreneurial intent is measured through potential entrepreneurs, who are the people of the adult population (18 to 64 years old) who show intention to start a new company in the next 3 years. It is interesting to note that the years in which the entrepreneurial intention is greater, 2012 with 12% of potential entrepreneurs, coincides with the peak of the unemployment rate, 26% in that year, so it can be deduced that the intention of undertake comes from the lack of work alternatives.

To measure entrepreneurship in Spain, we take as a reference the TEA Indicator; according to the Global Entrepreneurship Monitor [28], it is the Entrepreneurship Rate that reflects the entrepreneurial activity in the initial phase. Its calculation corresponds to the sum of the percentage of nascent entrepreneurs (less than 3 months) and new entrepreneurs (less than 42 months) developing a business project. In Figure 5, we can see the evolution of the TEA indicator in recent years, which reflects an increase in entrepreneurial activity in the initial phase, surpassing the 6.0% barrier for the first time since 2008, before the crisis, when the TEA was around 7.0%. This means that in 2017 in Spain 6 out of every 100 respondents between 18 and 65 years of age declare that they are launching an entrepreneurial initiative [3].

Figure 6 shows the evolution of male and female TEA, as well as the variation between them, highlighting that, like the trend in the evolution of the number of self-employed, the gap between men and women seems to be narrowing and the difference between female and male entrepreneurship tends to zero. In this way, in

	2005	2006	2007	2008	2009	2010	2011	2012	2013	2014	2015	2016	2017
Potenciales	5.90%	6.30%	6.70%	7.50%	5.50%	6.70%	9.70%	12.00%	9.30%	8.00%	6.10%	6.10%	6.80%
TEA	5.70%	7.30%	7.60%	7.00%	5.10%	4.30%	5.80%	5.70%	5.20%	5.50%	5.70%	5.20%	6.20%

FIGURE 5: Evolution of the entrepreneurial intention and of the entrepreneurial initiative in Spain during 2005–2017

Source [5].

2007, the gender difference reached its highest level at 4.2 points, also coinciding with the Tea level, which was higher by 7.6%. It is from then on that the variation between the male and female TEA decreases progressively until reaching its minimum in 2016, 1.1 points of difference between men and women. Despite these good data, it can be seen that the line that represents the male entrepreneurship rate is above the TEA and the female Entrepreneurship rate is below the TEA.

With respect to the trend of entrepreneurs who are consolidated, this is that their business project exceeds 42 months of activity, is decreasing since its peak in 2008, coinciding with the beginning of the economic crisis in Spain. In 2017, the rate of consolidated entrepreneurs stood at 7%.

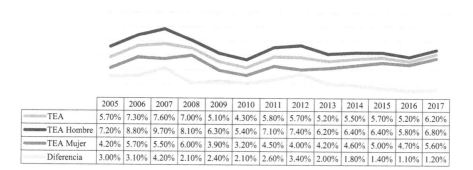

	2005	2006	2007	2008	2009	2010	2011	2012	2013	2014	2015	2016	2017
TEA	5.70%	7.30%	7.60%	7.00%	5.10%	4.30%	5.80%	5.70%	5.20%	5.50%	5.70%	5.20%	6.20%
TEA Hombre	7.20%	8.80%	9.70%	8.10%	6.30%	5.40%	7.10%	7.40%	6.20%	6.40%	6.40%	5.80%	6.80%
TEA Mujer	4.20%	5.70%	5.50%	6.00%	3.90%	3.20%	4.50%	4.00%	4.20%	4.60%	5.00%	4.70%	5.60%
Diferencia	3.00%	3.10%	4.20%	2.10%	2.40%	2.10%	2.60%	3.40%	2.00%	1.80%	1.40%	1.10%	1.20%

FIGURE 6: Evolution of the TEA index by gender in Spain during the period 2005–2017

Source: Own elaboration based on data from the GEM Report [5].

The group in which the female weight is greater is that of potential entrepreneurs, 49.1%, followed by those who initiate the idea, 44.9%, with fewer women who manage to consolidate their project, 40%. In Table 2, we can see the distribution of the different entrepreneurial groups by gender, but these data are not triangulated with the rest of criteria of age, level of education, specific training to undertake or motivation to undertake.

The age of the people involved in the entrepreneurial process tends to increase as they advance in the entrepreneurial process due to the accumulation of knowledge and experience over the years, keys for the identification of business opportunities [3]. We see this tendency in the average age of the different groups: potential entrepreneurs 38.4 years, start-up entrepreneurs 40 years and consolidators 49.7 years.

Education is one of the three fundamental pillars of the entrepreneurial process and reduces inequalities [40]; in fact, according to the 2016 Gem report [3], education and training is the main factor to promote entrepreneurship in Spain, and more specifically education in entrepreneurial skills [41]. In recent years, the profile most likely to be undertaken is adults with a higher education level followed by people with an average level of education. Entrepreneurs who start their entrepreneurial project have a higher level of education than potential or consolidated entrepreneurs, specifically 40.5% higher education and 9.3% postgraduate, while potential entrepreneurs have 34.1% and 6.1%, respectively, and consolidated 31% higher education and only 4.8% postgraduate.

The percentage of entrepreneurs that have specific training to start has increased in all groups compared to previous years. According to the different groups, 49.4% of the potential entrepreneurs have specific training to undertake, 49.2% of the entrepreneurs in the initial phase, and 43.8% of the entrepreneurs consolidated.

Entrepreneurs are increasingly trained and seek specific training to consolidate their projects, education and entrepreneurship, according to [42] are essential to promote entrepreneurial intent and develop the skills necessary to consolidate business projects. In addition, the difficult socioeconomic situation that Spain is

TABLE 2:   Distribution by gender of the entrepreneurial groups in Spain in 2017

	Spain	
	Men	Women
Potentials	50.9%	49.1%
Nascent	59.1%	40.9%
New	51.9%	48.1%
TEA	55.1%	44.9%
Consolidated	60.0%	40.0%
Abandonment	52.6%	47.4%

Source [3].

experiencing in recent years has increased the interest in promoting an entrepreneurial culture [13,43]. This has caused a notable increase in the number of entities, organizations and platforms that, in some way, give support to the entrepreneur in any of the phases of the entrepreneurial process. Entrepreneurship support entities can be classified according to the scope of action in National, regional, regional and local [43] or according to the origin of funds, in public bodies if the funding comes from government funds, private organizations are constituted with capital of companies and individuals. They can also be mixed bodies, with public and private funding [44]. The 2015 GEM report has produced a monograph on the organizations and measures to support the entrepreneur in Spain and through the following tables draw a map of public and private organizations in Spain which is reflected in Tables 3 and 4, respectively.

Taking into account the gender differences at the time of undertaking previously mentioned there are in Spain numerous entities that are dedicated to give service and support specifically to women. Among the organizations dedicated exclusively to the promotion of female entrepreneurship, we find the Ministry of

TABLE 3:   Map of public entities

Central administration	Ministry of Industry, Energy and Tourism (DGPYME)
	Ministry of Economy and Competitiveness
	Ministry of Health, Social Affairs and Equality (INJUVE and Women's Institute)
Regional Administration	Regional Development Agencies (ADR)
	European Business and Innovation Centers (CEEI)
	Employment Services, own offices distributed by all the Autonomous Communities and localities
Local Management	Local Development Agencies (ADL)
	Local Youth Information Centers
	Nurseries of municipal management company
	Delegations in all provinces
	Own business incubators
Chambers of Commerce	Delegations in all provinces
	Own business incubators
Public universities	Vicerrectorado de emprendimiento
	Employment Orientation and Information Centers (COIE)
	Incubation spaces and nurseries
	Awards
	Specific programs (Yuzz, e2 ...)
	Official titles and own entrepreneurship
	Chair of entrepreneurs
	Offices of Results Transfer Research (OTRI)

Source: GEM 2015, p. 141 [44].

TABLE 4:   Map of private entities

Business and Professional Organizations	Provincial Business Organizations: Confederations, federations and associations Business organizations of the social economy Self-employed organizations Association of Young Provincial Entrepreneurs Organization of Women Entrepreneurs Professional Associations of Professionals
Private University and Business Schools Foundations and non-profit organizations	Chair of Entrepreneurs School of Industrial Organization (EOI) Red Cross University Business Foundation Spanish Seniors for Technical Cooperation (SECOT) Repsol Foundation Everis Foundation UCEIF Foundation Rafael del Pino Foundation Telefónica Foundation Ernest & Young Foundation Tomillo Foundation Youth Bussines Spain Bankinter innovation foundation Initiator Foundation Entrepreneurship Shuttle Cajarural Foundation Castilla_La-Mancha CEL Foundation UPO undertakes

Source: GEM 2015, p. 143 [44].

Health, Social Affairs and Equality, to which the Institute for Women belongs, as a public body of the Central Administration, and the Organization of Women Entrepreneurs as a private entity [45]. details a list of programs and organizations to support women entrepreneurs, of which we highlight, for example, the Business Support Program for Women, the Chamber of Commerce of Spain, the Ministry of Health and Social Services (Instituto de la Woman for Equal Opportunities), the European Social Fund, the Support Services for Women Companies, the Ministry of Presidency and Equality, the Rural Women and Families Association or the Federation of Associations of Women Entrepreneurs of the Social Economy, among other specific resources.

If we look at specific data from the interviews with the participating women with respect to this dimension, we can highlight that the sample has an average age of approximately 42 years. 83.7% of women have a university education, compared to those who study professional training. All have specific training related to their business profiles, mainly services, such as business management, human resources, accounting or administration and finance, administrative assistant or secretariat. They are restless women who have continuous work experiences, some also in paid employment as Luisa and Elena. Others have progressively started entrepreneurship projects, such as the case of Esther, and choose to undertake mainly by necessity or forced before situations of unemployment and labor instability, specifically 68.5% are in this situation, compared to women who manifest a vocation enterprising Women whose profiles are consolidated have a more solid track record as entrepreneurs, although they consider themselves in development because they consider that they continue to learn. In his own words:

You should never be stuck, because then that project is like dying, the motivation must remain so that a business project is still alive.

(María)

It's like never believing that you know everything, being receptive to innovations, to changes ..., because there are always new needs in your company, or improvements that you can make.

(Lidia)

You must always reinvent yourself, even if you have a defined and relatively stable project, day by day and experience shows you where you should go walking, but it is also in you, you must anticipate these needs and be always thinking, valuing, creating ...

(Irene)

4.2 Predominant Reasons for Entrepreneurship in Women Entrepreneurs

There is some consensus in the literature about the motivations that lead people to undertake. The theoretical model of the GEM report [3,5] considers two fundamental reasons that explain entrepreneurial behavior, those that they undertake out of necessity because they have not found a better alternative in the labor market and those that undertake by opportunity or vocation, differentiating those that have found a pure business opportunity and an opportunity in part. Table 5 shows the reasons for undertaking distinguishing two profiles, entrepreneurs in transition or in the initial phase and the consolidated entrepreneurs, no significant differences between both groups.

Figure 7 represents the evolution of entrepreneurial behavior during the period 2005–2017 where it can be seen that for more than a decade the main motivation

TABLE 5:   The entrepreneurial process in Spain in
2017 according to the reason for undertaking

	TEA	**Consolidated**
Another reason	0,2%	0,7%
Need	1,8%	2,0%
Opportunity in part	1,0%	1,1%
Pure opportunity	3,2%	3,2%

Source: GEM 2017 [5].

of the entrepreneurial population in Spain, represented by the TEA, has been to
identify a business opportunity. The year 2017, with 68.5%, records together with
the years 2013 and 2014 the lowest figures of this period.

However, it is necessary to point out that since 2009, entrepreneurs in the
initial phase who have started out of necessity have almost doubled, representing
28.3% of the TEA in 2017, which according to [46] has a low impact on economic
development and which becomes means of individual survival. And in the case of
women it is more accentuated since they undertake 20% more out of necessity
than men, constituting, in addition, it is a difficult paradox to explain: when the
level of economic development increases the entrepreneurial participation of
women decreases [32]. A study carried out by [18] confirms that more women
than men have the motivation to start a business the impossibility of finding an
adequate job. There are differences in factor-based economies, where 35% of
women undertake by necessity, and in economies based on innovation, where it is
reduced to 21% [5].

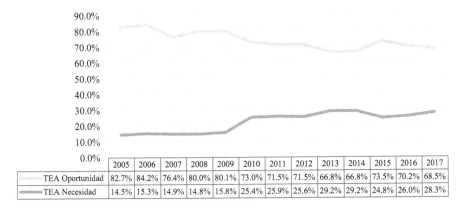

FIGURE 7: Evolution of motivation to undertake in the period 2005–2017 in Spain
Source: Prepared by the authors based on data from the GEM Spain 2017 Report [5].

Regarding the reasons that underlie entrepreneurs by chance in Spain, the main reason is to achieve greater independence, 57.1%, followed by the intention to increase revenues, 25.2% [5], while maintaining income or other cases represent only 9.7% and 8.1% respectively. Other studies also confirm that independence is the main motivation to undertake [47,48].

Considering the motivation of entrepreneurs to create a company in the different Autonomous Communities, we will refer to 2016 data as presented in Table 6. Madrid, with 81.5% and as in previous years, is the Community Autonomous that shows percentages of entrepreneurship by opportunity well above the national average located at 70.2%. At the other extreme, Catalonia, with a 50.7% motivation to undertake by chance, followed by a mixed motivation to undertake. As for the motivation to start based on need, Castilla La Mancha is the community that undertakes the most for this reason, 40.7% and Madrid the least with 15.9%.

These data are put in relation with others from interviews conducted with women entrepreneurs (Table 1), revealing some issues. On the one hand, we can corroborate that the main reason to undertake has to do with one's vocation, in addition to the economic factor (caused by an unemployment situation, whether maintained or unexpected). Let's see how the women themselves express it:

In my case, I decided to start because I wanted to see a project that I had been thinking about for years. Come on, I came from a family, my father started it and I wanted to continue it, especially to maintain a family project. He had the experience and the main resources, it was a pity to lose him.

(María)

My brother never followed the family business, but in my case it was the one closest to the family home, and it was logical that he felt it as an employment option.

(Gema)

When I've decided to start, it's always been by vocation, I like to think about projects that I can put into practice, but the truth is that I was later opened up to work for others and I tried, and this last business project came up of an unexpected situation of unemployment.

(Elena)

Actually I always feel more capable to face new challenges, and that happens to be my own boss, which allows other options, for example flexibility, maybe all women look for this in self-employment, which is also to think. do not? Of course working as an entrepreneur gives you autonomy, that independence I value it a lot, although it also has its own things.

(Julia)

TABLE 6: Motivation of TEA by communities in 2016

	Entrepreneurship by opportunity	Entrepreneurship by necessity
Spain	70,20%	26,00%
Andalucía	–	–
Aragón	60,80%	35,70%
Asturias	–	–
Baleares	–	–
Canarias	–	–
Cantabria	73,0%	27,0%
Castilla la Mancha	53,20%	40,70%
Castilla León	–	–
Cataluña	50,7%	22,9%
Comunidad Valenciana	47,80%	36,40%
Extremadura	–	–
Galicia	66,2%	30,0%
Madrid	81,5%	15,9%
Murcia	65%	30%
Navarra	65,8%	34,2%
País Vasco	74,3%	24,2%
La Rioja	56,10%	25,12
Ceuta	–	–
Melilla	–	–

Source: Own elaboration based on the data of the Regional GEM reports of the Autonomous Communities that elaborate it. (Asturias, Balearic Islands, Canary Islands, Ceuta and Melilla do not elaborate Regional GEM Report) Castilla León has not published it, usually in previous years. Andalusia and Extremadura use another way to measure motivation, and Extremadura so it cannot be compared to the rest.

If we delve into the reasons that drive entrepreneurship, as we see in the case of Julia and other women interviewed, temporary flexibility is placed in first place. Also the feeling of owning their own business, which at the same time gives a feeling of independence and control and job security, they feel that the progress of the company depends more on themselves and not so much on other people, which it provides them with security while also serving as a stimulus.

For a self-employed person, be it a woman or a man, the company depends on one, nobody will come to solve the problems, but not to take the profits, although there is a lot to pay and more aid and less tax increases are needed.

(Luisa)

Being autonomous gives me power, as security that my work depends on me, and if one day I do less for some reason, the other I know I can do more, or the other way around, although in general you can not sleep because every day it's a new challenge.

(Julia)

In my case, I come from a very humble family and saw how my father could dominate his future with his work, whether he won or lost depended on him, and that is the model that I followed and can prosper economically.

(Vanesa)

What gives a freelance is above all the flexibility, although in our case it is often a hoax, it depends on how you take it and the help you have also to take your house and your company; learning to manage and delegate is fundamental.

(Monica)

We find women whose decisions to undertake link the professional project of the couple. Such is the case of Irene. Her husband is currently going through a period of unexpected unemployment that forces him to reorient his career. She bets to help him, -this to the development of his own career in another direction-, giving a boost to a business project in which he adopts a secondary role (taking the reins of the company) to support his partner.

On another level, simply because of my decision to undertake ... is there another issue of gender than my reason for commitment to help my husband? Due to this reason that led me to undertake, I have my life paused during this year and it is possible that during the next one as well. If it had not been like that, I would probably have started in another sector, another type of company more related to my professional identity.

(Irene)

4.3 Determinants of Female Entrepreneurship: Lights and Shadows

Considering the discourse of women, in general, it is appreciated how they feel that they have more difficulties than their male colleagues in reconciling personal life, family and work. This is mainly due to how they signify their roles as women, where there is still an unequal socialization process that values traditional roles in women to a greater extent than in men and vice versa, labor roles in men in higher values are valued as in women. Thus, Silvia's words are significant when she states that

> *conciliation is always easier in men because, in general, they do not*
> *usually conciliate; it is easier to separate them from their children and*
> *they have assumed a more diverse set of roles, for example the need for*
> *leisure, sports or going with their friends or colleagues.*

Women also put us on the table an obsolete labor system, not really prepared for women to work and be mothers on equal terms with their male partners. Mother-hood and fatherhood are not lived equally or require the same requirements for one and for others. As Julia puts it

> *no matter how much you want it is not the same, and this can be seen in*
> *positive and negative, in positive by the experience of being a woman*
> *and a mother, and negative not so much for us but for society, which*
> *should value women and establish support systems to give real equality.*

Women state that self-employment is so absorbing and requires so much presence, that a company is not something that can be delegated; posing the paradox that self-employment allows more flexibility for women but at the same time requires presence. In regard to Elena, she posed the following:

> *Maybe the company, your company, is a friendlier means to the extent*
> *that you can establish more favorable spaces for women, for example,*
> *I took my baby to the company when I needed it and that you can not do*
> *in another work context, or you allow yourself certain needs to other*
> *women so that they can reconcile, while the work is covered, for example*
> *at the level of schedules, work by objectives or from home sometimes,*
> *which I suppose that can occur more in some companies than in others,*
> *according to their characteristics, areas, demands for work, etc., but in*
> *my case this helped, although sometimes it was also particularly hairy*
> *when setting personal and family limits.*

Returning to the statistics and literature to use, we find that gender differences are aggravated according to the sectors where it is undertaken and the characteristics of them. As can be seen in [5], the gap between men and women is much more evident in the technological field where female representation is much smaller. According to [5] the lower presence of women in technological entrepreneurship is due to three variables: a) A more competitive nature with greater difficulty in undertaking; b) Conflicts between the rigidity of dedication and family responsi-bilities; and, c) High investment requirements due to the associated high risk.

Taking into account the information thrown by the interviews in this dimen-sion, we find some gender determinants felt by the women themselves. Among them, the family business culture is noteworthy, which as we saw can be a facilitator but also a major obstacle. At the moment of starting an entrepreneurial career, the family business culture, in the opinion of women, facilitates the creation of a company, either as a continuation of the previous or new creation. Here we have facilities such as

> *having a relatively solid or solid contact portfolio, knowledge of access to resources and potential clients, a ready-made clientele that generally shows confidence in previous entrepreneurs and serves as your endorsement, even if you already have experience in the management although it has been like aid to the parents or relatives.*

(Mónica)

And, many women start from child in the family business helping their parents although there is no contractual relationship itself. Thus, some women suggest that the main conditioning factor for them to decide to undertake has been this family culture, which they have lived since they were child.

On the other hand, the character of the person seems to be another conditioning factor in the face of entrepreneurship, and here are included the characteristics of a family socialization process, with general and specific characteristics for each woman, which has also shaped her identity. Some women tell us about a series of 'innate' qualities that predispose entrepreneurship, which at the same time can be reinforced by the business/entrepreneur family context, specifically if we refer to entrepreneurship by chance or by vocation (speeches change markedly when it comes to entrepreneurship), of necessity/forced entrepreneurship). These innate qualities are referred to as ways of being or being placed before professional actions and choices, even to signify as a woman, and are reinforced by the education received. Thus, for example, Vanesa and Lidia state that '*their mothers have already given birth to women entrepreneurs, with qualities and traits characteristic of women entrepreneurs*'.

However, a recurring theme in the interviews and where, in general, the women interviewed coincide, has been in the conciliation of roles as a conditioning factor (negative) for entrepreneurship. Which is minimized with external help, usually from other women who are in charge of the roles related to the care and maintenance of domestic life. And, it is that, women tell us that it is they who '*continue to have greater difficulties to reconcile personal life, with family and work*', and that the situation is complicated when they are entrepreneurs and managers of their own company and staff, because this requires a dedication to permanent time, at the same time that the family environment also demands when they have children or dependents dependent on them. Like Vanesa and Carmen, they pose graphically to us:

> *Reconciliation today does not exist, it remains unreal in daily practice (...)*
> *On the one hand, work as an entrepreneur is more flexible than others that require specific working hours, but women suggest that this is a hoax, as conciliation remains practically a women's issue, and for women.*

(Mónica)

María insists on this issue by contributing some more elements:

> *Although the truth is that being a businesswoman has its good things,*
> *because it allows you greater flexibility, many times, when I have*
> *needed, I have taken the children to work, of course you can not*
> *always do it, but at a specific moment that is not you have to travel*
> *and they get sick, or you do not have anyone to leave them with ... it's*
> *more relaxed than if you work somewhere else; But in the end everything*
> *is for you, and the solution lies in how you manage it, because it is still*
> *considered 'yours' as 'woman' in most cases, or the most important*
> *weight you still carry as a woman; and I'm talking about cases in which*
> *there is some awareness on the part of men as is my case.*
>
> (María)

Other women give us in their speeches more questions that abound in these barriers, as we can see, that manifest themselves affecting personal decisions such as having a partner and/or being mothers with them or alone.

These data show us the feeling of a scarce coresponsibility with couples in matters of management and maintenance of life, as well as an internal fear on the part of women faced with the difficulty of attending to traditional roles and work demands at the same level. Let's see how the women interviewed narrate it:

> *I do not see any kind of conciliation and I will not be able to have a family,*
> *because if I have a couple I would have to get involved in the care of the*
> *baby, not in a sporadic way but in a real way, as an equal; by friends I know*
> *that this is not real, it seems that today parents help, it is not like before, but*
> *something else is needed, the guide is still carried by the woman, not only*
> *with the children, but also with the house and domestic issues.*
>
> (Esther)

> *It is now that I do not have a family and I have problems with my*
> *personal conciliation, there are many hours dedicated to work and*
> *I hardly have time for myself, and now leisure ... it is difficult for the*
> *woman today, perhaps because we intend to cover a lot, I do not*
> *know ..., or because we do not know or do not want to delegate, I do*
> *not know ...*
>
> (Lidia)

In general, women argue that this type of difficulties not only occurs in the female entrepreneur but in all women, at the social level, remaining, according to them, nowadays barriers that continue to make invisible the real role that women perform in society:

> *Gender differences not only occur in women entrepreneurs, but at the*
> *level of society as a whole and it is reflected in us, we can see it*

differently but in general in all women, whether they are aware or not, it is something that happens.

(Gema)

There are structural gender differences, it's clear. For example, the company is mine and my husband's, in spite of it, I created it, and he is the director, and for the clients he is the authority and I am the secretary (...). Because of my gender and my position as a human resource of the company, people asume two things: I do not have responsibilities in the company and I do not have knowledge or skills, and this affects the day today

(Irene).[2]

What I do not have is the money to pay someone to do this work and so I dedicate myself to running the company, and it's not that I do not do things at home, or that I dedicate myself to my children, it's not that, it's the carry the load, I do not know if you understand me, all the decisions, the managements, the going ahead of necessary basic things that if you do not do them they are not done because they do not look, I do not know if I explain myself.

(María)

Given the difficulties felt by women, solutions seem to come from having external resources or favoring networks (mainly women).

In another order of things, the findings show how in some cases women officially adopt secondary roles in business management, '*the bosses are them*' (Irene), when in reality they are the ones who manage, organize and they lead. On these datas we should think about as society.

---

5   Conclusions and Discussion

Considering the findings found, the following can generally be concluded:

1) Some women choose to undertake in the absence of options in the labor market for others; others, on the other hand, do so because of the illusion of creating their own professional project that they can develop throughout their working life (work identity, entrepreneurial vocation);

2) The careers of women entrepreneurs in transition are more flexible and innovative than those of women entrepreneurs with more experience/con-solidated, where there are interrelated variables of a personal and family nature that can explain it, and where we see associated gender stereotypes

('scissors effect', which also occurs in the entrepreneurial career), at least as reflected by the enterprising women interviewed.

3) There continue to be structural gender barriers that affect entrepreneurship, identifying an unequal starting point biased by gender factors that are at the base. These are maintained by a patriarchal model that, in spite of reinforcing the work trajectory of women and establishing 'compensatory' actions to reduce these differences, continue to occur, perhaps because of an important element of awareness and awareness that women interviewed show and that it still remains, not recognizing its real role that in many cases remains stable in terms of the reproduction of traditional roles as women. Here is the model of women as superwoman, which entails danger due to the conflict of roles, and on which we must work in these, and especially in the new generations, having to be attentive to the new models of women -and of men- that are being transmitted subliminally. Perhaps this has to do with other barriers, such as access to high positions, management or business management, which at a certain time women do not care or compensate them. This is an important element that opens up for debate. In coherence with the above, women show barriers to reconcile the personal, family and work dimensions of the life project, which also makes gender mediate in professional/labor decision making.

Deepening the general conclusions, and with the intention of contributing some elements to the discussion, we can see a clear unequal situation in terms of entrepreneurship. The literature tends to agree that there are certain characteristics more typical of women, such as that they have less confidence in themselves; women feel that they do not possess the required skills [49], which limit their aspirations in the development of their career. This lack of confidence of women about their entrepreneurial skills and abilities may be because the entrepreneurial attributes are seen socially as masculine [50]. However, in terms of proactivity, the female gender is associated to a greater extent with attributes related to responsibility, discipline and independence and masculine to initiative and leadership positions [51].

According to the study of [22] there are gender differences also when seeking advice for entrepreneurship, although men and women resort more to informal sources than to contracted professionals, women resort to the advice of family and friends while men resort to well-known professionals. On the other hand, the main support of women entrepreneurs is the family (the husband) or other nearby women (networks of family and friends), while the main support of the men entrepreneurs are the consultants as lawyers or accountants, the wives are Secondly. According to [51] the female gender is more adverse to risk and considered less innovative. This can be due to the greater weight in the care of the family that makes it look for stability and security, leaving the man who is the one who risks.

With respect to the motivations and decisions that drive entrepreneurship, in the case of women, these are more of necessity or forced given the few, nefarious and discriminatory offers and possibilities of employment for others. Women undertake 20% more out of necessity than men, in fact, women's entrepreneurship has grown in times of crisis [28] posing a difficult paradigm to explain and that is, when the level of economic development of a country grows the participation of women decreases. Maybe it's because the women who do not need them prefer to enjoy their motherhood and the care of their children instead of starting out of necessity. Similarly, we obtain that independence is an aspect that stimulates women to undertake, which coincides with [48], as does labor flexibility [47].

Alluding to the constraints for entrepreneurship, it is concluded that one of the main barriers faced by women when it comes to undertaking is the reconciliation of work and family life, which coincides, for example, with the study of [50], who states that although men can also find themselves with this same problem, since the dedication to their professional career can mean a renunciation of the care of their family, it is the women who are most affected by this issue, especially because of how they understand the cares and resignations in one and in another case. In the first place, for motherhood, since the first months in the care of a child are irreplaceable; second, because they are less willing than men to give up this motherhood. That is why the refusal to develop a professional career is more common in women [29] if they want to start a family. The woman has to face her professional and vital development from the social role that indicates that she is, as a woman and mother, who mainly has to take charge of the family, showing for her models of specific working women that have and will have their repercussion partner -labour in these and following generations of women (including the maternal role).

6 Some Implications and Final Considerations for Entrepreneurial Professional Theory and Practice

The conclusions raised lead us to questioning the mechanisms that are operating in the entrepreneurial professional development of women (also men). Manifest situations that show an unequal starting situation in the entrepreneurship of the women interviewed with respect to their male counterparts, the need arises to integrate a gender perspective in the design and management processes of the entrepreneurial career.

We have identified numerous public and private organizations that support the entrepreneur, especially in the valuation of their business project, and not so much in the management of the same or in the construction and development of their professional and vital entrepreneurial project, which involves considering habits and vital styles, at the same time as the daily management of the different roles that people (women) play. This has a number of implications at the training level, going through the necessary work around the construction of professional projects in entrepreneurship based on the conviction and personal awareness about the motivations, itineraries and conditions that affect entrepreneurial development, including the factors of gender and social exclusion that may be mediating.

It is assumed that entrepreneurship is considered as a strategy to promote employment and combat unemployment [12]. Many family policies focus only on women, reinforcing the idea that child care and family problems concern only women [34], which is why it is proposed that the measures should be aimed at the family unit and not only women, although it will be necessary to consider those measures in order to balance unfair situations of departure.

As stated [10,18], programs to support female entrepreneurial activity should take into account the stages of work and personal life. Measures aimed at reducing the rigidity of the career, and in working hours, could favor the development of female entrepreneurship, as long as they are required at the family level and responsibilities related to domestic tasks and care are shared in a responsible manner, which does not mean measuring the times in an exact way, but rather that there is real co-responsibility in the family and that the working women do not have the same weight, doubling and tripling the day. It will be necessary to assess with this the real work load that is demanded according to the sector, the business objectives to be covered and the responsibilities assumed in each case.

In this sense [22], states that institutions and society should provide better support systems for the care of children, which we understand should also be aimed at supporting the family unit instead of men or women individually. Measures such as parental leave equated to maternal leave would break the social stereotype that it is the woman who has to take care of the children, giving rise to a more equitable and egalitarian context where men and women are on equal terms and where you can exercise paternity and maternity without renouncing the development of professional career. This has been an issue that is clearly affecting women entrepreneurs and that conditions their careers.

On the other hand, solutions to promote the career of women need to be adapted to their particular situations [22]. This goes through evidence with segregated data (not always accessible or existing) the reality of both sexes against entrepreneurship in order to make gender gaps visible and work them. From education, it is necessary to work on the psychological barriers [19] that prevent women from developing their entrepreneurial career, and also about the barriers that society maintains and reproduces from a patriarchal social model still in force. Programs to support female entrepreneurial activity should take into account the stages of work and personal life [10,18], as well as the different moments of the entrepreneurial career, where different needs are revealed. In coherence, labor institutions should establish clear criteria for promotion and development, encouraging women to aspire to leadership positions and establishing policies that ensure equal conditions for women and men entrepreneurs.

Studies such as [22] make a series of recommendations to achieve equal career development between men and women and achieve a more equal academic landscape. Some of these proposals are considered in light of the conclusions of this work. On the one hand, we need to have specialized training in gender issues in labor organizations [30], especially in the initial stages and at times of transition of the entrepreneurial career.

Similarly, when designing training programs or guidance, the above mentioned issues should be considered, because we need to create from the bottom a social and labor model more equitable, fair and socially responsible, which inevitably happens through the education of future generations. Contents such as values, stereotypes and gender barriers should be present in school content, to work specifically on professional guidance actions in school settings, secondary education, professional and university training, in relation to professional decisions, specifically in entrepreneurship.

We should also contemplate realities that are present and that we cannot avoid, such as the entrepreneurial activity sectors, the types of businesses they develop, the roles and positions they occupy, their career aspirations and limitations, etc., where efforts should be directed to motivate entrepreneurship; how to help overcome barriers and threats to entrepreneurial success; what competencies/training can be promoted; what resources would be necessary; what institutions can contribute/help; etc.

With all this, we understand that this study provides some relevant clues to guide and develop entrepreneurship respecting the entrepreneurial identity and equal opportunities between women and men in the business world. We contribute with a series of exploratory results, because this work is part of a broader study, at this time in development. And, we understand that, like any study, it has its own limitations and complexity, in this case, mainly related to its wide scope and the multiplicity of factors that intervene in the career of women entrepreneurs, also taking into account the diversity of profiles and situations that characterize their personal and professional trajectories.

As a prospective, we appreciate the continuity of this work integrating in the analysis of the motivations and conditioning of women's senses, perceptions about daily business behavior (for example, applying the shadow technique in the daily life of women entrepreneurs). Also in the development and implementation of concrete actions in entrepreneurship, so that both women and men entrepreneurs become aware of the gender factors present in their careers, and jointly identify possible responses to gender gaps. We understand that the elimination of these stereotypes must come hand in hand with the dialogue between the sexes to eradicate stereotypes that have been constructed on the basis of an unequal model of and between the sexes, and that still remains affecting the different vital spheres in which we develop, and limiting us in both cases.

Notes

1 Partial results of the R & D Project, Career Design and Management of Entrepreneurial Talent are presented, with a national dimension, financed by the Ministry of Economy and Competitiveness in the 2013 call for the 2013–2016 State Plan Excellence, with Reference: EDU2013-45704-P. Sustituir por: Developed between 2014–2018.
2 In some cases of companies shared by men, interviews were also conducted with their male colleagues (whose data are not included in this work). Specifically in this case, and by way of example, we indicate that these difficulties have been perceived in the speeches of women, not in that of men. They come to admit gender barriers if they develop roles that are typically considered feminine, for example taking children to the company if necessary, or benefiting from parental leave.

References

1 Alemany, L. and Urriolagoitia, L. (2014): *Iniciativa Emprendedora y Jóvenes en España.* In ICE EmpleoJuvenil, p. 881.

2 Fernández-Laviada, A., Peña, I., Guerrero, M., González-Pernia, J. L., and RubioBañón, A. (2015): *Global entrepreneurship monitor, Informe GEM España 2014,* Graduate S, p. 155. Global Entreprenership Research Association.

3 Gutiérrez-Solana, F., Fernández-Laviada, A., Peña, I., Guerrero, M., y González-Pernía, J. L. (2017): *Global entrepreneurship monitor. Informe GEM España 2016.* Global Entreprenership Research Association.

4 Reyes Recio, L. E., Pinillos Costa, M. J., and Soriano Pinar, I. (2014): Diferencias de género en la orientación emprendedora. In *Esic Market Economics and Business Journal,* 45(3), pp. 441–460. doi:10.7200/esicm.149.0453.1e

5 Gutiérrez-Solana, F., Fernández-Laviada, A., Peña, I., Guerrero, M., González-Pernía, J. L., Montero, J., and Sánchez de León, J. (2018): *Informe GEM España 2017.* USA/UK. Global Entreprenership Research Association.

6 Alemany, L., Alvarez, C., Planellas, M., y Urbano, D. (2011): *El libro blanco de la iniciativa emprendedora.* Barcelona: ESADE.

7 Carree, M. A., y Thurik, A. R. (2006): *Entrepreneurship and economic growth.* Cheltenham, UK: Edward Elgar.

8 Carter, N. M., Gartner, W. B., Shaver, K. G., y Gatewood, E. J. (2003): The career reasons of nascent entrepreneurs. In *Journal of Business Venturing,* 18(1), pp. 13–39.

9 Serrano-Bedia, A. M., Pérez-Pérez, M., Palma-Ruiz, M., and López-Fernández, M. C. (2016): Emprendimiento: Visión actual comodisciplina de investigación. Un análisis de los números especiales publicados durante 2011–2013. In *Estudios Gerenciales,* 32(138), pp. 82–95.

10 Sánchez Cañizares, S. M. y Fuentes García, F. J. (2010a): Análisis del perfil emprendedor: Una perspectiva de género. In *Estudios de Economía Aplicada,* 5731(3), pp. 1–28.

11 Pérez Camarero, S., Hidalgo Vega, Á., Balaguer García, S., y Pérez Cañellas, E. (2009): Emprendimiento económico y social en España. In *Guía De Recursos Para Jóvenes Emprendedores/As.*

12 Castro, B. y Santero, R. (2014): Caracterización del emprendimiento autónomo en España. Un análisis desde la perspectiva de género. In *Esic Market Economics and Business Journal,* 45(3), pp. 487–514.

13 Ministerio de Economía Industria y Competitividad. (2017): *Retrato de la PYME (Pequeña y mediana empresa) a 1 de Enero de 2017.* Madrid: Ministerio de Empleo y Seguridad Social. Gobierno de España.

14 Ministerio de Empleo y Seguridad Social. (2017): *Perfil de los trabajadores autónomos en España a 31 de diciembre de 2017.* Madrid: Ministerio de Empleo y Seguridad Social. Gobierno de España.

15 Conroy, T. y Weiler, S. (2016): Does gender matter for job creation? Business ownership and employment growth. In *Small Business Economics,* 47, pp. 397–419.

16 Holienka, M., Jančovičová, Z., y Kovačičová, Z. (2016): Drivers of women entrepreneurship in visegrad countries: GEM evidence. In *Procedia—Social and Behavioral Sciences,* 220, pp. 124–133.

17 Bönte, W. y Piegeler, M. (2013): Gender gap in latent and nascent entrepreneurship: driven by competitiveness. In *Small Business Economics,* 41(4), pp. 961–987.

18 Sánchez Cañizares, S. M. y Fuentes García, F. J. (2010b): Gender differences in entrepreneurial attitudes. In *Equality, Diversity and Inclusion: An International Journal*, 29(8), pp. 766–786.

19 Sánchez Cañizares, S. M. y Fuentes García, F. J. (2013): Mujer y emprendimiento: Un análisis en el contexto universitario español. In *Revista De Ciencias Sociales (RCS)*, XIX (1), pp. 140–153.

20 Comisión Europea. (2018): *Report on equality between women and men in the UE.* European Union: European Commission.

21 Comisión Europea. (2015): *She figures handbook 2015. Research and Innovation.* Brussels: European Commission.

22 Salinas, P. C. y Bagni, C. (2017): Gender equality from a European perspective: myth and reality. In *Neuron*.doi:10.1016/j.neuron.2017.10.002

23 Cheraghi, M. and Schøtt, T. (2015): Education and training benefiting a career as entrepreneur. Gender gaps and gendered competencies and benefits. In *International Journal of Gender and Entrepreneurship*, 7(3), pp. 321–343.doi:10.1108/IJGE-03-2013-0027

24 Consejo Superior de Investigaciones Científicas, CSIC. (2017): *Informe mujeres investigadoras. Comisión Asesora de Presidencia "mujeres y ciencia" 2018.* Madrid: CSIC.

25 Pons Peregort, O., Calvet Puig, M. D., Tura Solvas, M., y Muñoz Llescas, C. (2004): Análisis de la Igualdad de Oportunidades de Género en la Ciencia y la Tecnología: Las carrerasprofesionales de lasmujerescientíficas y tecnólogas. In *Intangible Capital*, 9(1), pp. 65–90.

26 Pons-Peregort, O., CalvetPuig, M. D., Tura, M., y Muñoz Illescas, C. (2013): Analysis of equal gender opportunity in science and technology. The professional careers of women scientists and technologists. In *Intangible Capital*, 9(1).

27 Pérez Quintana, A. y Hormiga Pérez, E. (2012): La influencia de los estereotipos de género en la orientación emprendedora individual y la intención de emprender. Investigación Y Género, Inseparables En El Presente Y En El Futuro: IV Congreso Universitario Nacional Y Investigación Y Género», Sevilla, 21 y 22 de junio de 2012.

28 Kelley, D., Brush, C., Greene, P. G., Herrington, M., Ali, A., y Kew, P. (2015): *GEM special report: women's entrepreneurship 2015.* USA/UK: Global Entreprenership Research Association.

29 Leung, A. (2011): Motherhood and entrepreneurship: gender role identity. In *International Journal of Gender and Entrepreneurship*, 3(3), pp. 254–264. doi:10.1108/17566261111169331

30 Moreno Calvo, A. (2016): *Las mujeres en las organizaciones empresariales: Unescenariopara el desarrollo de su proyecto profesional y de vida.* Tesis doctoral inédita. Universidad de Sevilla.

31 Luque Salas, B. (2008): El itinerario profesional de las mujeres jóvenes: Unacarrera de obstáculos. In *Anuario De psicología/The UB Journal of Psychology*, 39(1), pp. 101–107.

32 Kelley, D., Baumer, B. S., Brush, C., Greene, P. G., Mahdavi, M., MajbouriMarciaCole, M. and Heavlow, R. (2016): *Women's entrepreneurship 2016/2017 report global entrepreneurship monitor.* USA/UK: Global Entreprenership Research Association.

33 González-Pernía, J. L. (2013): Género y actividad exportadora de los emprendedores en España. In *Economía Industrial*, 383, pp. 95–110.

34 Portillo Navarro, M. J. y Millán Jiménez, A. (2016): Moderators elements of entrepreneurship. Gender differences. In *Suma de Negocios*, 7(15), pp. 47–53.

35 Maes, J., Leroy, H., y Sels, L. (2014): Gender differences in entrepreneurial intentions: a TPB multi-group analysis at factor and indicator level. In *European Management Journal*, 32, pp. 784–794.

36 Santos, F. J., Roomi, M. A., y Liñán, F. (2016): About gender differences and the social environment in the development of entrepreneurial intentions. In *Journal of Small Business Management*, 54(1), pp. 49–66.

37 Elam, A. y Terjesen, S. (2010): Gendered institutions and cross-national patterns of business creation for men and women. In *European Journal of Development Research*, 22(3), pp. 331–348.

38 Dempsey, D. y Jennings, J. (2014): Gender and entrepreneurial self-efficacy: a learning perspective. In *International Journal of Gender and Entrepreneurship*, 6(1), pp. 28–49.

39 Karimi, S., Biemans, H. J. A., Lans, T., Chizari, M., Mulder, M., y Mahdei, K. N. (2013): Understanding role models and gender influences on entrepreneurial intentions among college students. In *Procedia—Social and Behavioral Sciences*, 93, pp. 204–214.

40 Wilson, F., Kickul, J., and Marlino, D. (2007): Gender, entrepreneurial self-efficacy, and entrepreneurial career intentions: implications for entrepreneurship education. In *Entrepreneurship Theory and Practice*, 860, pp. 713–731.doi:10.1111/etap.12051

41 Marina, J. A. (2010): La competencia de emprender. In *Revistade Educacion*, 351, pp. 49–71.

42 Fayolle, A. y Gailly, B. (2015): The impact of entrepreneurship education on entrepreneurial attitudes and intention: hysteresis and persistence. In *Journal of Small Business Management*, 53(1), pp. 75–93.

43 Ministerio de Economía, Industria y Competitividad. (2010): *Servicios de apoyo a la persona emprendedora*. Madrid: Ministerio de Economía, Industria y Competitividad. Gobierno de España.

44 Peña, I., Guerrero, M., y González-Pernía, J. L. (2016): *Global Entrepreneurship monitor: Informe GEM España 2015*. Madrid: Editorial de la Universidad de Cantabria.

45 Castro Mora, J. (2015): *Guía Persán para emprendedores 2016*. Sevilla: Fundación Persán.

46 Marulanda Montoya, J. A., Correa Calle, G., y Mejía Mejía, L. F. (2009): Emprendimiento: Visiones desde las teorias del comportamiento humano. In *Revista EAN*, 66, pp. 153–168.

47 Hessels, J., Van Gelderen, M., y Thurik, A. R. (2008): Entrepreneurial aspirations, motivations, and their drivers. In *Small Business Economics*, 31(3), pp. 323–339.

48 Thurik, A. R., y Wennekers, S. (2004): Entrepreneurship, small business and economic growth. In *Journal of Business and Enterprise Development*, 11(1), pp. 140–149.

49 Suárez-Ortega, M. and Gálvez-García, M.R. (2016): Motivations and decisive factors in women's entrepreneurship. A gender perspective in education and professional guidance. In *Procedia—Social and Behavioral Sciences*, 237(2017), pp. 1265–1271.

50 Braches, B. and Elliott, C. (2017): Articulating the entrepreneurship career: a study of German women entrepreneurs. In *International Small Business Journal: Researching Entrepreneurship*, 35(5), pp. 535–557. doi:10.1177/0266242616651921

51 Robinson, S. and Stubberud, H. A. (2009): Sources of advice in entrepreneurship: gender differences in business owners' social networks. In *International Journal of Entrepreneurship*, 13(1), pp. 83–101.doi:10.1177/097135570801800101

Index

For Product Safety Concerns and Information please contact our EU
representative GPSR@taylorandfrancis.com
Taylor & Francis Verlag GmbH, Kaufingerstraße 24, 80331 München, Germany

www.ingramcontent.com/pod-product-compliance
Ingram Content Group UK Ltd.
Pitfield, Milton Keynes, MK11 3LW, UK
UKHW021611240425
457818UK00018B/494